Interpreting Governance, High Politics, and Public Policy

Interpreting Governance, High Politics, and Public Policy offers the latest perspectives on the interpretive approach to governance and public policy research.

This book commemorates more than a decade of governance research by Mark Bevir and R. A. W. Rhodes, the leading exponents of interpretive political science in the United Kingdom. It explains how insights from the interpretive perspective may be used to advance the study of governance and public policy. Featuring contributions from major scholars in the field, both inside and outside the interpretivist fold, the authors critically reflect upon interpretivism and consider how aspects of the interpretive approach apply to their own research. The authors debate the significance of Bevir and Rhodes's work and develop future directions for interpretive governance research. The chapters link one of the most innovative contemporary perspectives in political science with the latest empirical studies.

Contributing towards setting the governance research agenda, *Interpreting Governance, High Politics, and Public Policy* is an excellent resource for the study of interpretive policy analysis.

Nick Turnbull is Lecturer in Politics at the University of Manchester, where he researches political communication and political rhetoric, public policy and governance, and the philosophy of social science. He is a specialist in the philosophy of questioning, applied to the social sciences.

Routledge Studies in Governance and Public Policy

University of Plymouth
Charles Seale Hayne Library
Subject to status this item may be renewed
via your Primo account

http://primo.plymouth.ac.uk
Tel: (01752) 588588

Interpreting Governance, High Politics, and Public Policy

Essays Commemorating *Interpreting British Governance*

Edited by Nick Turnbull

Routledge
Taylor & Francis Group

NEW YORK AND LONDON

First published 2016
by Routledge
711 Third Avenue, New York, NY 10017

and by Routledge
2 Park Square, Milton Park, Abingdon, Oxon OX14 4RN

Routledge is an imprint of the Taylor & Francis Group, an informa business

© 2016 Taylor & Francis

Library of Congress Cataloging in Publication Data
A catalog record for this book has been requested

ISBN: 978-1-138-77728-6 (hbk)
ISBN: 978-1-315-77275-2 (ebk)

Typeset in Times New Roman
by Wearset Ltd, Boldon, Tyne and Wear

MIX
Paper from
responsible sources
FSC
www.fsc.org FSC® C013056

Printed and bound in Great Britain by
TJ International Ltd, Padstow, Cornwall

Contents

Illustrations

Figures

Tables

Contributors

Perri 6 is Professor in Public Management at Queen Mary University of London. His work on decision making among ministers and officials focuses on thought styles cultivated by distinct forms of informal social organisation. He has made major contributions to developing the neo-Durkheimian institutional framework. His recent books include *Explaining Political Judgement* (Cambridge, 2011) and *Principles of Methodology* (with Christine Bellamy, Sage, 2011). He has published widely on joined-up government, privacy, personal social networks, behaviour change, and health and social policy.

Christine Bellamy is Emeritus Professor of Public Administration at Nottingham Trent University and has research interests in e-government, data-sharing and privacy. She is currently working on the history of the British 'information state', focusing on personal record systems in health and social administration. She is co-author with Perri 6 of *Principles of Methodology* (Sage, 2011), and has served on the ESRC's Research Evaluation Committee and its International Benchmarking Study of Politics, on the sub-panel for Politics and International Relations in the 2008 Research Assessment Exercise, and on the Academy of Social Sciences' Nominations Committee.

Mark Bevir is Professor of Political Science at the University of California, Berkeley. He is the author of a number of books, including, most recently, *The Making of British Socialism* (Princeton University Press, 2011), *Governance: A Very Short Introduction* (Oxford University Press, 2012), and *A Theory of Governance* (University of California Press, 2013).

David Craig is Lecturer in History at Durham University. He is the author of *Robert Southey and Romantic Apostasy: Political Argument in Britain 1780–1840* (2007) and editor, with James Thompson, of *Languages of Politics in Nineteenth Century Britain*. He is currently working on the language of liberalism in the nineteenth century.

Patrick Diamond is Lecturer in Public Policy at Queen Mary, University of London. His most recent books are *Governing Britain: Power, Politics and the Prime Minister* (IB Tauris, 2013) and *Transforming the Market: Towards a New Political Economy* (Civitas, 2014).

Paul Fawcett is Associate Professor at the Institute for Governance and Policy Analysis at the University of Canberra. His research is focused on theories of governance with related empirical interests in central agency reform, political participation, and policy transfer. He has published in journals including *Administration & Society, Government and Opposition, Policy & Politics* and *The Australian Journal of Political Science*.

R. A. W. Rhodes is Professor of Government at the University of Southampton (UK). He is the author or editor of some 37 books including recently: (with Anne Tiernan) *Lessons of Governing* (Melbourne University Press, 2014); *Everyday Life in British Government* (Oxford University Press, 2015, paperback); and with Mark Bevir, *The Routledge Handbook of Interpretive Political Science* (2015). He is a Fellow of the Academy of the Social Sciences in both Australia and the UK.

David Richards is Professor of Public Policy at the University of Manchester. He has previously held posts at the Universities of Strathclyde, Birmingham, Liverpool, and Sheffield. He is the author of numerous articles and books on British politics, governance and public policy including, most recently, N*ew Labour and the Civil Service: Reconstituting the Westminster Model* and (ed.) *Institutional Crisis in 21st Century Britain*.

Emily Robinson is Lecturer in Politics at the University of Sussex. She is the author of *History, Heritage and Tradition in Contemporary British Politics* (Manchester University Press, 2012) and is currently writing a history of the political and cultural meanings of the word 'progressive' in modern Britain.

Martin Smith is Anniversary Professor of Politics at the University of York. Previously he was Professor of Politics at the University of Sheffield and has also taught at the Universities of Essex, Kent, and Brunel. He has published 14 books and over 100 articles and chapters. He has received research grants from a number of funding bodies including the ESRC and the EU. He was appointed as a member of the Academy of Social Sciences in 2010. His main research interests are British politics, public policy, and state transformation.

Helen Sullivan is Professor and Foundation Director of the Melbourne School of Government, University of Melbourne. Her research and teaching focuses on changing state–society relations and modes of interaction including collaboration and citizen participation. She has published widely on public policy, public governance, and public service reform. Her latest book (with C. Skelcher and S. Jeffares) is *Hybrid Governance in European Cities: Neighbourhood, Migration and Democracy* (Palgrave Macmillan, 2013).

Andrew Taylor is Professor of Politics at the University of Sheffield. His interests include EU enlargement into South East Europe, the politics of state failure, and political rhetoric. His most recent books are *State Failure* (Palgrave Macmillan, 2013) and *The European Union and South East Europe: The Dynamics of Europeanization and Multi-level Governance* (with Andrew Geddes and Charles Lees, Routledge, 2012).

Nick Turnbull is Lecturer in Politics at the University of Manchester, where he researches political communication and political rhetoric, public policy and governance, and the philosophy of social science. He is the author of a recent work of philosophy, *Michel Meyer's Problematology: Questioning and Society* (Bloomsbury, 2014) and is co-editor of *Rhetoric in British Politics and Society* (Palgrave Macmillan, 2014).

Hendrik Wagenaar is Professor at the Department of Urban Studies and Planning at the University of Sheffield, where he is also Associate Director of the Crick Centre for Understanding Politics. He publishes in the areas of participatory democracy, prostitution policy, interpretive policy analysis and practice theory. He is author of *Meaning in Action: Interpretation and Dialogue in Policy Analysis* (Routledge, 2011), and co-editor of *Practices of Freedom: Decentered Governance, Conflict and Democratic Participation* (Cambridge University Press, 2014).

Acknowledgements

This collection was produced from a series of special panels held by the Interpretive Political Science Specialist Group of the Political Studies Association of the UK at the 63rd Annual Conference in Cardiff, 25–27 March 2013. Sixteen scholars were invited to present their thoughts on interpretive political science to commemorate the tenth anniversary of Mark Bevir and R. A. W. Rhodes's ground-breaking book, *Interpreting British Governance* (Routledge, 2003). I would like to thank the Political Studies Association and the organisers of the 2013 Cardiff conference for their support in hosting these panels, as well as all those scholars who participated and agreed to share their ideas in contributing to this volume. I would like to give special thanks to Professor Matthew Flinders and the PSA for generously donating funds for essential pre-publication legal advice. My thanks also go to the other presenters who were unable to find time to write for this book or whom I was unable to include in the final version for reasons of space and coherence: Jonathan Davies, Peter Feindt, Jonathan Floyd, and Andrew Hindmoor.

I would sincerely like to thank my colleagues at the University of Manchester, Leeds Beckett University, and the University of Sydney who very kindly donated their time to read and review chapters and provide excellent suggestions on how to improve the book: Karen Clarke, Daniel Fitzpatrick, Francesca Gains, Anika Gauja, Robin Redhead, David Richards, Liz Richardson, Gabriel Siles-Brügge, and Ariadne Vromen.

Finally, I would like to thank Natalja Mortensen, Lilian Rand, Darcy Bullock and all the staff at Routledge for their tolerance and continuing support for this project.

Abbreviations

ADP	Automatic Data Processing
BPT	British Political Tradition
CSO	Central Statistical Office
DES	Department of Education and Science
EC	Executive Council
FA	Football Association
FoIA	Freedom of Information Act
GRO	General Register Office
HIP	Hillsborough Independent Panel
LEA	Local Education Authority
MRC	Medical Research Council
MH	Ministry of Health
MPNI	Ministry of Pensions and National Insurance
NCCL	National Council for Civil Liberties
NHS	National Health Service
NHSCR	National Health Service Central Register
NI	National Insurance
NR	National Register
O&M	Organisation and Methods
PAYE	Pay as You Earn
PMDU	Prime Minister's Delivery Unit
PMSU	Prime Minister's Strategy Unit
PSA	Public Service Agreement
SDP	Social Democratic Party
SYP	South Yorkshire Police
SYPF	South Yorkshire Police Federation
TNA	The National Archives
UK	United Kingdom

Introduction
Interpreting Governance, High Politics, and Public Policy

Nick Turnbull

Interpretive approaches to political analysis have gained significant ground over the last decade. Not yet mainstream, interpretivism, conceived broadly, is a perspective that has sought to challenge many established conventions of political science. Interpretive political science takes quite a different view from the most common approaches, both in theory and method. It highlights contingency in its explanations, working from alternative philosophical traditions to reject the logic of cause and effect. It seeks to offer a more holistic view, claiming to produce more comprehensive and more relevant explanations of social reality. It places great emphasis on meaning, articulating the myriad ways in which language and ideas construct the political world and how these are always in competition with alternative readings. It uses different methods, aimed at revealing everyday political practice and uncovering the effects upon it of culture and tradition, amorphous concepts but nonetheless vital contributors to the texture of political life. In short, interpretivists have put forward a serious case for an alternative analytical approach to political science. This approach has been applied across the many subdisciplinary areas of politics, but most notably in governance and public policy, the subject of this collection.

Interpretive social science has been around a long time. But in the United Kingdom (UK), the interpretivist flag in political science has been carried most prominently by Mark Bevir and R. A. W. Rhodes, who, since the publication of *Interpreting British Governance* in 2003, have made great strides in building their vision of interpretive political analysis. They have developed a rigorous and wide-ranging interpretive approach, from theory to methodology, through a research programme that aims to articulate a fresh understanding of government and governance. The scope of their published research is testament to their rigorous scholarship and unbounded enthusiasm. And few scholars have been so willing to engage in direct debate with critics.

This edited collection on their work marks ten years since that publication, a milestone in interpretive studies of governance and public policy in the UK. It is the product of the Interpretive Political Science Specialist Group of the Political Studies Association of the UK, arising from a series of panels held at the 2013 Conference at Cardiff University. But this book is no *Festschrift* for Bevir and Rhodes. Rather, it continues the critical engagement with their work by both fellow-travellers and critics, with a determined eye towards the future contribution of interpretivism to governance research. The authors in this collection engage with Bevir and Rhodes's ideas about governance, high politics and political history, and public policymaking, reflecting on them, criticising them and going beyond them to ascertain what interpretivism contributes to other perspectives as well as to develop further the interpretive analytical framework. It is neither a summation nor an end point, but instead a marker for the future, setting out continuing controversies as well as new avenues of inquiry for interpretive political science.

Interpretivism and Theory in British Political Studies

The interpretive political science research programme of Bevir and Rhodes can be read in two main ways. First, it can be interpreted as an endeavour to do something interesting and innovative in British political science, particularly in the often dry field of governance, public policy, and public administration. Bevir and Rhodes introduced new theoretical concepts and an innovative methodology to paint an altogether original picture of the everyday life of government, aiming to liven up the field and free it from the strictures imposed by an empiricist tradition. Second, their work can be read as an altogether more challenging and confrontational effort to establish interpretivism as an analytical framework, one which rejects some of the established and valued aspects of British political science. In this reading, Bevir and Rhodes propose interpretivism to be a superior perspective to other analytical frameworks, which they criticise as representing the conventional practices of positivism or modernist empiricism, which are argued to be weaker on both theoretical and empirical grounds. Here, they situate themselves in a broad, if loose, family of interpretive approaches they class as anti-foundational (Bevir and Rhodes, 2010). The varied reactions to their work hinge on which way critics lean in regard to these two interpretations of the contribution of interpretivism in British political studies. Both readings are represented in this collection.

Perhaps the main impact of interpretivism has been to prompt scholars of British government to take theory more seriously. A decade before the interpretive controversy, Gamble (1990) made a strong case that British political science had for a long time, to its great detriment, eschewed theory in favour of a conservative reliance upon accepted concepts, fused with a strong empiricism. He noted that theoretical developments were opening up the field to a diversity which provided exciting critical possibilities. *Interpreting British Governance* subsequently became part of that trend towards a new emphasis on theory, particularly within the field of public administration. Bevir and Rhodes injected a measure of theoretical depth and originality to public administration scholarship, taking it beyond what some regarded as the 'mindless empiricism' of much research and a journalistic approach which offered little in the way of critical analysis (Marsh, 2011). Interpretivists asked new questions about governance, transcending the tired approaches and breathing new life into the discipline. Even the much disputed claim of an empirical shift in the British state from 'government to governance', put forward by Rhodes before his interpretive work, is also best seen in this light – to question, to innovate, to generate new ideas and approaches, to be radical and shake things up. Anyone who has seen Rhodes present his research in person will understand this about his character. Hence, although depicted as travelling a road to Damascus upon meeting Mark Bevir and 'converting' from institutionalism to interpretivism, we should not be surprised that he was looking to make further innovations. Seeking out this trajectory is, for him, crucial in rendering the subject of public administration interesting for students as much as it is for himself as a researcher. *Interpreting British Governance* reflected the new plurality of positions on political analysis and Bevir's and Rhodes's subsequent work has contributed vitally to the sea change in theorising governance and public administration.

Interpretivism has thus generated new conversations that rarely took place 20 years ago. It has painted a picture of the governance world that is rich in meaning, animated by individuals working in collective cultures, rather than merely described in terms of institutional boxes. Throughout the many levels of governance, these individuals are engaged in a continuous dialogue of ideas, generating narratives to explain themselves and their policy responses to political problems. This cultural approach is also grounded in a political history, explaining continuity through the various competing traditions to which elected officials and civil servants refer when interpreting and responding to political events. It gives us fresh ways to explain governance processes and to understand what they mean for the individuals concerned. This is, importantly, a conception that these individuals are always acting in time, located in a context that renders each problem and each response different. The impact of this picture can be seen in how strongly it resonates beyond academia for practitioners themselves, as a realistic account of governing practice far more relevant to them than academic explanations based in institutional rules or rationalist conceptions of political action, and presented as schematic models of the policy process. Interpretivism asks new questions about governance by seeking to understand the meaning of problems for the actors, how they interpret the questions they face and how the ideas found in shared culture impact upon their responses, beyond the instrumental–rational conception of goal-seeking behaviour or institutionally driven action. In short, interpretivism aims to bring forward the contingency of political life and the agency of individuals in responding to it.

In terms of the novelty of interpretive empirical research, it is certainly the case that interpretive accounts of governance look very different from conventional depictions. Drawing on ethnographic methods in particular, Bevir and Rhodes drew dramatic pictures of the everyday life of government, told as stories about ministers, civil servants, and special advisors negotiating daily political and administrative problems. From travelling in cars with Ministers to frantic meetings preparing for a grilling by a parliamentary committee or late night strategising, their research brought governing to life as an activity. Interpretive governance is animated. These accounts are more reminiscent of the television dramas *Babylon, The Thick of It* and *Yes Minister* than conventional political science. But drama, as a narrative medium, has always spoken to us more effectively than the sciences because human societies are constructed through narrative accounts. So we should not be surprised at the resonance of interpretive accounts of political life for readers, including political insiders themselves. Ethnographic methodology to uncover and explain narratives is thus a key component of the interpretive approach. Given the richness of this interpretive data, along with other interpretive analyses of policymaking conducted at close quarters (see, for example, Shore and Wright, 1997), it would now be difficult to develop theory that leaves out a place for the cultural dimensions of the state and policy networks as important aspects of scientific explanations of governance processes and outcomes.

While interpretive political science has aimed to establish itself as a general approach to political science, it has most of all, in the field of public administration, directly targeted the relevance of the Westminster model as an explanation of British government. Smith has described well the persistence of this concept as the 'eternal return' of the Westminster model (Smith, 1999). He noted that this traditional idea has been so dominant that the teaching of government has lagged far behind reality, with textbooks on British governance haunted by the Westminster model ghost, leading them to pursue a descriptive rather than analytical course, insulated from conceptual developments in research. Indeed, Bevir and Rhodes (2003) have used the term 'governance' as a general signifier of an alternative to the Westminster model, in that it not only offers a theory of governing through networks but also through interpretive practices. In the 'new governance', characterised by a 'differentiated polity', they argue that the unitary state and integrated administration have been replaced by 'a maze of institutions and a complex pattern of decentralized functions. Governance is thus fragmented between organizations that cover different territories or deliver different functions. It occurs in and through networks composed of the relevant governments, departments, agencies, and other social and political actors' (Bevir, 2007: 227). In this environment, the production of meaning is also pluralised and more difficult to manage, such that exchanges between competing interpretations become more widespread. The differentiated polity is thus said to offer a more accurate organising perspective of the British system of government than the Westminster model, and interpretivism brought in as an analytical framework to study it.

Non-British readers of interpretive research often fail to appreciate the pervasiveness of the Westminster model as an entrenched historical ideal – Bevir and Rhodes may advance their programme internationally by doing more to extend their frame of reference beyond the British case to the analysis of dominant traditions in other polities – but entrenched it is, both in textbooks on British politics and in the corridors of Whitehall itself as an explanation of what government is about. Interpretivism takes on this shibboleth, aiming to explain both its redundancy as an analytical construct and its survival as an internal narrative within the civil service by reinterpreting it for its role in governance practice; it is a historical tradition for civil servants, one that tells them how to interpret and act in response to events, even when those events fail to conform to the Westminster ideal. However, it is not a good explanation of governance activity itself, which looks quite different when examined at close quarters. Of course, this depiction of radical change has been contested. Marsh *et al.* (2003)

argue that Bevir and Rhodes's differentiated polity model is inherently pluralist and propose an alternative that builds in structured power imbalances, the 'Asymmetric Power Model'. Bell and Hindmoor (2009) argue that governance does not necessarily mean decentred power, rather that the state has developed new strategies to enhance its capacity to govern. The nature of the state in the age of the new governance remains in question, and the interpretive theory of it is explored further in the chapters in this collection.

This conceptual shift is typical of interpretivism: to reject the Westminster model as a theory of governance and, instead, theorise it as a tradition. In other words, it historicises governance in order to show its contingency, its use in practice, and the possibility of alternatives. Although a novel claim, this historicisation resonates well with the classical conception of British politics as grounded in a historical approach (see Gamble, 1990), in contrast with the formal models common to American political science. Here, we can see the 'Britishness' of Bevir and Rhodes's interpretivism, and how its apparent radicalism for traditionalists may indeed be exaggerated. From this viewpoint, Bevir and Rhodes are simply doing differently what has always been a key aspect and strength of British political studies. Under interpretive scrutiny, the Westminster model is rendered contingent, but *one* tradition, set in competition with others.

This is where the strong view of interpretivism enters, as an epistemological programme. Much of the interpretive controversy has concerned Bevir and Rhodes's definition of the status quo. They label a broad swathe of public administration research as 'modernist empiricism' or 'positivism', to the chagrin of those so labelled, ranging from those who feel this misrepresents them to those who see the representation itself as a straw man depiction. A core element of interpretive scholarship has been to engage in philosophical debates about the basis of political science explanations, particularly in the advocacy of 'anti-foundational' epistemologies. Nevertheless, the nature of Bevir and Rhodes's interpretivism has perhaps not been entirely clear to scholars of public administration, who are sometimes quite unfamiliar with, if not resistant to, varieties of interpretive thought. Debates persist as to how much of Bevir's and Rhodes's work is derived from analytic philosophy and how much from continental thought. For example, they have been described as putting forward a 'hermeneutics' of public administration, given that they do use this term (Hay, 2011; see also Finlayson, 2007). But they themselves reject this classification. This is made clear by Bevir (1999: 17) in his major philosophical work, the *locus classicus* of interpretivism, *The Logic of the History of Ideas*, and later explained by both Bevir and Rhodes in regard to other interpretive approaches (Bevir and Rhodes, 2010). Others have described their approach as another version of idealism, along with its requisite limitations (McAnulla, 2006a). But Bevir and Rhodes have rejected this characterisation as well. Their work might also be understood as akin to post-structuralism, given their anti-foundational philosophy and references to social theorists such as Foucault. In this regard, although they stress that it is important to engage with post-structuralist accounts, they explicitly reject the radical epistemology of post-structuralism as irrational (Bevir, 1999: 6) and post-structuralists have distanced themselves in turn

(Glynos and Howarth, 2008). To add to this, Bevir and Rhodes's extensive use of ethnomethodology has interpretive–pragmatist origins in American symbolic interactionism. However, Smith (2008) points out that, in fact, they implicitly reject much of the conceptual toolkit of this strand of interpretive sociology.

Despite some similarities with all these perspectives, the philosophical basis of their work is quite different and quite specific: it is grounded in 'post-analytic' philosophy. So, although hermeneutics and phenomenological methods have influenced them, Bevir and Rhodes reject continental approaches and remain firmly post-analytic. While such an epistemological orientation is clearly at odds with many political scientists' natural instincts, it does situate them within a strong and influential current of contemporary thought, one which is practised in philosophy departments around the world and which has produced many significant recent philosophers, including Hilary Putnam, Donald Davidson, W. V. Quine, John Rawls, and Sheldon S. Wolin.

The Interpretive Analytical Framework of Bevir and Rhodes

It is their post-analytic philosophy and origins in the History of Ideas school that make Bevir and Rhodes's approach a uniquely British interpretivism, distinct from other interpretive perspectives in political science. This specificity stands out most of all in their strongly individualist ontology, which demarcates them sharply from constructivist approaches in the continental *verstehen* tradition – which I note is hardly marginal in the social sciences, given that Weber (1978) unproblematically describes social science as interpretive in the subtitle and very first pages of *Economy and Society* – as well as variants of post-structuralism, which similarly take a more holistic approach to the analysis of discourse. This is not to say that Bevir and Rhodes do not use aggregate concepts – they refer conventionally to cultures, narratives, and traditions as the source of shared meaning (2005). It is just that they do so with remarkable caution and concern about reification (Bevir and Rhodes, 2010: 88), always returning home to their central theme of explaining political action in terms of the *beliefs of individuals*. From the very beginning, with the publication of *Interpreting British Governance*, it was this claim that proved controversial, with Keith Dowding raising significant objections to it at the time (Finlayson *et al.*, 2004). And it continues to be what separates Bevir and Rhodes from their constructivist cousins, such as Hay, and others who are more sociologically or at least holistically inclined (6, 2014a; see also Leggett, 2011; Smith, 2008). Their entire approach is built upon this central philosophical precept and they have consistently maintained it, despite modifying various aspects of their framework over time through critical encounters with other scholars.

To locate them within a broader perspective, one can affirm that, in general, while interpretive approaches come in many colours, all 'Interpretive approaches to political science focus on the meanings that shape actions and institutions, and the ways in which they do so' (Bevir and Rhodes, 2003). Bevir and Rhodes's work thus sits within the larger family of interpretive political science, but their interpretivism is distinguished by the particular claim that:

We can understand and explain practices and actions adequately only by reference to the beliefs and desires of the relevant actors. Hence to study political life adequately we have to engage in the interpretation of the beliefs and desires of those we study.

(Bevir and Rhodes, 2003: 18)

They insist that this basic claim cannot be bypassed, neither by reference to pre-supposed assumptions about human behaviour as utility maximising nor by objective facts about individuals' social position, defined by class, gender, or race, nor even by social norms or institutional rules. The traditional concepts of social science are thus 'decentred' and the subjective, individual actor is placed at the heart of the action. This decentring applies to institutions in particular, which are reduced in standing to simply being one element of the context in which political actors operate, the effects of which are only manifested through political actors' subjective perspectives. The decentred account leads them away from functionalist, rule-driven explanations in terms of institutional imperatives, towards situating institutions as one element of a set of political *practices*, 'the contingent products of numerous actions inspired by competing narratives' (Bevir and Rhodes, 2003: 38). I note that, although their understanding of prac-tices in terms of individual beliefs is distinctly different from contemporary soci-ological theories of practice (for a critique, see Wagenaar, Chapter 7 this volume, and 2012), this allocation of priority to practices over institutions shares at least a common *aim* with the work of critical scholars in sociology, such as Beck and Bourdieu, who aim to reveal and replace the presumption of a bureaucratic thinker who operates entirely through the institutional categories of the nation-state (Turnbull, 2011). Instead, actors are posited as being embroiled in 'situated practices', actions conceived as interpretations in context. Nonetheless, Bevir and Rhodes do indeed diverge sharply from the more holist perspectives on prac-tice that one finds in contemporary sociology, with the individualist ontology of interpretivism giving a much stronger weight to individual agency, such that it aims to 'repopulate' the state with individuals engaged in dynamic interactions which generate collective meaning (Bevir and Rhodes, 2010).

What they propose is thus quite a radical rethinking of political analysis and a very different form of explanation of political behaviour. Bevir and Rhodes's anti-foundational epistemological position – that there is no reflexively secure starting point for knowledge upon which to anchor interpretations of social facts – necessitates a more modest perspective on knowledge of the political world. Instead of hypotheses and models, institutional frameworks and concomitant interests, or social categories and attendant action-orientations, we find narrative explanations: 'We account for actions, practices and institutions by telling a story about how they came to be as they are and perhaps also about how they are preserved' (2003: 20; see also Bevir and Rhodes, 2006). Interpretivists make interpretations of the interpretations of political actors (Hay, 2011) and, consist-ently, produce explanations of their thinking and behaviour by way of narratives. For inspiration, interpretive political science thus looks away from the natural sciences towards other humanities. A key point about their method is that they subject their perspective to their own method of analysis, locating and explaining the emergence of interpretive political analysis within British political science, thereby exhibiting a concern for reflexivity espoused by too few authors (the question of philosophical consistency is often neglected altogether by many political scientists, or conveniently waved away by some unjustified, pragmatic sleight of hand).

Individual beliefs about governance are located in reference to governing *traditions*, competing historical narratives from which actors draw their beliefs and to which they contribute in turn through their actions. Here again, one might easily confuse this with the hermeneutic conception of tradition, which is a kind of historical episteme that defines an era (Gadamer, 1975). This is the lineage of constructivist approaches, which emphasise more strongly the structuring effects of historical patterns of ideas and norms. This shares some similarities with the concept as it is used in British interpretivism; however, Bevir and Rhodes are careful to distinguish themselves from this view by giving much greater weight to contingency in the effect of traditions (Bevir and Rhodes, 2003: 34). They think of tradition as a source of historical continuity in the weakest sense, as a set of ideas and beliefs which have built up over time, upon which political actors may draw in the process of interpreting and responding to events. They are careful to assert that traditions are not fixed, and therefore not as structuring as norms: traditions are highly contingent and carried only by individuals, who exercise their own agency in bringing them to life (Bevir and Rhodes, 2003: 33).[1] Interpretive traditions are historical narratives that serve as sources of knowledge which enable individual political actors to respond to *dilemmas* encountered in the practice of governance. A dilemma is not an objective account of a political problem, but rather indicates a disjunction between an individual's beliefs and perceptions of policy failure. A dilemma prompts individuals to reflect upon their own beliefs and seek a source of resolution from competing traditions (Bevir and Rhodes, 2003: 64). Thus, dilemmas, once responded to, may in turn reconstruct a historical tradition so as to change its meaning. This also means that events cannot be explained by specific epistemes or ideologies, but rather result from the questioning of, and competition between, a plurality of traditions. The use of traditions is thus pragmatic; they are interpreted and reinterpreted in specific contexts in response to dilemmas. To reiterate the point above, this is a most contingent and even hesitant affirmation of an aggregate concept. The strong emphasis on the beliefs and desires of individuals, and the cautious construction of meta-level concepts in the form of traditions as webs of belief, leads them to prefer the term 'patterns' over social 'structures' when describing consistency in governance practices.

Interpreting British Governance

In their first book, *Interpreting British Governance*, Bevir and Rhodes set out the basis of interpretive political science and applied it to the analysis of the new governance. They examined how the introduction of New Public Management was experienced quite differently in Britain and Denmark because of differences in beliefs and because it produced different dilemmas. Whereas, in Britain, the aim was to increase political control but also deal with the unintended consequences of the proliferation of networks, in Denmark, the key dilemma was to maintain democracy and accountability. Going into more depth about the British case, they argued that Thatcherism was not a uniform phenomenon but had been interpreted through four main, overlapping traditions: Tory, Liberal, Whig, and Socialist. Thatcherism was thus a set of practices that responded to key dilemmas – of welfare dependency, overload, inflation, and globalisation – with each interpreted differently according to the different traditions. Moving on to the New Labour government, they interpreted it as a response to Thatcherism which drew on the British socialist tradition to create a vision of the enabling state, one which aimed to reconstruct the idea of social democracy. Thus, they concluded that, despite the broad coherence of neo-liberal ideas on governance, they were far from uniform in practice, thanks to contingent responses to dilemmas, the reinterpretation of traditions, and the many unintended consequences of reforms. They also analysed the responses of civil servants to the new governance, providing a thick description of individual experiences in the civil service elite, showing that they handled the dilemmas of civil service reform by drawing on tradition, but also that their beliefs changed over time. On the whole, they explain the reform of British governance as a variety of responses to dilemmas that drew on, and amended, a series of overlapping and competing traditions. The combined methodologies of the analysis of webs of meaning, reflected in historical analysis and practices, reveal a patterned but also contingent set of activities, one which is continuously shifting and evolving.

Over the subsequent period, British interpretivism was extended to new research questions, encompassing new cases and, most importantly, involved more in-depth empirical research. In particular, *Governance Stories* (Bevir and Rhodes, 2006) provided an ethnographic analysis of much greater scope. This included rejecting ideas of the 'Blair presidency' in favour of a more nuanced, contingent account of the New Labour government. Bevir and Rhodes showed how conflicts within policymaking fields – in their case study, the National Health Service (NHS) – arise from, and are expressed through, conflicting sets of beliefs. They also added significant weight to their argument for the importance of the unintended consequences of decisions, explaining consistency in police reform not in terms of culture – the popular explanation – but as resulting from the many actions of individuals in response to the dilemmas of contradictory management reforms and expectations. Ultimately, they conclude that governance is not a top-down process, but a bottom-up one, the collective product of many individuals exercising their agency in contingent circumstances. For political science, this is a marked challenge. Governance stories:

> challenge the craving for generality that characterizes comprehensive theories and definitions of contemporary governance. The craving for generality appears in attempts to explain the highly diverse practices of contemporary governance in terms of a monolithic social logic or law-like regularity. In contrast, our governance stories explain diverse practices of contemporary

governance by reference to various contingent actions rooted in overlapping and competing traditions.

(Bevir and Rhodes, 2006: 164)

They later went on to develop a similarly bottom-up depiction of the state, challenging the new institutionalism by controversially declaring it to be 'the stateless state' (Bevir and Rhodes, 2010). Along with a prolific output of joint articles, Bevir produced interpretive theoretical analyses of New Labour (2005), British socialism (2011), governance (2013), and democracy (2010), while Rhodes delivered a comparative analysis of Westminster governance (Rhodes *et al.*, 2009) and an extended ethnography of governance practices (Rhodes, 2011).

Throughout this period, interpretive political science more generally developed in many other directions. But it was in Britain that a continuous contestation has taken place between the British interpretivists and their critics outside the interpretive fold. An essential element of Bevir's and Rhodes's research programmes has been to debate with others in the pages of scholarly journals. The exchanges are too numerous to discuss in detail, but they do cover a wide ground and are instructive for anyone seeking to understand the contours of the interpretive controversy. The history of interpretive British governance studies is a series of disputes over interpretivism and the validity of its interpretations. Aside from single articles that critically address interpretive governance theory (see, for example, 6, 2014b; Colebatch, 2009; Goodwin and Grix, 2011; Marsh, 2009, 2008; Marsh and Hall, 2007; McAnulla, 2006a, 2006b; Peters, 2011; Wagenaar, 2012), symposiums in academic journals dealing with their work can be found on the following topics: governance and public administration (*Australian Journal of Public Administration* 2014 73(3); *British Journal of Politics and International Relations* 6(2); *British Politics* 2011 6(2); *Political Studies Review* 2008 6(2); *Public Administration* 2009 87(1) and 2011 89(1)); Labour party politics (*History of the Human Sciences* 2006 19(1)); and the history of ideas (*History of European Ideas* 2002 28(1–2); *History of the Human Sciences* 2002 15(2); *Intellectual History Review* 2011 21(1); *International Journal of Organization Theory and Behavior* 2011 14(4); *Journal of the History of Ideas* 2012 73(4); *Rethinking History: The Journal of Theory and Practice* 2000 4(3)). Taken together, these amply demonstrate the extent of intellectual engagement between supporters and critics of the British school of interpretive political science.

Interpreting Governance, High Politics, and Public Policy

This volume was produced to mark ten years since the publication of *Interpreting British Governance*. It is an opportunity to consider what mark the interpretive research agenda has made on the field, which of its concepts remain essentially contested by critics, and where interpretive governance research might progress from here. The chapters in this volume continue the conversation between Bevir and Rhodes, and their critics and supporters. The contributions represent a range of opinions about interpretive political science, from those who employ the ideas in their own research to those who reject interpretivism as an analytical framework. In Part I, contributors debate the contribution of interpretivism to research on governance and metagovernance. Patrick Diamond, David Richards, and Martin Smith agree with Bevir and Rhodes that traditions and interpretation are important in understanding political behaviour. However, they argue against the interpretive reading of traditions, contending that the British Political Tradition remains a central influence in determining the shape of the British state. And, against the interpretive finding that power has been decentralised in the differentiated polity, they argue that the dominant institutional arrangements in the UK maintain power in an elite group, occupying power in a centralised state and supporting top-down forms of governance. So, while acknowledging a role for traditions, they reject the view that decentred traditions and beliefs exert so much influence, maintaining instead the importance of institutions in the exercise of state power. Paul Fawcett also makes positive use of the concept of tradition, but explains the benefits of an integrated view which takes in the path dependency effects of traditions along with those of institutions and politico-economic factors as well. He also raises a most interesting question about how interpretive theory has not addressed the implicit, and problematic differentiation between conscious and unconscious actions, and what this means for interpretive theory regarding the interchange, for individuals, between belief and tradition. He broadens the idea of steering the state beyond the use of narratives, including proposing an alternative form of storytelling, *parrhēsia*, for its ability to make a contribution to critical democratic practice. In Chapter 3, Andrew Taylor draws on interpretive concepts in considering the state's response to the Hillsborough football disaster of 1989. He employs the interpretive concept of narrative analysis, but, like Fawcett, aims to broaden and deepen interpretivism, this time by examining how the standard story of the disaster differed from the deeper reality, in which entrenched state powers used public office to construct a narrative that deflected blame on to football supporters. Like Diamond *et al.*, he also aims for an analysis informed by a greater concern for political power. He also departs from interpretivism in using interpretive concepts to develop explanations of cause and effect. In sum, while the authors of all three chapters concede the importance of tradition and narrative in British politics, each continues to take issue with some aspects of Bevir and Rhodes's framework for analysing governance, particularly concerning the place of traditional institutions and the distribution of power in governance systems.

The chapters in Part II consider the role of interpretive research in the study of high politics and political history. Within this subfield, the premises of interpretivism are more readily accepted. Rod Rhodes presents his own current research on high politics, in which he investigates the essential contingency of leadership arising from the problematic relationship between leaders and cabinet colleagues. He elaborates the particularities of the interpretive conception of high politics, which shifts emphasis from institutions to individual leaders located in a contingent political history. Rhodes reinterprets Bulpitt's conception of statecraft, moving away from a realist conception to propose an interpretive reading of high politics as 'court government'. His aim is to blur the genres of the new political history and the political scientific study of the executive in order to provide a better explanation of how elites construct traditions and respond to the dilemmas of leadership. In doing so, he shows the prospective benefits of looking beyond political science to engage more directly with ideas drawn from other humanities. David Craig extends upon a similar theme in his chapter. He provides an engaging intellectual history of the work of John Dunn, noting the resonances of his writing with Bevir and Rhodes's interpretivism so as to better appreciate the underlying philosophical bases of interpretivism and also to show what an interpretive account can contribute to political history and political theory. This chapter clarifies much about the basis of interpretive thought and its location within the history of the field. Also on the topic of political history, Emily Robinson's chapter examines the historical variation in ideas about 'progressive' and 'conservative' politics. She contests this common, contemporary, oppositional definition of British politics, historicising these concepts and rethinking them by reflecting upon how political actors have used and created particular historical narratives that serve as forms of historicised memory (from Pierre Nora). Hence, she is able to introduce a role for emotion in connecting with the past and explaining how this contributes to the propagation of traditions. In so doing, she shows that interpretivism has perhaps been too restricted in its notion of tradition, which itself evinces historical variation in its practical use. For Robinson, traditions are rhetorical devices, holding more or less persuasive appeal for political actors in the present, depending on their emotional experience of the resort to tradition. Here again, Robinson shows the benefits of looking beyond political science to the new political history, sociology, and cultural studies. She shows that interpretivism has much to gain from interdisciplinary engagement.

Finally, in Part III, authors debate the contribution of interpretivism to the study of policymaking. Hendrik Wagenaar comes from a different tradition of interpretive policy analysis, one which is influenced more strongly by continental variants of interpretive theory and methods, as well as interdisciplinary perspectives. Wagenaar offers a thoroughgoing defence of interpretive policy analysis, and in particular of Bevir and Rhodes's version of it. He takes on some of the key criticisms of interpretivism and offers his own rebuttal by looking at Bevir and Rhodes's theoretical framework through an alternative interpretive lens. Specifically, he rejects what he sees as the opposition between belief and action in their work, advocating instead the benefits of a performative theory of social practice. He considers how time, actions, and the objects of political interventions are intermingled in a performative understanding of practice, such that the policymaking world appears constructed from a variety of sources beyond the beliefs of individuals. He points the way to a more practice-informed interpretive political science and explanation of policymaking. Perri 6 and Christine Bellamy fall within the camp of those taking a strong stance against Bevir and Rhodes's epistemological critique of realism. They engage in a robust critique of interpretivism, rejecting its fundamental basis in individual beliefs and desires and its rejection of causal logic. Instead, they defend a realist approach, stressing the primacy of social relations and their institutionalisation in explaining the beliefs and desires of individuals. They argue that interpretivism suffers from methodological individualism, thereby bringing out one of the key points of demarcation between interpretivism and its rivals. They elaborate their position by analysing the history of the effort to develop a single identifying number for each person in the UK, arguing that an interpretive analysis would miss the three main explanatory factors in the case: objective constraints, informal institutions, and styles of thought. Finally, Helen Sullivan agrees with Bevir and Rhodes that interpretivism constitutes a major alternative to the dominant frameworks in public policy research. She locates their work within a broader perspective on interpretive public policy studies, explaining how one of interpretivism's central contributions is to enhance the practical utility of public policy scholarship. She explains how the concept of tradition offers important explanations of community leadership in the transformation of local government, in so far as the process took on multiple meanings for different stakeholders, contributing to a reform process which progressed in multiple, complex trajectories. What emerges is the clear conclusion that the making of meaning in a policy process is equally as important as policy design, showing that policymaking is a contested account of reality, not a programmatic function of top-down administrative edicts.

Finally, Bevir and Rhodes reflect upon the themes of the chapters and set out a direction for the future of interpretive governance research. They reiterate that the primary contribution of interpretivism to understanding governance and public policy is to show they are defined by political contests between a plurality of contingent meanings. Interpretive political science aims to highlight what has been left out by mainstream approaches and to challenge them directly by showing their limited explanatory power. Bevir and Rhodes's research agenda continues to be informed by the '3Rs' of 'rule, rationalities, and resistance'. In rule, the focus is on the high politics of the court and the traditions that inform the perspectives of elite actors within the fragmented world of the new governance. The interpretive study of rationalities refers to understanding the expert managerial technologies which aim to govern conduct within the new governance world, in particular how they produce consistency within an increasingly complex and plural reality. Resistance refers to the agency possessed by actors within this differentiated polity, and thus future research should aim for better accounts of local traditions and practices. Ultimately, they conclude that the way forward for interpretive political science is to blur genres even further by turning more towards the humanities for innovative conceptual and methodological tools. This entails more use of qualitative methods, notably archival research and ethnography.

In an era in which the capacity of government has been called into question by the pluralisation of the actors engaged in governance and public policymaking, the increasing complexity of societies and the intrusion of global forces into local affairs, interpretive political science offers an important means of understanding the fluid dynamics and possibilities of the new governance. Over more than a decade, the robust and unapologetic interpretive political science developed by Bevir and Rhodes has issued a challenge of major significance to the mainstream as a rival account of governance and public policymaking. Interpretivism is currently extending in new directions, regenerated by ideas from the humanities and taking on new questions across political science. Highlighting the variability of meaning for actors in a pluralised world means that even those holding to an institutionalist account cannot ignore the role of the beliefs and ideas of individuals in influencing political behaviour and outcomes, as we see reflected in the chapters in this collection. And by bringing out the agency of individuals across networks, interpretivists show that explanations of even the most bureaucratised political activity cannot be reduced to institutional rules or instrumental–rational action. The future of interpretive governance research will continue to be controversial, but other analytical frameworks must now reckon appropriately with the central features of interpretive accounts.

The chapters in this collection also pose some strong challenges to the interpretive framework, both from without and within the interpretive camp, suggesting that further theoretical refinement is necessary for its advance. What emerges from these debates, the common ground of this collection, and what it shows most forcefully, is that the integration of analytical frameworks is essential. In the future, it will be hybrid models – those that cross epistemological as well as disciplinary demarcations – which offer the most promising avenues for improving scientific explanations of political behaviour.

Note

1 Critics have argued that their typology of traditions is incomplete, particularly in excluding the 'British Political Tradition' (Marsh *et al.*, 2003; Marsh and Hall, 2007; Marsh *et al.*, 2014). Others have argued that they do not go far enough and should give even more room for the uncertain and contested nature of traditions in practice (Finlayson, 2007).

References

6, P. (2014a) 'Explaining Unintended and Unexpected Consequences of Policy Decisions: Comparing three British governments, 1959–74', *Public Administration*, 92(3): 673–91.

6, P. (2014b) 'If Governance is Everything, Maybe it's Nothing', in A. Massey and K. Johnston (eds), *The International Handbook of Public Administration and Governance*, Cheltenham, UK: Edward Elgar.

Bell, S. and Hindmoor, A. (2009) *Rethinking Governance: The centrality of the state in modern society*, Port Melbourne: Cambridge University Press.

Bevir, M. (1999) *Logic of the History of Ideas*, Cambridge: Cambridge University Press.

Bevir, M. (2005) *New Labour: A critique*, London: Routledge.

Bevir, M. (2007) *Encyclopedia of Governance, Volume I*, Thousand Oaks, CA: Sage.

Bevir, M. (2010) *Democratic Governance*, Princeton, NJ: Princeton University Press.

Bevir, M. (2011) *The Making of British Socialism*, Princeton, NJ: Princeton University Press.

Bevir, M. (2013) *A Theory of Governance*, Berkeley, CA: University of California Press.

Bevir, M. and Rhodes, R. A. W. (2003) *Interpreting British Governance*, London: Routledge.

Bevir, M. and Rhodes, R. A. W. (2005) 'Interpretation and Its Others', *Australian Journal of Political Science*, 40(2): 169–87.

Bevir, M. and Rhodes, R. A. W. (2006) *Governance Stories*, London: Routledge.

Bevir, M. and Rhodes, R. A. W. (2010) *State as Cultural Practice*, Oxford: Oxford University Press.

Colebatch, H. K. (2009) 'Governance as a Conceptual Development in the Analysis of Policy', *Critical Policy Studies*, 3(1): 58–67.

Finlayson, A. (2007) 'From Beliefs to Arguments: Interpretive methodology and rhetorical political analysis', *British Journal of Politics and International Relations*, 9(4): 545–63.

Finlayson, A., Bevir, M., Rhodes, R. A. W., Dowding, K., and Hay, C. (2004) 'The Interpretive Approach to Political Science: A symposium', *British Journal of Politics and International Relations*, 6(2): 129–64.

Gadamer, H. G. (1975) *Truth and Method*, London: Sheed & Ward.

Gamble, A. (1990) 'Theories of British Politics', *Political Studies*, 38(3): 404–20.

Glynos, J. and Howarth, D. (2008) 'Structure, Agency and Power in Political Analysis: Beyond contextualised self-interpretations', *Political Studies Review*, 6(2): 155–69.

Goodwin, M. and Grix, J. (2011) 'Bringing Structures Back In: The "governance narrative", the "decentred approach" and "assymmetrical network governance" in the education and sport policy communities', *Public Administration*, 89(2): 537–56.

Hay, C. (2011) 'Interpreting Interpretivism Interpreting Interpretations: The new hermeneutics of public administration', *Public Administration*, 89(1): 167–82.

Leggett, W. (2011) 'The Analytical and Political Limits to "Interpreting" Governance', *British Politics*, 6(2): 241–51.

Marsh, D. (2008) 'Understanding British Government: Analysing competing models', *British Journal of Politics and International Relations*, 10(2): 251–68.

Marsh, D. (2009) 'Keeping Ideas in Their Place: In praise of thin constructivism', *Australian Journal of Political Science*, 44(4): 679–96.

Marsh, D. (2011) 'The New Orthodoxy: The differentiated polity model', *Public Administration*, 89(1): 32–48.

Marsh, D. and Hall, M. (2007) 'The British Political Tradition: Explaining the fate of New Labour's constitutional reform agenda', *British Politics*, 2(2): 215–38.

Marsh, D., Hall, M., and Fawcett, P. (2014) 'Two Cheers for Interpretivism: Deconstructing the British Political Tradition', *Australian Journal of Public Administration*, 73(3): 340–48.

Marsh, D., Richards, D., and Smith, M. (2003) 'Unequal Plurality: Towards an asymmetric power model of British politics', *Government and Opposition*, 38(3): 306–32.

McAnulla, S. (2006a) 'Challenging the New Interpretive Approach: Towards a critical realist alternative', *British Politics*, 1(1): 113–38.

McAnulla, S. (2006b) 'Critical Realism, Social Structure and Political Analysis: A reply to Bevir and Rhodes', *British Politics*, 1(3): 404–12.

Peters, B. G. (2011) 'Response to Mark Bevir and Benjamin Krupicka, Hubert Heinelt and Birgit Sauer', *Critical Policy Studies*, 5(4): 467–70.

Rhodes, R. A. W. (2011) *Everyday Life in British Government*, Oxford; New York: Oxford University Press.

Rhodes, R. A. W., Wanna, J., and Weller, P. (2009) *Comparing Westminster*, Oxford: Oxford University Press.

Shore, C. and Wright, S. (eds) (1997) *Anthropology of Policy: Critical perspectives on governance and power*, New York: Routledge.

Smith, M. (1999) 'Institutionalising the "Eternal Return": Textbooks and the study of British politics', *British Journal of Politics and International Relations*, 1(1): 106–18.

Smith, M. (2008) 'Re-centring British Government: Beliefs, traditions and dilemmas in political science', *Political Studies Review*, 6(2): 143–54.

Turnbull, N. (2011) 'Interpretivism and Practice in Governance Studies: The critique of methodological institutionalism', *British Politics*, 6(2): 252–64.

Wagenaar, H. (2012) 'Dwellers on the Threshold of Practice: The interpretivism of Bevir and Rhodes', *Critical Policy Studies*, 6(1): 85–99.

Weber, M. (1978) *Economy and Society: An outline of interpretive sociology*, Volume 1, Berkeley, CA: University of California Press.

Part I

Governance and Metagovernance

1 Re-centring the British Political Tradition

Explaining Contingency in New Labour's and the Coalition's Governance Statecraft

Patrick Diamond, David Richards, and Martin Smith

Bevir and Rhodes's work, in particular *Interpreting British Governance* (2003), has contributed significantly to understanding British government, especially the way in which tradition and interpretation have influenced political behaviour.[1] Our research has paid considerable attention to how political traditions shape the nature of British politics, the state and the policymaking process (see Diamond, 2013; Diamond and Richards, 2012; Marsh *et al.*, 2001, 2003; Richards, 2008; Richards *et al.*, 2014). The core argument presented in this chapter is that, despite more than 30 years of reform in central government, the British Political Tradition (BPT) has continued to powerfully shape the way in which the UK state operates.[2] Hence, whilst we are sympathetic to the work of Bevir and Rhodes in recognising the centrality of tradition in shaping the political process, our interpretation of traditions and their impact on political life is fundamentally different.

Bevir and Rhodes draw on a long-established interpretivist scholarship (Berger and Luckman, 1967; Garfinkel, 1967; Goffman, 1969) which embraces an approach that prioritises the role of individuals in interpreting traditions. This, in turn, shapes their overall understanding of government. Conversely, in our view, political actors are often shaped by a material reality, in which tradition is understood as a form of political practice, not merely a narrative interpretation of events (McAnulla, 2006).

We would argue traditions contribute to, and are reinforced by, particular institutional arrangements. Moreover, the nature of the institutional arrangements are not neutral, but in the UK context support a particular form of elite government where power is centralised within the executive, based on limited forms of participation and accountability. Our aim in this chapter is to illustrate that, while the 1997–2010 Labour governments and the Coalition government up to September 2014 have presented apparently distinct governing projects, in practice there were strong commonalities between them, each having drawn on a deeply embedded aggregated tradition based on a series of centralising tendencies ineluctably associated with the BPT. So while all parties throughout this period have made rhetorical commitments to localism, the reality of governing has been the continuation of a centralised, top-down and elitist form of government. From this perspective, this aggregate-tradition has shaped the process of governmental practice in the UK and in so doing offers a contrasting understanding of British governance than that presented by Bevir and Rhodes's 'decentred' approach.

The Ambiguity of Tradition

Bevir and Rhodes present a 'decentred' analysis which aims to disaggregate various traditions and interpretations, focusing on the diverse actions and practices inspired by those traditions in the processes of governance. The decentring of British government is intended as a corrective to the misleading impression conveyed by the Westminster model and positivist accounts of governance, which are portrayed as reifying human action, viewing government as hermetically sealed within the central institutions of the state (Judge, 2006). A decentred approach highlights, 'a more diverse view of state authority and its exercise', and focuses on how, 'patterns of rule arise as the contingent products of diverse actions and political struggles informed by the varied beliefs of situated agents' (Bevir and Rhodes, 2010: 16).

Bevir and Rhodes's analysis rejects the premise of earlier narratives of the state that institutions can fix human actions and practices, along with what they regard as 'unhelpful phrases' such as 'path dependency' which ignore the beliefs of situated agents and the role of tradition in explaining why actors perform particular actions (Bevir and Rhodes, 2010: 17). In addition, the approach conveys 'shared truths' about the shift from markets and hierarchies to networks which has apparently occurred over the last three decades through the New Right and New Labour (Bevir and Rhodes, 2001: 26).

There is, nonetheless, an ambiguity in Bevir and Rhodes's interpretivism and the decentred approach illustrated in their analysis of traditions. Traditions are placed at the centre of their analysis, but the meaning of 'tradition' remains somewhat elusive. Bevir and Rhodes claim that 'traditions persist', as indeed they must, but traditions are initial beliefs that people hold, and 'every strand of tradition is in principle open to change' (2003: 33); this inevitably raises the question of when it becomes a different tradition. They argue:

> We define traditions, therefore, as a set of understandings that someone receives during socialization. A governmental tradition is a set of inherited beliefs about the institutions and history of government. Although tradition is unavoidable, it is so as a starting point, not as something that determines later performance. We are cautious about representing tradition as an unavoidable presence in everything people do in case we leave too slight a role for situated agency.... (W)e see tradition mainly as a first influence on people.
>
> (2006b: 7)

Tradition, then, is a concept that does an enormous amount of work for Bevir and Rhodes. It is a process of socialisation, a form of 'inherited belief' (different from other types of beliefs), the basis of institutions and a set of power relations. Although tradition is unavoidable, it is not, 'an unavoidable presence'. While presumably it is transmitted through socialisation, those who are doing the transmitting must have some agency to act outside of the tradition. Exactly what tradition is doing, and what it is sustaining in the political world, is at times difficult to discern: the causal relationship between traditions and beliefs is left ambiguous in Bevir and Rhodes's analysis (Hay, 2004: 146).

There is no doubt that traditions have different interpretations of governance; there are a variety of ways of narrating and understanding changes that have occurred. However, it is questionable what particular traditions or narratives actually tell us about the process of change. Bevir and Rhodes identify, for instance, a 'socialist' tradition in the work of Mandelson and Liddle (1996), highlighting 'joined-up' government as the narrative. One question that arises is why these authors should be identified as representing a 'socialist' tradition, and why joined-up government is prioritised as the key narrative of Labour's approach to public sector reform? Bevir and Rhodes (2003: 197) claim that 'New Labour rejects the command bureaucracy of Old Labour with its emphasis on hierarchy, authority and rules'.

There can be little doubt that rhetorically New Labour rejected Old Labour, but again, in government, New Labour did anything but eschew, 'hierarchy, authority and rules' (Richards, 2008) and in practice there were considerable similarities (Smith, 2014). Hierarchy, authority, and rules are the 'iron cage' of the modern world. Even governance networks are networks of hierarchies and not flat, decentralised organisations. Labour has often resorted to hierarchy and rules as a mechanism for policy delivery: it is revealing, for example, that, after the 2001 'Foot and Mouth' crisis, Blair contemplated the idea of using the military as the most effective mechanism for delivering his goals; it seemed to be the only organisation able to deal with the crisis decisively (McConnell and Stark, 2002).

The narrative of New Labour was about reforming public services to improve delivery and alter social behaviour, again raising the question of how we assess a particular set of ideas as emblematic of a tradition. Given their emphasis on decentring, it is somewhat surprising that Bevir and Rhodes claim New Labour's tradition is socialist, rather than a melded blend of traditions and political ideologies drawing on the Westminster model, New Public Management, social liberalism, ethical socialism, and social democracy (Richards and Smith, 2004a). Joined-up government was not a new idea that developed within the socialist tradition, but something first alluded to in the 1950s during the Churchill Administration and more recently deployed by the Major government in relation to welfare policy (Kavanagh and Richards, 2001). Joined-up government was a pragmatic response to fragmented governance and a weak Cabinet Office, a relatively small part of the reform process that emanated from a Labour government attempting to overcome a historical reputation for failing to deliver in office.

Power Relations and a Centrist Tradition

As Bevir and Rhodes point out, the Westminster model is a legitimising myth; because politicians and officials believe in the myth, it can sometimes explain their behaviour. For instance, Bevir and Rhodes (2006a: 119) ask a permanent secretary what he wants of a minister and the reply is, 'clear leadership ... engagement with us on the really difficult issues. I want a Minister to be very influential with their colleagues'. These are stock answers found in numerous studies of the civil service (Marsh *et al.*, 2001). They reflect how far officials are socialised into the view that ministers are the key actors, but they must have a symbiotic relationship with officials, based on trust.

As a myth, the Westminster model may represent how officials and ministers perceive the political system, but, however strong their beliefs, it does not offer an accurate picture of how power operates in Britain. We need, as Dowding (2004: 140) highlights, to distinguish between myth and the material reality; while there is no doubt that myth is important in explaining how the system works, it does not represent the material reality about either the power of ministers or officials; this is what political science needs to investigate. Moreover, Bevir and Rhodes do not adequately address the issue of power; Rhodes (2007: 1250) states that for him, 'power is structured in a few competing elites'. For Rhodes, power is not positional but, 'is contingent and relational; that is, it depends on the relative power of other actors' (2007: 1247). Of course, there is a degree to which power is indeed structural. Having a certain position provides potential powers, resources, and capabilities (Stones, 1996: 34). Being Chancellor of the Exchequer, for example, gives an individual greater influence over economic policy than other ministers.

We are not convinced that Bevir and Rhodes' theoretical and methodological framework allows them to explore the multiple and fluid layers of power relations. This is partly explained by the interpretivist underpinnings of their approach, and with it the ostensible rejection of structure. In relation to power, there is an almost conscious avoidance of the issue; the only real discussion of power is the argument that tradition does much of the work of power in a post-structuralist sense – but Bevir and Rhodes strongly imply that they do not see tradition as related to power (Richards and Smith, 2014). The focus on traditions and beliefs does not adequately explain the nature of power relations, nor how they are shaped. Instead, we discern an essentially co-constitutive relationship between traditions and institutions: institutions reflect and embody certain power relations which are legitimised by, and reinforced through, an appeal to particular traditions. Hence, the key example we focus on in this chapter is how the institutions which reinforce the BPT are deployed to reassert the power of the central elite in controlling access to the policymaking process.

Centring Tradition in British Politics and Institutional Layering

There is a need for a 'centred' approach to the BPT and the Westminster model that examines the processes of institutional 'layering' in the restructuring of the state, and the asymmetrical power relations that constitute the British political system. The notion of a decentred or 'differentiated' polity (the word 'model' was discreetly dropped more than a decade ago) defines the work of Bevir and Rhodes but over-emphasises the diffuse nature of power, and the extent to which the British state has been 'hollowed out' (see Richards, 2008; Diamond, 2013). The nature of change in the British state over the last three decades has been powerfully conditioned by deeply embedded institutional processes. Since the early 1980s, at the material level, there has been structural continuity in the evolution of the state (Tant, 1993; Ling, 1998; Marsh *et al.*, 2001; Evans, 2003; Hall, 2011). From an institutionalist perspective, 'institutions shape actors' strategic choices' (Steinmo, 2010: 14). Thatcher, Blair, and Cameron as political leaders may have had a particular vision of how they wished to transform the state, but the decisions their governments made were shaped, though not necessarily determined, by inherited institutional practices and rules of the game. As a consequence, changes have been generally evolutionary rather than radical, based on a process of institutional layering (Steinmo, 2010).

As such, institutional theory illustrates the difficulty of reforming institutions and, more particularly in the UK case, the degree to which path dependency shapes policy outcomes, a concept dismissively rejected by Bevir and Rhodes. To explain path dependency it is useful to invoke the concept of hybridity, as crystallised by Thelen's understanding of institutions, highlighting the:

> remarkable resilience of some institutional arrangements even in the face of huge historic breaks, and, on the other hand, ongoing subtle shifts beneath the surface of apparently stable formal institutions that, over time, can completely redefine the functions and political purposes they serve.
>
> (2002: 101)

Deeply embedded institutions, as in the case of the UK, exhibit considerable resilience even when confronting potential critical junctures. Thelen (2002: 101) points out that: 'even "sticky" institutions that persist over long stretches of time undergo subtle but significant changes in terms of their form and functions'. In Britain, the context of reform over time has been characterised by growing pressures for change, alongside commitment to major structural reform of the state. What emerges then, rather than radical change, is a process of 'institutional layering':

> New coalitions may design novel institutional arrangements but lack the support, or perhaps the inclination, to replace pre-existing institutions established to pursue other ends. While each individual change is consciously designed to serve specific goals, the layering of successive innovations results in institutions that appear more haphazard than the product of some overarching master plan.
>
> (Schickler, 2001: 15)

In this context, institutional layering can be understood as path dependent, rather than a critical juncture leading to a paradigmatic shift. The options for institutional reform are inevitably assessed within the context of existing organisational arrangements, constitutional conventions, and rules of the game (Diamond, 2013). In the UK, this approach can be used to explain why reforms are usually not constructed on the basis of 'new' institutions replacing 'old' ones, but instead new institutional forms are layered on top of existing systems. Richards and Smith's (2004a) notion of a 'hybrid state' in the UK can be understood as part of a layering process that stems from the scale of sunken resources within deeply embedded institutions. For the political class, it is much less costly to adapt existing governance forms rather than to develop new arrangements (Alexander, 2001: 254). This is an approach that has been highlighted in the two main Westminster parties' immediate responses to the fallout from the 2014 Scottish referendum, guided by a desire to graft reform on to the existing Westminster model, rather than overhaul it.

More importantly within the British context, there has been a strong institutional incentive over the last three decades for politicians to offload responsibility for policy delivery, while ensuring that their resources remain untouched at the centre. Steinmo (2010) illustrates how capitalist democracies evolve and adapt, arguing they do so within an existing historical and institutional context. Consequently, while the post-2008 financial crisis pressurised states to reform, how this occurred was shaped by a variety of contingent forces associated with distinct institutional pathways. After 2008, the post-crisis response in Britain can be understood as an attempt to adapt to changed circumstances (not least the fiscal crisis of the welfare state and constitutional reform after the Scottish referendum), conditioned by a particular set of inherited (*sticky*) institutional forms and traditions.

The BPT as an Aggregate Concept: The Dominant Tradition in British Politics

From our perspective, an aggregated understanding of the BPT as the dominant tradition in British politics helps explain why both New Labour and the Conservative–Liberal Democrat Coalition up until 2014 have been drawn back to a state-centric model of governance, despite at the outset offering a rhetorical appeal to change and reform. In the UK, the nature of reform is strongly shaped by the ideas and institutional framework associated with the BPT. British politics is organised around an ideational framework advocating an essentially uniform, elitist and top-down system that delivers strong, seamless, but accountable government (Oakeshott, 1962; Birch, 1964; Greenleaf, 1983a, 1983b, 1987). The British political system derives its character from specific historical processes reflecting elitist notions of responsible and representative government (see Tant, 1993; Evans, 2003; Marsh and Hall, 2007; Richards, 2008; Hall, 2011).

Crucially, this led to the perpetuation of a 'power-hoarding' governance paradigm (Barry, 1965; Richards and Smith, 2004b; King, 2007). The argument is that the BPT has a unique shaping effect: the political class – ministers and civil servants – are socialised into a tradition predicated on preserving centralised power and resources. The paradox of this tradition is that, in the last three decades, different governments have been rhetorically committed to reducing the role of the state and devolving power from the centre in response to a perceived crisis in state–society relations (Richards *et al.*, 2014). However, each has retained the belief that a strong state is crucial for achieving their governing aspirations (Gamble, 1994; Richards, 2008; Hall, 2011). This reveals the extent to which Britain's institutional framework is constructed by a 'power-hoarding' rather than a 'power-dispersing' model, with strong incentives operating for the retention of power at the centre (Richards and Smith, 2004b). From this perspective, up until the 2014 Scottish referendum, reforms have not led to a significant dispersal of power away from the centre, but instead reflect a process of overlaying new, often contradictory, governance processes on to existing institutional forms. We illustrate this empirically by drawing on a comparative case study of the statecraft projects pursued by the post-1997 New Labour Government, and the post-2010 Coalition administration.

The Ideational Framework: The Third Way and the Big Society

The role of ideas in governance and statecraft is important, and Bevir and Rhodes consistently emphasise the role of the ideational in structuring political outcomes. 'The Third Way' and 'The Big Society' are the labels most routinely attached to the ideational framework around which the statecraft projects of New Labour and Cameron's Conservative party have respectively coalesced. There are, of course, obvious distinctions between these approaches, but also striking similarities. As we shall see below, in both cases pluralising instincts have been checked by the material reality of a state-centric mode of governance which trenchantly protects the Westminster model.

The Third Way and the New Labour Governments 1997–2010

Anthony Giddens' *Third Way* argued that, since the 1970s, the growth of economic and political internationalisation combined with greater diversification in society had undermined the ability of the traditional state to control social and economic outcomes. Rigid hierarchical state structures, most often associated with Weberian models of bureaucracy and welfare provision, were no longer capable of meeting the aspirations or fulfilling the needs of an increasingly heterogeneous society. The Third Way sought to resolve a crucial dilemma within the Labour Party – the need to accept some of the key reforms that had been initiated by Thatcherism, while not turning its back on Keynesian welfarism. New Labour had to come to terms with this shift, reappraising its traditional understanding of a society based on a hierarchical, bureaucratic state. The rhetorical solution sought by the Third Way was to move beyond the statist approaches of the 1970s and the market-led policies of the 1980s. The Third Way advocated the idea of networks of institutions and individuals cooperating together in mutually beneficial partnerships based on trust in order to deliver public goods. As such, the Third Way approach to governance inspired the search for alternative models of state delivery, as Labour came to power in 1997 after 18 years in the opposition wilderness.

Labour's Reform Programme Mark I: 'Wiring Up' the British State and Modernising Government

Initially, the emphasis after 1997 was on 'joining-up' government to improve policy coordination, combined with initiatives to modernise the civil service. Labour's programme sought to overcome debilitating Whitehall turf wars which led to disputes between departments over territory, resources and power. *Next Steps* reforms delegating delivery to 'arms-length' agencies were consolidated by the New Labour government, although *Next Steps* did not address the weakness of Whitehall policy coordination (Richards and Smith, 2004a).

The *Modernising Government* White Paper (Cm 4310, 1999) committed the civil service to major changes: New Labour was concerned not only with improving efficiency, but redefining the role of Whitehall as a delivery agent. However, the capacity of departments to work together was constrained by the doctrine of ministerial accountability. Moreover, New Labour was mistrustful of large sections of the civil service. This was not ideological mistrust, a belief that Whitehall mandarins had a hidden agenda. The concern was that civil servants lacked the capacity to effectively develop and implement policy: as such, New Labour procured policy advice from a range of external agents and institutions. A plethora of tsars, taskforces, and ad hoc bodies were created, curtailing officials' monopoly of advice, alongside the appointment of unprecedented numbers of special advisers (Seldon, 2006; Blick and Jones, 2010; Richards, 2009; Smith, 2011).

The granting of executive powers to Jonathan Powell (Number Ten Chief of Staff) and Alistair Campbell (Number Ten Director of Communications) to instruct civil servants, alongside the creation of the Strategic Communications Unit in Number Ten, were attempts to consolidate the centre's grip over the machinery of state. One senior minister in the New Labour years argued vociferously; 'It was an inspired decision ... creating a Chief of Staff who would act within Number Ten as a pivotal point between the civil service, the political advisers, the communications staff, and government relations'.[3] As Blair remarked, 'I was conscious of the fact that if you didn't have a strong centre, you weren't going to be able to enforce the culture of New Labour throughout the system'.[4]

Nonetheless, there was growing frustration at the inertia of the state bureaucracy, an acknowledgement that the centre needed to push even harder for change. In 1998–99, the NHS experienced one of the worst 'winter flu crises' for half a century, focusing attention on Labour's failure to deliver sustained improvements in public sector performance (Riddell, 2006; Barber, 2007). This made a 'command bureaucracy' attractive to frustrated, apparently impotent, politicians operating the 'rubber levers' of the traditional Whitehall machine. The levers were pulled with ever greater force after 1997. However, there was a dawning realisation that too often they were not connected to anything.[5]

Labour's Reform Programme Mark II: State-centric Core Executive
'Command and Control'

As a consequence, New Labour's second term entailed further changes in the political and administrative machinery of the state. The Number Ten Policy Unit more than doubled in size, re-established as the Prime Minister's Policy Directorate after the 2001 election. The Directorate's role was not only to provide policy advice to the Prime Minister, but to oversee departments through a network of ministers and special advisers. Within the Cabinet Office, an array of prime ministerial units was created, including the Prime Minister's Delivery Unit (PMDU) and the Prime Minister's Strategy Unit (PMSU). The PMDU coordinated bi-monthly meetings between the Prime Minister, the Treasury and the Secretary of State, agreeing the indicators by which success should be measured through Public Service Agreements (PSAs). This created a line of accountability directly to the centre in 10 Downing Street.

The aim of the reforms was to shift the balance of power towards the centre, institutionalising departmental dependency on Number Ten over politics and policy. This was combined with an approach to public sector restructuring designed to improve productivity and outcomes through centralised control, including sanctions and targets (Newman, 2005). The centralisation of core executive capacity is justified by one of Blair's ministerial allies:

> Blair thought the Cabinet and large swathes of the civil service would have blocked what he was trying to do. And therefore what you had to do was step around them … operate a sort of *force majeure* that didn't give them the chance to fight back.[6]

Number Ten enhanced its implementation role by establishing direct relationships with front-line providers and local agencies, launching delivery initiatives from street crime to school truancy that bypassed departments (Barber, 2007; Blair, 2010). In relation to education, the Academies initiative was conceived in 10 Downing Street; Number Ten advisers continued to directly manage and oversee the programme alongside departmental officials (Blair, 2010; Adonis, 2012). There was little confidence that the Department for Education and Skills had the capacity to deliver reforms.

The post-1997 Labour Administration argued that the traditional public sector model did not provide the most effective delivery of public goods; it was rigid ('one-size fits all'); cumbersome to reform; often focused more on the producer than the consumer. The challenge was that the delivery of public services was too often controlled by producers: public servants were 'knaves' as well as 'knights', motivated by self-interest as much as altruism (Le Grand, 2003). Labour sought to control public sector producers by increasing consumer choice, together with strengthened core executive oversight. For example, it enhanced central capacity over delivery, establishing the PMDU as a mechanism for ensuring that public services did what the government wanted. Labour sought pluralism in public services, but within a highly controlled context. This hybrid between the marketisation of neo-liberal public management, and the retention of a hierarchical state, became increasingly explicit during the post-1997 period (Richards, 2011). Labour layered a pluralised notion of policy delivery on to the traditional institutions of the Westminster model, reconstituting the core executive, notably by strengthening the centre through a period of concerted unit-building (Richards and Smith, 2006). The cumulative impact of New Labour's reforms over 13 years were significant changes in the nature of the state and the UK core executive:

- Under Blair and Brown, there was a fundamental change in the size and influence of the centre (Heffernan, 2003; Marquand, 2004; McAnulla, 2006; Richards, 2008).
- There were major alterations in the nature of the policymaking process, which became more empirical and guided by performance data (Barber, 2007; Richards, 2008).
- Performance indicators within PSAs meant that departments were increasingly held to account by the centre (Barber, 2007).
- The structure of dependency shifted: Number Ten had direct contact with front-line providers at 'street-level' (Marinetto, 2003; Richards, 2008). The role of the centre went beyond coordination, intervening directly in the process of implementation (Richards, 2008; Smith *et al.*, 2011).

What is striking, however, is the determination of New Labour ministers to preserve and uphold the ethos of strong government, elitist political rule, and executive dominance (Judge, 2006; Marsh and Hall, 2007). Despite the radical constitutional reform agenda and the rhetoric of transferring power back to localities, it is important to consider how far the Westminster model acted as a constraint diminishing the impact of structural and institutional change in the British polity.

The Big Society and the Conservative–Liberal Democratic Coalition Government

In opposition, Cameron's Conservatives argued that New Labour had failed to translate the rhetoric of the Third Way into reality. The notion of the 'Big Society' was presented as an alternative to what was portrayed as New Labour's centralised, state-oriented approach. Nonetheless, the 2008 financial crisis created a dilemma for the Conservative Party: there was an apparent need for fiscal retrenchment, more market-oriented strategies, and a reduction in the role of government. At the same time, the continuing popularity of universal, 'free at the point of use' public services, particularly in the core areas of health and education, was consistently emphasised by voters. The Big Society offered an alternative conception of the state. A reduction in the provision of public goods would be substituted by social action involving voluntary and civic associations. Social enterprise and the private sector would deliver public services, a 'post-bureaucratic society' reconciling the tension between reducing spending and maintaining welfare (Cameron, 2010).

Nonetheless, since 2010, the programme has achieved mixed results and the Big Society narrative increasingly disappeared from the Coalition's political lexicon. According to Philip Blond, a figure closely associated with the early Cameron project:

> The Big Society has – while not fatally but certainly tragically – become identified with the cuts and politics of the deficit agenda.... The Treasury ... regard the Big Society with amused indifference – consequently the agenda they are following looks like Thatcherism redux with salami slicing of services and pushing cuts out to the front line.
>
> (Blond, 2011)

Rhetorically, the Coalition government initially reacted against what it saw as the development of a centralised core executive under New Labour, appealing to the notion of a re-invigorated Westminster model (HM Government, 2012). The Government stated (Cm 7996, 2011: 8): 'Across Government we are committed to ending top-down decision making and the tendency in Whitehall to develop one-size-fits-all solutions which ignore the specific needs and behaviour patterns of local communities'. In the first 12 months, the Coalition's approach was to re-establish 'cabinet government' in riposte to New Labour's supposed 'sofa-style'. This relied on reducing the role of special advisers and restoring power to departments and minsters. At the same time, it reaffirmed one of the core tenets of the Westminster model: 'Policy will be decided by ministers alone, with advice from officials. Boards will give advice and support on the operational implications and effectiveness of policy proposals, focusing on getting policy translated into results' (Cabinet Office, 2010). The PMDU and the PMSU were abolished, replaced by a new Efficiency and Reform Group, chaired by the Cabinet Office Minister, Francis Maude. Significantly, unlike the New Labour model, central policy capacity under the Coalition was to be provided by civil servants, not political advisers. Paradoxically, this could be understood as reinforcing the traditional Westminster model: a core executive built round the minister–civil servant relationship.

Governing at the Centre

There are elements of the Coalition's agenda, nonetheless, which ostensibly challenge key tenets of the Westminster model. *The Civil Service Reform Plan* (HM Government, 2012) illustrates how the government is re-envisioning the central state. It has committed itself to a 23 per cent reduction in the civil service by 2016; in meeting this goal, by March 2014, the number of civil servants was 407,000, a fall of 24 per cent since its most recent peak in early 2005 (see Figure 1.1).

In addition, like the previous government, there is a desire to radically pluralise the policy process, first, in terms of policy formulation by moves to further break up Whitehall's traditional monopoly over policy advice through the introduction of a Contestable Policy Fund as a mechanism to 'draw directly

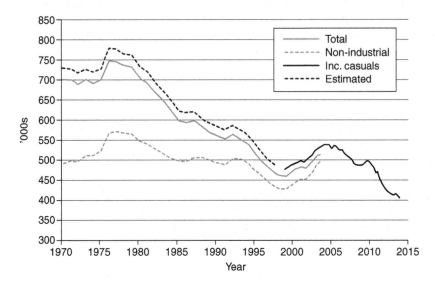

Figure 1.1 Civil Service Headcount 1970–2014 (source: Civil Service Statistics Bulletin, 5 November 2014. Available at www.parliament.uk/briefing-papers/sn02224. pdf [accessed 25 March 2014])

on thinking, evidence and insight from experts beyond Whitehall' (HM Government, 2012). The *Civil Service Reform Plan* (HM Government, 2012) heralded the introduction of 'Extended Ministerial Offices', incorporating increasing numbers of political advisers and outside 'experts' appointed on fixed term contracts. Second, in terms of policy delivery, replacing 'the old binary choice between monolithic in-house provision and full scale privatisation by … joint ventures, employee-owned mutuals and entering into new partnerships with the private sector' (HM Government, 2012: 8).

Moreover, the Coalition rhetorically abandoned a key element of New Labour's governance statecraft – the use of targets to retain central control over a more pluralised model of public sector delivery. After May 2010, the Government set about formally abolishing the use of targets in criminal justice, education, housing, local government, and the health service. PSAs and Departmental Strategic Objectives were replaced by Departmental Business Plans that were presented as offering a different form of control and accountability, eschewing the language of targets. *Priorities* and *transparency* became the accepted *lingua franca* of public services: the government's new mantra was a shift from 'bureaucratic accountability' to 'democratic accountability' predicated on a distinctive mode of governance – that of direct accountability to the public through enhanced transparency:

to enable the public to hold politicians and public bodies to account; to reduce the deficit and deliver better value for money in public spending; and to realise significant economic benefits by enabling businesses and non-profit organisations to build innovative applications and websites using public data.

(Cameron, 2010)

In particular, data transparency through government's use of the Internet was seen as an alternative to target-based, central bureaucratic control, acting as the key medium to deliver a new form of democratic accountability. Nonetheless, the use of targets in everything but name soon re-emerged. An analysis of the Coalition's Departmental Business Plans identified that the number of 'strategic objectives' had actually risen relative to the last year of the New Labour Administration (see Table 1.1 below).

Contained within the 2012 *Civil Service Reform Plan* was a detailed set of objectives for each Departmental Permanent Secretary over a designated period, specifying business delivery objectives, performance measures, and milestones (see Gov.UK, 2012). So, while the rhetorical appeal to 'targets' was formally removed from the Whitehall lexicon, their use, firmly established by the New Labour Administration as a tool to retain state-centric control over public service delivery, had not disappeared under the Coalition. From the centre downwards, a vibrant 'cascading culture of target-setting' remained intact (Gains, 2003; Richards, 2008; Talbot, 2013).

Table 1.1 Breakdown of Departmental Targets 2010–12

Department	New Labour Targets (2010)	Coalition Targets (Average for 2011 and 2012)	Increase in Number of Targets
Education	6	25	+19
Treasury	2	24	+22
Home Office	7	35	+28
Defence	3	24	+21
Justice	5	36	+31
HMRC	3	5	+2
Foreign Office	10	17	+7
Health	3	33	+30
Energy and Climate	7	18	+11
Work and Pensions	8	37	+29
Transport	4	17	+13
International Development	7	21	+14
Environment	8	17	+9
Culture, Media, Sport	4	27	+23
Local Government	6	37	+31
Business	6	49	+43
Cabinet Office	6	35	+29
TOTAL	95	453	+358
AVERAGE	6	27	21

Source: Talbot (2013).

Reform, New Localism, and Devolving Power from the Centre

Elsewhere, the Coalition has attempted to pursue its commitment to the Big Society through its 'new localism' agenda. Both parties have expressed a strong commitment to return power to local communities. This commitment materialised in the 2011 Localism Act. Lowndes and Pratchett (2012) argue that the Act is a radical measure granting a 'general power of competence': local government can in theory undertake any policy initiative it chooses. This is a reversal of the previous Westminster model definition of local government acting within a framework set by Parliament. Local government is being given greater control over local services and, with the abolition of the Regional Development Agencies, economic development has passed to Local Enterprise Partnerships which allow local authorities to lead on the growth agenda. The Chancellor, George Osborne, has spoken of creating a 'Northern Powerhouse' with 'devo-max' and elected mayors for English cities.

Nonetheless, while the Coalition has demonstrated a rhetorical commitment to localism, it is played out within the structured context provided by the British constitution and the BPT – sovereignty formally resides in Westminster; decisions on the direction of policy are determined at the centre. Localism is pursued in an environment where local government is undergoing a sizeable retrenchment in the budget it receives from the centre. The 2010 Comprehensive Spending Review outlined a 27 per cent (£5.5 billion) reduction in the local government budget – from £29.7 billion in 2010–11 to £24.2 billion in 2014–15 (HM Treasury, 2010: 81). The Comprehensive Spending Review in 2013 implied real terms cuts of 33.2 per cent in the period between 2011 and 2018, as local government is a 'non-protected' department. One of the consequences is the large number of job cuts; the Chair of the Local Government Association identified 200,000 local authority redundancies by 2013 (see also, Institute for Fiscal Studies, 2013). Lowndes and McCaughie argue that after 2017 more severe cuts will occur:

> particularly as the percentage of the population over 65 rises to above 20%. National debt looks set to hit 90% of GDP by 2016, which is more than twice pre-crisis levels.... The LGA [Local Government Association] estimates that the costs of adult social care will absorb 90% of council expenditure by 2020, suggesting the services most popular with the public (libraries and leisure facilities) could effectively wither on the vine.
>
> (2013: 534)

Central government is specifying the scale of retrenchment at the local level, but deflecting criticism, arguing that it is up to local government to determine how the available money should be spent. Councils have responded by making substantial cuts to key services, sometimes in contentious areas; for example, care of the elderly and in children's services relating to the Sure Start programme. This created tensions with the centre on the grounds that such cuts challenge the Government's commitment to protect 'front-line' services, but also that cuts were seen as 'politically driven and too deep' (Cameron, 2011).

A further irony is that the Government's attempt to pluralise policy delivery has permanently altered the relationship between central and local government. In education policy, this has meant the establishment of more Academy schools independent of Local Education Authorities (LEAs) in England based on bilateral, contractual arrangements with the Department for Education in Whitehall. Following the 2010 Academies Act, the number of academies increased from 203 to 2083 by February 2014. In addition, the Coalition has supported 'free schools' set up by parents or third sector organisations, but funded by central government. Accountability for the performance of 'free schools' resides directly with the department, rather than at the local authority level. This highlights the 'layering' of new institutional forms, but also tensions in the Coalition's strategy between devolving and pluralising policy, alongside a well-worn tendency to revert back to centralised management.

What we can see within the British political system is that politicians continue to draw on the Westminster model and BPT in defining, shaping, and legitimising their behaviour (see Richards, 2008). In so doing, interventionism has remained their dominant modus operandi. The political imperative is the view of ministers that they need to deliver 'results' using the interventionist, top-down precepts of the BPT to drive through policies that will secure their re-election.

The irony is that while the Coalition has been determined to stress a vibrant new localism agenda devolving powers away from the centre across an array of policy areas, the reform programme between 2010 and 2015 has been enacted in a highly centralist style, true to the exigencies of the BPT. As Jones (2010) observes: 'Ministers are essentially promoting sub-localism, taking powers from councils allegedly to give to 'Big Society' actors below the local-authority level, but ineluctably sucking up key control functions to Whitehall at the same time'. In a sense what is more significant is the development of a contradictory notion of the state that emerged within the Coalition. The Conservatives exhibit strong opposition to the 'Nanny State' and 'welfare dependency', reinforcing their belief that the size and scope of the UK state should be drastically reduced. Indeed, some Conservative MPs have called for further large-scale cuts in public expenditure. At the same time, the Coalition is prepared to use the power of the Westminster model to impose spending cuts, maintaining a cohesive 'national' polity through a strong, centralising state but qualifying the localism agenda.

Conclusion

The interpretive analysis of British politics and government originating in Bevir and Rhodes's *Interpreting British Governance* (2003) has underlined the centrality of tradition to our understanding of political life. The governing strategy of both Labour and Conservative administrations has offered ample evidence of a continuing commitment to a distinctive political tradition manifested in the Westminster Model. Rather than delivering on the rhetorical claim of a 'bottom-up revolution', familiar governance patterns emerge, built around a strong core executive. In light of this, Bevir and Rhodes's decentred analysis appears somewhat inadequate for understanding this period of governance. Such an approach cannot illuminate the contingency underlying New Labour and the Coalition government's statecraft. Nor is there an adequate theorisation of power relations and the role of institutions which can explain the ongoing commitment to a 'power-hoarding' model: the tendency of both New Labour and the Coalition to revert to a state-centric conception of governance has been marked. New Labour was committed to reforming the state and returning power to communities, but pursued its strategy through a top-down approach concerned with reinforcing the capacity of the centre, revealing the ongoing resonance of the BPT. The desire for political success, both in electoral and policy terms, led Labour to reinforce the power of the centre.

The Coalition Government argued that the need to respond to the 2008 crisis opened up a 'window of opportunity' to recalibrate the British state. As New Labour did in 1997, it appealed to a narrative of the need for a 'new politics' as part of a 'bottom-up revolution' (Richards, 2011). Yet the initial rhetorical claims that the Coalition's reforms would signal the death knell of the BPT, delivering the 'biggest shake-up in British democracy since 1832' (Clegg, 2010), subsequently appeared for much of the Coalition's period in office as little more than post-election hubris.

In a climate of austerity, the pressure for strong, powerful, potentially unpopular, political leadership premised on 'command and control' is considerable. This chapter highlighted why the Coalition, like New Labour, succumbed to pressures to strengthen central bureaucratic and ministerial power through the centre of British government. Hierarchical command is a key characteristic of the Westminster model's formal and informal code of governing. In contrast to Bevir and Rhodes, we argue that focusing on the long-established 'power-hoarding' model drawn from ideas associated with the BPT offers a richer explanatory framework to address the patterns of governance in the UK during these two periods of government. This approach is underpinned by an aggregate concept of political tradition in which long-embedded forms of hierarchy continued to structure and shape the contemporary British state.

Nevertheless, paradoxically, the September 2014 Scottish referendum may retrospectively come to be seen as an exogenous shock to this aggregate tradition of a central, power-hoarding approach. The response of both the main parties in the aftermath of the referendum reveals a series of contingencies potentially challenging the key tenets of the BPT. Crucially though, both parties are attempting to shape constitutional reform to suit their own interest, the Conservatives by focusing on 'English votes for English laws' as a way of preserving the Westminster model in the context of devolved powers and in that way maintaining their dominance. Meanwhile, Labour chose to concentrate on themes of regional and city devolution. Neither has been willing to set out a clear framework concerning how the process of reform should develop, nor identify whether it is predominantly a matter of grafting further reform onto the existing constitutional system. Of course, what this chapter's analysis of recent history reveals in relation to both devolution and constitutional reform is a default setting on the part of both main parties to revert to the path of ad hoc-ery and incrementalism as a means of preserving the founding premises of the BPT.

Notes

1 We are grateful to the editor and an anonymous reviewer for very helpful comments on this chapter.
2 Of course, given the events of the September 2014 Scottish referendum and the subsequent political response, there are at the time of writing a whole set of contingencies concerning the future of the BPT.
3 Interview with a former Cabinet minister, 23 October 2011.
4 Interview with a former Number Ten special adviser, 12 October 2011.
5 Interview with a former Number Ten official, 15 September 2011.
6 Interview with a former Cabinet minister, 23 October 2011.

References

Adonis, A. (2012) *Education, Education, Education: Reforming England's schools*, London: Biteback Publishing.

Alexander, G. (2001) 'Institutions, Path Dependence and Democratic Institutions', *Journal of Theoretical Politics*, 13(3): 249–70.

Barber, M. (2007) *Instruction to Deliver: Tony Blair, public services and the challenge of achieving targets*, London: Politicos.

Barry, B. (1965) *Political Argument*, London: Routledge and Keegan Paul.

Berger, P. and Luckman, T. (1967) *The Social Construction of Reality*, Penguin: Harmondsworth.

Bevir, M. and Rhodes, R. A. W. (2001) 'Decentring Tradition: Interpreting British government', *Administration and Society*, 33(2): 107–32.

Bevir, M. and Rhodes, R. A. W. (2003) *Interpreting British Governance*, London: Routledge.

Bevir, M. and Rhodes, R. A. W. (2006) 'Interpreting British Governance', *British Journal of Politics and International Relations*, 6: 2–8.

Bevir, M. and Rhodes, R. A. W. (2006a) *Governance Stories*, London: Routledge.

Bevir, M. and Rhodes, R. A. W. (2010) *The State as Cultural Practice*, London: Routledge.

Birch, A. (1964) *Representative and Responsible Government*, London: Allen & Unwin.

Blair, T. (2010) *A Journey*, London: Hutchinson.

Blick, A. and Jones, G. (2010) *Premiership: The development, nature and power of the office of the British Prime Minister*, Exeter: Imprint Academic.

Blond, P. (2011) 'The Big Society: Innovation or slogan?' *Independent*, 9 February 2011.

Cabinet Office (2010) Cabinet Office Structural Reform Plan, June. Available at www.gov.uk/government/uploads/system/uploads/attachment_data/file/60804/srp-cabinet-office_3.pdf [accessed 13 March 2015].

Cameron, D. (2010) *Big Society versus Big Government*, Speech 19 April 2010. Available at www.conservatives.com/News/Speeches/2010/04/David_Cameron_Big_Society_versus_Big_Government.aspx.

Cameron (2011) 'Prime Minister's Question Time', Hansard Col. 955 16 February 2011. Available at www.publications.parliament.uk/pa/cm201011/cmhansrd/cm110216/debtext/110216-0001.htm [accessed 18 August 2011].

Clegg, N. (2010) 'The New Politics: Nick Clegg's speech on constitutional reform', 19 May 2010, City and Islington College Centre for Business, Arts and Technology: London. Available at www.cabinetoffice.gov.uk/media/408354/new-politics.pdf [accessed 18 August 2011].

Cm 4310 (1999) *Modernising Government*, London: Stationary Office.

Cm 7996 (2011) *Creating Growth, Cutting Carbon: Making local sustainable transport happen*, London: Stationary Office.

Diamond, P. (2013) *Governing Britain: Power, politics and the prime minister*, London: IB Tauris.

Diamond, P. and D. Richards (2012) 'The Case for Theoretical and Methodological Pluralism in British Political Studies: New Labour's political memoirs and the British political tradition', *Political Studies*, 10(2): 177–94.

Dowding, K. (2004) 'Interpretation, Truth and Investigation: Comments on the interpretative political Science of Bevir and Rhodes', *British Journal of Politics and International Relations*, 6(2): 136–42.

Evans, M. (2003) *Constitution-Making and the Labour Party*, Basingstoke: Palgrave Macmillan.

Gains, F. (2003) 'Surveying the Landscape of Modernisation: Executive agencies under new Labour', *Public Policy and Administration*, 18(2): 4–20.

Gamble, A. (1994) *The Free Economy and the Strong State*, London: Macmillan.

Garfinkel, H. (1967) *Studies in Ethnomethodology*, Oxford: Polity Press.

Goffman, E. (1969) *The Presentation of Self in Everyday Life*, Harmondsworth: Penguin.

Gov.Uk (2012) 'Permanent Secretaries Objectives Published for the First Time', Available at www.gov.uk/government/publications/permanent-secretaries-objectives-published-for-the-first-time [accessed 13 March 2015].

Greenleaf, W. (1983a) *The British Political Tradition: The rise of collectivism, Volume 1*, London: Methuen.

Greenleaf, W. (1983b) *The British Political Tradition: The ideological heritage, Volume 2*, London: Methuen.

Greenleaf, W. (1987) *The British Political Tradition: A much governed nation, Volume 3* (Parts 1 and 2), London: Methuen.

H. M. Government (2012) *The Civil Service Reform Plan*, London: The Stationary Office.

H. M. Treasury (2010) *The 2010 Comprehensive Spending Review*, London: The Stationary Office.

Hall, M. (2011) *Political Traditions and UK Politics*, Basingstoke: Palgrave Macmillan.

Hay, C. (2004) 'Taking Ideas Seriously in Explanatory Political Analysis', *British Journal of Politics and International Relations*, 6(2): 142–49.

Heffernen, R. (2003) 'Prime Ministerial Predominance? Core executive politics in the UK', *British Journal of Politics and International Relations*, 5(3): 347–72.

Institute for Fiscal Studies (2013) *The IFS Green Budget*, London: IFS.

Jones, G. (2010) 'The Coalition Government's "New Localism" Decentralisation Agenda may well Undermine Local Government. A new agreement is needed', *London School of Economics Blog*, 22 November 2010. Available at http://blogs.lse.ac.uk/politicsand-policy/archives/5615 [accessed 13 March 2015].

Judge, D. (2006) *Political Institutions in the United Kingdom*, Oxford: Oxford University Press.

Kavanagh, D. and Richards, D. (2001) 'Departmentalism and Joined-Up Government', *Parliamentary Affairs*, 54(1): 1–18.

King, A. (2007) *The British Constitution*, Oxford: Oxford University Press.

Le Grand, J. (2003) *Motivation, Agency and Public Policy: Of knights and knaves, pawns and queens*, Oxford: Oxford University Press.

Ling, T. (1998) *The British State Since 1945*, London: Polity Press.

Lowndes, V. and McCaughie, K. (2013) 'Weathering the Perfect Storm? Austerity and institutional resilience in English local government', *Policy and Politics* 41(4): 533–49.

Lowndes, V. and Pratchett, L. (2012) 'Local Governance Under the Coalition Government: Austerity, localism and the 'Big Society', *Local Government Studies*, 38(1): 21–40.

Mandelson, P. and Liddle, R. (1996) *The Blair Revolution: Can New Labour deliver?*, London: Faber.

Marinetto, M. (2003) 'Governing Beyond the Centre: A critique of the Anglo-Governance School', *Political Studies*, 51(3): 592–608.

Marquand, D. (2004) *The Decline of the Public*, Cambridge: Polity Press.

Marsh, D. and Hall, M. (2007) 'The British Political Tradition: Explaining the fate of New Labour's constitutional reform agenda', *British Politics*, 2(3): 215–38.

Marsh, D., Richards, D., and Smith, M. J. (2001) *Changing Patterns of Governance*, Basingstoke: Palgrave.

Marsh, D., Richards, D., and Smith, M. J. (2003) 'Unequal Power: Towards an asymmetric power model of the British polity', *Government and Opposition*, 38(3): 306–22.

McAnulla, S. (2006) *British Politics: A critical introduction*, London: Continuum.

McConnell, A. and Stark, A. (2002) 'Foot-and-Mouth 2001: The politics of crisis management', *Parliamentary Affairs*, 55(4): 664–81.

Newman, J. (2005) *Remaking Governance: Peoples, politics and the public sphere*, Bristol: Policy Press.

Oakeshott, M. (1962) *Rationalism in Politics and Other Essays*, Indianapolis, IN: Liberty Press.

Rhodes, R. A. W. (2007) 'Understanding Governance: Ten years on,' *Organization Studies*, 28(08): 1243–64.

Richards, D. (2008) *New Labour and the Civil Service: Reconstituting the Westminster model*, Basingstoke: Palgrave Macmillan.

Richards, D. (2009) 'New Labour and Special Advisers: Examining a model of resource dependency', *Political Education Forum Journal*, 2(2).

Richards, D. (2011) 'Changing Patterns of Executive Governance', in P. Cowley, C. Hay, and R. Heffernan (eds), *Developments in British Politics 9*, Basingstoke: Palgrave Macmillan, pp. 29–50.

Richards, D. and Smith, M. J. (2004a) 'The Hybrid State: Labour's response to the challenge of governance', in S. Ludlam and M. J. Smith (eds), *Governing as New Labour: Policy and politics under Blair*, Basingstoke: Palgrave Macmillan, pp. 106–25.

Richards, D. and Smith, M. J. (2004b) 'Interpreting the World Of Political Elites: Some methodological issues', *Public Administration*, 82(4): 777–800.

Richards, D. and Smith, M. J. (2006) 'Central Control and Policy Implementation in the UK: A case study of the Prime Minister's Delivery Unit', *Journal of Comparative Policy Analysis*, 8(4): 325–46.

Richards, D. and Smith, M. J. (2014) 'Introduction', in D. Richards, M. J. Smith, and C. Hay (eds), *Institutional Crisis in Twenty-First Century Britain*, Basingstoke: Palgrave Macmillan, pp. 1–14.

Richards, D., Smith, M. J., and Hay, C. (2014) *Institutional Crisis in Twenty-First Century Britain*, Basingstoke: Palgrave Macmillan.

Riddell, P. (2006) *The Unfulfilled Prime Minister*, London: Politicos.

Schickler, E. (2001) *Disjointed Pluralism*, Princeton, NJ: Princeton University Press.

Seldon, A. (2006) *Tony Blair*, London: Harper Collins.

Smith, M. J. (2011) 'Tsars, Leadership and Innovation in the Public Sector', *Policy and Politics*, 39(3), 343–59.

Smith, M. J. (2014) 'Globalisation and the Resilience of Social Democracy: Reassessing New Labour's political economy', *British Journal of Politics and International Relations*, 16(4): 597–623.

Smith, M. J., Richards, D., Geddes, A., and Mathers, H. (2011) 'Analysing Policy Delivery in the United Kingdom: The case of street crime and anti-social behaviour', *Public Administration*, 89(3): 975–1000.

Steinmo, S. (2010) *The Evolution of Modern States: Sweden, Japan and the United States*, Cambridge: Cambridge University Press.

Stones, R. (1996) *Sociological Reasoning: Towards a past-modern sociology*, London: Macmillan.

Talbot, C. (2013) *Strategy in Government: From growth to austerity*, Georgetown: Georgetown University Press.

Tant, A. (1993) *British Government: The triumph of elitism. A study of the British Political Tradition and its major challenges*, Aldershot: Dartmouth.

Thelen, K. (2002) 'The Explanatory Power of Historical Institutionalism', in R. Mayntz, (ed.), *Akteure–Mechanismen–Modelle*, Frankfurt: Campus Verlag.

2 Critical Encounters with Decentred Theory

Tradition, Metagovernance, and *Parrhēsia* as Storytelling

Paul Fawcett

Public policy has long been criticised for being overly rationalistic (e.g. Cole-batch, 2009). The post-positivist turn that has followed has opened up a new terrain within which interpretivist and constructivist approaches have become particularly influential.[1] Of course, interpretivist and constructivist approaches come in a variety of different forms, some of which are reflected in the contributions to this volume (Wagenaar, 2011). However, an extended analysis of Bevir and Rhodes's particular form of interpretivism – decentred theory – is more than warranted due to the particularly influential role that it has played in shaping the fields of political science, public policy, and governance. Relatedly, it also makes sense to go back to *Interpreting British Governance* (2003) as this was Bevir and Rhodes's first book-length attempt to set out their approach. It is an argument that they have elaborated on in numerous other journal articles and several books, most notably *Governance Stories* (2006) and *The State as Cultural Practice* (2010). The wide-ranging debates generated by these contributions provide ample evidence of the influential and substantial contribution that decentred theory has made on both policy-related research and the discipline of political science more broadly construed. It is also one of the principal reasons why the study of governance has become ubiquitous within much public policy discussion and research.

Decentred theory's overall argument is that individuals act on their beliefs, which are made in the context of a set of traditions that colour but do not determine an agent's actions. This makes traditions particularly important because they provide the means by which situated agents use their local reasoning consciously and subconsciously to modify their contingent heritage (Bevir and Rhodes, 2006: 9). So, situated agents govern themselves through the beliefs that they hold, which are loosely tied to the traditions within which they are situated. Change occurs when a situated agent's beliefs evolve in response to a dilemma or set of dilemmas.

This approach has had a very significant impact on how we understand and study governance and public policy. Even those who remain sceptical about its core claims (e.g. James, 2009) can no longer ignore its growing influence on the profession, particularly amongst younger scholars. Theoretically, Bevir and Rhodes have set out a coherent alternative to 'modernist empiricism' (notably rational choice and new institutionalist approaches) and distinguished themselves from other anti-foundationalist approaches (particularly post-structuralism) by bringing the ideas of 'post-analytic philosophy' into the analysis of policy and governance (Bevir and Rhodes, 2010: 64).[2] Methodologically and empirically, they have also shown how decentred theory can be used to help inform our understanding of policy, politics, and the polity. Yet, at the same time, I remain dubious that Bevir and Rhodes's decentred approach offers all the answers.

It is in this spirit that I am taking the opportunity presented by this chapter to reflect on three different ways in which I have benefited from engaging with decentred theory, either by incorporating elements of it into my own work or by taking an alternative direction following an engagement with it. These critical encounters centre on: the concept of tradition; Bevir and Rhodes's engagement with the literature on metagovernance; and *parrhēsia* as a particular form of storytelling. This chapter is structured around these three themes.

Tradition[3]

Interpretation is the obvious starting point for most, if not all, interpretivist and constructivist approaches. Most interpretivist approaches use a range of mid-level concepts to describe a more or less embedded idea, or set of ideas, ranging from discourses to frames and norms (for a review see Schmidt, 2008). Decentred theory rejects these concepts in favour of meaning, belief, situated agency, tradition, and dilemma. Bevir and Rhodes (2010: 78) elaborate on this point in *The State as Cultural Practice*: 'A tradition is the ideational background against which individuals come to adopt an initial web of beliefs. It influences (without determining or – in a strict philosophical sense – limiting) the beliefs they later go on to adopt'. Change occurs when traditions are challenged by dilemmas, which are defined as 'any experience or idea that conflicts with someone's beliefs and so forces them to alter the beliefs they inherit as a tradition' (Bevir and Rhodes, 2006: x). Accordingly, Bevir and Rhodes argue that their version of interpretivism is inherently contingent and open to change.

Bevir and Rhodes (2003: 107–08) apply decentred theory in *Interpreting British Governance* to study the changing nature of governance in the UK. They identify four traditions and show how each tradition underpins a distinct analysis of Thatcherism. First, the Tory narrative focuses upon strong, authoritative government, which bypasses intermediate institutions. Second, the Liberal narrative emphasises the need to marketise public services, thus reducing state control and the power of intermediate institutions. Third, the Whig narrative is strongly associated with the Westminster model and argues for the reinvention of the organic constitution and a focus on gradual change. Finally, the Socialist narrative emphasises the need for more participation, trust, and negotiation. However, Bevir and Rhodes also argue that there are several other 'sub-traditions' within each of the four 'major' traditions. For example, they further divide the Tory tradition into 'One Nation' and 'Statecraft' strands. There is not the space to examine these traditions in detail here, but three points are important.

First, Bevir and Rhodes are quick to claim and defend their position as distinctive even compared with those approaches that are relatively aligned with their own. So, modernist empiricism, new institutionalism, and most other anti-foundationalist approaches (except those based in post-analytic philosophy) are all criticised for either essentialising concepts and/or reifying ideas. This critique applies broadly (but for different reasons), from Greenleaf's notion of a British political tradition (Bevir and Rhodes, 2003: 35) to the work of constructivist institutionalists (Bevir and Rhodes, 2010: Chapter 4). The overall effect is that decentred theory 'others' a large number of alternative approaches.

I would argue that this can be partly explained by the radical position that decentred theory takes towards agency, meaning, and belief in which it is argued that traditions, as meanings, cannot exist independently of individual subjects.[4] The result is that institutions and ideas are co-constituted in decentred theory. Institutions do not exist independently of ideas; they are narrated, whilst agents are seen as the interpreters of traditions that do not exist independently of agents – i.e. it is their interpretations which shape outcomes. This is what marks decentred theory out as both distinctive but also different from most other approaches (see Hay, 2011).

However, contra Bevir and Rhodes's claim that approaches other than their own suggest that meanings exist independently of individual subjects, I would contend that most other approaches actually see patterns of meanings as shared, that meanings are inscribed in institutions and processes, and that both affect, but certainly do not determine, agents' behaviour. By arguing that traditions are inscribed in institutions and processes, I suggest that we can maintain the view that agents interpret traditions at the same time as those same interpretations are constrained by the way in which those traditions are inscribed in institutions, processes, and narratives.

This brings me onto my second point. The basic argument here is that path dependency does not mean path determinancy. A great deal of debate has been provoked by arguments over the relative 'stickiness' of institutions and the appropriate role for ideas and agency in explaining change, particularly between historical and constructivist institutionalists (see, for example, Bell, 2011; Hay, 2006; Marsh, 2010). In particular, many historical institutionalists have sought to incorporate a greater role for agency and incremental change (Bell, 2011; Mahoney and Thelen, 2010).

However, I would argue that we also need to understand how institutional and political–economic path dependencies shape outcomes. So, by analytically distinguishing between discursive, institutional, and political–economic structures as three different forms of path dependency, we can examine the different ways in which all three enable and constrain the actions of different agents without determining them (see also Marsh and Hall, 2015). Change will occur as a result of the actions of agents, in the context of discursive and political–economic contestation, within an institutional path dependency. From this point of view, decentred theory can play an important role by highlighting the value of interpretation in political analysis, particularly how traditions establish a discursive path dependency that helps to shape but not determine policy outcomes. Thus, whilst I would argue that we need to acknowledge that traditions can, and do, change, this needs to be combined with an understanding of how that change takes place within a strategic context that enables and constrains certain types of change over others. This means that we need to find better ways of connecting aggregate-based analyses with individually driven analyses, the nature of the links that exist between these two forms of analysis, and any associated mid-level concepts.

Relatedly, my third point is that, whilst Bevir and Rhodes identify four traditions, they do not fully explain why they have chosen to focus on these four in particular nor the relationship between them.[5] We get a better sense of the beliefs that inform the actions of particular individuals in Bevir's and Rhodes's later work (Bevir and Rhodes, 2006; Rhodes, 2012). In earlier work, they note that the distinction between aggregate and individual analysis is 'artificial' (Bevir and Rhodes, 2003: 2). For example, they argue that researchers need to be wary not to 'neglect the differences in the beliefs of the individuals lumped together in a tradition', but they argue that this can be guarded against by decentring a tradition, so as to highlight its diversity (2003: 2). In other words, traditions are 'aggregate concepts' that allow one to 'scale up' an analysis beyond the level of individual meaning, but beliefs themselves never exist anywhere other than at the individual level.

It is within this context that labelling a set of beliefs as a tradition is clearly an important act of recognition. However, this does not address the broader question about the point at which the researcher is justified in labelling one particular set of beliefs as one tradition compared with another. For example, Bevir and Rhodes identify several 'sub-traditions' whilst others have defined and categorised their own different set of traditions (e.g. Greenleaf, 1983). Relatedly, Bevir and Rhodes do not really consider the relationship between these traditions and, particularly, the common elements in various traditions. So, as I and others have argued at further length elsewhere (Marsh et al., 2014), only some elements of the socialist tradition have any emphasis on participation, whereas nearly all of the other traditions identified by Bevir and Rhodes have strong elitist tendencies. As Evans (2003: 313) puts it, UK politics is dominated by an 'elitist conception of statecraft which has informed the development of the modern British state and its political institutions'. This suggests that some beliefs may be more important than others, because they are able to travel across more than one tradition.

Metagovernance

Rhodes has identified *Interpreting British Governance* as an important shift in his own intellectual trajectory from the networked governance approach – that he had developed in the preceding years – to the decentred approach that has underpinned his work since (Marsh, 2011; Rhodes, 2007; Rhodes, 2011a). The implications of this shift have been particularly evident in Bevir and Rhodes's work on the state. They (2010: Chapter 5) now characterise this earlier work as 'first wave' governance theory. First wave governance theory often conflated governance with networks and held that governance was replacing government in many contemporary polities (Rhodes, 2011a: 198). Marsh (2011: 34) argues that aspects of the same argument can be found in *Interpreting British Governance*. For example, he quotes a passage in which Bevir and Rhodes argue that 'governance as networks is a common and important development in advanced industrial societies where the relationship between state and civil society has changed dramatically' (Marsh, 2011: 34). Governance scholars often linked these changes with the notion that society was transitioning into a period of late modernity marked by increased complexity, reflexivity, individualism, dynamism, and diversity. Advocates of this view supported their argument with reference to various trends, such as: the transition from government to governance; the replacement of hierarchy by networks (or networks and markets); the 'hollowing out' of the state; the proliferation of more complex and multiple identities that were no longer rooted in distinct cleavages such as class, ideology, gender, or ethnicity; and higher levels of individual self-reflexivity, manifested in declining levels of mainstream political participation and a shift from 'duty norms' towards 'engagement norms'.

Bevir and Rhodes (2010: 87–90) have since criticised the first wave on various grounds, including: its shared modernist empiricist description of the characteristics of network governance; its concern to provide 'policy advice' on network governance based on the shared assumption that the state is there to manage the networks of service delivery; its use of a reified notion of structure; and its desire to provide comprehensive and general accounts of networks and network governance.[6] In contrast, one of their key aims in *The State as Cultural Practice* was to show how a decentred approach and the aggregate concepts discussed above could be applied to understand the empirical shifts in, and debates about, the changing nature of 'the state' (Bevir and Rhodes, 2010: 79). This has helped revitalise an extremely welcome debate about how we should conceptualise and study 'the state'. It was not so much that the state had disappeared altogether in first wave governance approaches, rather it was more that it was accorded an altogether secondary role compared with the language of governance and networks. It is within this context that Bevir and Rhodes's decentred approach has been instrumental in reintroducing discussions about the state, even if their overall argument is that we need to decentre it!

Decentring the state means that the institutions of the state are explored as: 'the contingent meanings that inform the actions of the individuals in all kinds of practices of rule' (Bevir and Rhodes, 2010: 91). Decentred theory refuses to treat the state as uniform. It argues that it has no defined metaphysical nature, rather studying the state is about examining, 'the ways in which patterns of rule, including institutions and policies, are created, sustained, and varied by individuals' (Bevir and Rhodes, 2010: 91). Thus, state authority itself is constantly being 'remade, negotiated, and contested in widely different ways within widely varying everyday practices' (Bevir and Rhodes, 2010: 93–94). In short, if we refer to 'the state', we are referring to an aggregate descriptive term for a vast array of meaningful actions that coalesce into contingent, shifting, and contested practices. It follows that studying the state is about telling stories about the 'everyday' performance of governance at the micro-level (see Rhodes, 2014).

My work has critically engaged with a decentred approach to the state by using the concept of metagovernance. Bevir and Rhodes classify metagovernance approaches as part of a 'second wave' of governance research. However, the literature on metagovernance is perhaps better seen as one of the main contemporary alternative approaches to questions about the changing form of the polity. This would seem to be supported by the rising number of studies that have used a perspective based in metagovernance to examine empirical shifts in, and debates about, the changing nature of 'the state'. But, it is also reflected in the different theoretical approaches that have used metagovernance and the variation that exists between them on fundamental questions, such as: who can metagovern; whether metagovernance takes place within particular modes of governing or across and between them; and why it is important and necessary to metagovern (see Sørenson and Torfing, 2007; Meulemann, 2008: Figure 5; Jessop, 2011: 108–12). This diversity makes an 'authoritative' account of the literature on metagovernance challenging. Whilst some accounts examine metagovernance from a more macro-perspective of the 'whole governance system' (e.g. Kooiman and Jentoft, 2009; Jessop 2011) others take a more meso- or micro-level perspective by examining who steers particular governance networks and how they go about it. Most fundamentally, the meaning ascribed to metagovernance changes according to how governance is defined and understood.

Nevertheless, a common starting point is to define metagovernance as the 'governance of governance' (Kooiman 2003). This often involves analysing the role, capacity, and legitimacy of formal public organisations to exercise control over the more devolved and decentralised forms of decision making characteristic of network governance. Thus, Bevir (2013: 56) defines metagovernance as 'an umbrella concept that describes the role of the state and its characteristic policy instruments in the new world of network governance'. Whilst many studies of metagovernance would certainly fall within this definition, there remains a significant subset of the literature that retains the possibility that metagovernance can be performed by a political authority other than the state.

This diversity within the literature on metagovernance is recognised by Bevir and Rhodes, but I would argue that there is actually more difference than they acknowledge. Taking my own point of departure from this work as well as alternative classifications such as the one offered by Sørenson and Torfing,[7] I would argue that there are actually three major approaches within the literature on metagovernance: pluralist, neo-Weberian, and neo-Marxist. Pluralist approaches place a particular emphasis on the state's role as a 'network manager' (Klijn and Edelenbos, 2007; Sørenson and Torfing, 2009; Torfing et al., 2012). The overall argument is that the state needs to steer networks in order to ensure that effective and legitimate policy outcomes are delivered. However, it is also an approach that is underpinned by the notion that networks have become the dominant mode of governing. As such, the argument is that the shift to networks means that metagovernors cannot revert back to traditional forms of hierarchical steering. As Torfing et al. (2012: 132) argue, 'metagovernors must respect the capacity for self-regulation of the interactive governance arenas in order to preserve the commitment of the public and private actors'. By contrast, neo-Weberian approaches use metagovernance to refer to the state's capacity to govern (Bell and Hindmoor, 2009; Dahlström *et al.*, 2011). They do this by arguing that the state has effectively responded to changes in the policymaking environment by implementing strategies that protect, perhaps even extend, its capacity to act. For example, Bell and Hindmoor (2009) argue that two developments have been particularly important in this context. First, they claim that the state has access to a much broader range of policy instruments than in the past, ranging from 'traditional' hard policy instruments to a series of 'softer' policy instruments. Second, they argue that the state has augmented its relational capacity by 'reaching out' and developing stronger and closer links with non-state actors. Finally, there are a number of neo-Marxist approaches that use metagovernance to refer to changing patterns of state power, strategy, and intervention. There is often an attempt within these approaches to locate governance within a broader socio-economic, political, and institutional context (Davies, 2011; Jessop, 2011; Kjær, 2011).

One example of a neo-Marxist approach to metagovernance is Davies's (2011) approach to network governance theory, which is inspired by Gramsci's notion of hegemony. Davies (2011: 144) argues that 'the study of networks should be placed squarely in the political economy tradition, examining how they reproduce and embed power asymmetries or generate conflict and resistance.' In contrast to the 'network-boosterism' that Davies and Spicer (2015: 225) associate with a 'tendency to attribute excessive analytical and normative weight to the role of networking in organizing and regulating relationships between governments, corporations and citizens', network governance is better understood as a key element of neo-liberalism's hegemonic project and its 'visionary regulative ideal' (Davies, 2012: 2688). This reflects a broader scepticism within neo-Marxist approaches towards arguments about the proliferation and ascendancy of networks.

Sharing several aspects of this argument, my own approach to metagovernance has argued that we should study how hierarchy, market, and network coexist and interact with one another.[8] Jessop (2004: 61) makes this point when he argues that most governance arrangements will be hybrids of all three modes of governing. In other words, no one mode of governing – hierarchy, market, or network – is privileged over another. Moreover, modes of governing will coexist with one another – networks are unlikely to exist without hierarchy and market, markets are unlikely to function without hierarchy and networks, etc. (Grote, 2012). Thus, governance is defined as the 'the structures and practices involved in coordinating social relations that are marked by complex, reciprocal interdependence' and metagovernance becomes 'the coordination of these structures and processes' (Jessop, 2011: 108). This is achieved by 'judiciously mixing the balance of hierarchy, markets and networks in order to achieve the best outcome from the viewpoint of those engaged in metagovernance' (Jessop, 2004: 70). But, this will take place within a structurally inscribed strategically selective context that asymmetrically privileges some outcomes over others. As such, we can expect that institutionally inscribed asymmetries of power, differences in capacity between social forces, and the extent to which interests and ideas align with one another will lead to 'heterogeneous patterns of government and/or governance, with patterns varying with the objects of state intervention, the nature of policy fields, the changing balance of forces in and beyond the state, and so on' (Jessop, 2004: 63).

Jessop's argument is similar to the agnostic approach to governance recently advocated by Davies and Spicer (2015). Davies and Spicer begin by arguing that networks have become a 'revered mode of governance' and setting out the reasons why they believe that this should not be the case.[9] They conclude that governance is multi-modal and that network-based forms of governance may be appropriate in particular settings, but only when they are combined with other modes of governance (Davies and Spicer, 2015: 223). They argue that their agnostic approach has advantages over other approaches because it: (a) avoids the 'fetishisation' of any particular mode of governing, particularly networks; (b) inductively treats 'hierarchy, market and network as "inputs" or building blocks rather than "outcomes" or "types" of institution' (Davies and Spicer 2015: 234); and (c) entails a more detailed consideration of the 'appropriateness' of hierarchy, markets and networks, their mechanisms and the different settings in which they can be useful (see Crouch, 2011).

Neo-Marxist approaches have therefore placed a particular emphasis on how hierarchical power relations remain crucial to understanding how we are governed by challenging the argument that we are moving from a logic of structures to a logic of flows. This is illustrated by the way in which Jessop has highlighted how governance takes place in a strategically selective context that privileges some outcomes over others, rather than a narrower set of concerns about how to manage issues of 'strategic coordination'. Relatedly, Davies has placed more emphasis on explaining the rise of network governance ideology, its embodiment in everyday practice and its relation to neo-liberal hegemony.

Parrhēsia as Storytelling

Tied into the growing interest in metagovernance, a considerable literature has now emerged around the different ways in which governance can be implemented and performed (e.g. Baker and Stoker, 2013). Bevir and Rhodes (2010: 85–7) identify three different approaches in their review of the literature. A metagovernor can set the rules of the game, tell stories, and distribute resources. Here, I want to focus on the second of these approaches for several reasons. The first is the important role that storytelling plays in Bevir and Rhodes's work.[10] The second is that I think that we can see ways in which storytelling is growing in importance in an era of 'communicative abundance', yet it has received relatively limited attention in the literature on metagovernance, particularly amongst some of the neo-Marxist variants that I have discussed above (Hajer, 2009; Keane, 2013). Finally, storytelling is an extremely fruitful way to analyse how metagovernance can be performed by actors outwith the state, at the same time as it can provide ways for administrators and politicians to rethink how they communicate with the political communities that they serve.

Stories and storytelling perform a particularly important function in decentred theory; they spell out shared meanings and shared understandings, but they are also provisional and unfolding, come in many versions, and have no clear beginning or end (Rhodes, 2011b: 288). The importance of stories and storytelling is a point that Bevir and Rhodes underscore at various points in their work (Bevir, 2011; Bevir and Rhodes, 2006; Rhodes, 2011b: 130–1 and 288–90).[11] Here, I argue that stories and storytelling perform at least three functions in decentred theory.

First, decentred theory uses stories and storytelling as an alternative to formal theory building. As Bevir and Rhodes (2010: 95) argue, 'Studying the changing state is not about building formal theories; it is about telling stories about other people's meanings; it is about narratives of their narratives'. Relatedly: 'we argue that the state is constructed differently by many actors inspired by different ideas and values. Our stories construct and reconstruct the stateless state' (Bevir and Rhodes, 2010: 99). An emphasis on stories and storytelling therefore underscores a broader epistemological point:

> Political scientists cannot make predictions. All they can offer are informed conjectures that seek to explain practices and actions by pointing to the conditional connections between actions, beliefs, traditions and dilemmas. Their conjectures are stories understood as provisional narratives about possible futures.
>
> (Bevir and Rhodes, 2006: 26)

Second, storytelling is what situated agents do in their 'everyday life'. For example, Rhodes (2011b: 289) argues that storytelling has at least three characteristics – a language game, a performing game, and a management game – in which officials are invited to tell a story, test its plausibility, and judge how it will play out publicly (Rhodes, 2011b: 131). These games also play an important role in helping an organisation to define itself:

> Top civil servants and ministers learn through the stories they hear and tell one another and such stories are a source of institutional memory, the repositories of the traditions through which practitioners filter current events. The basis for much advice is the collective memory of the Department, its departmental traditions or philosophy. It is an organized, selective retelling of the past to make sense of the present. Permanent secretaries explain past practice and events to justify recommendations for the future.
>
> (Rhodes, 2011b: 130)

Third, stories and storytelling can also help promote learning. For example, Bevir and Rhodes argue that:

> Because governance is constructed differently, contingently and continuously, we cannot have tool kits with which to manage it. Hence an interpretive approach encourages us to foreswear management techniques and strategies but, and the point is crucial, *to replace such tools with learning by*

telling stories and listening to them.... No matter what rigour or expertise we bring to bear, all we can do is tell a story and judge what the future might bring.

(2006: 26, emphasis added)

Bevir (2011: 191) argues that stories and storytelling can also be directed towards enlarging our sympathies: 'Meaning holism can remind us that public administration resembles fiction.... Public administration needs the imagination to create a new sense of the world that enlarges our knowledge and sympathies.' He argues that this is important because it is the means by which new research agendas are generated, neglected themes are brought to the fore, new questions are opened up, and bridges are built to other ways of thinking.

Following Bang (2009, 2010a, 2010b, 2011, 2012, and 2015), I would argue that we can more clearly position the shift towards stories and storytelling as part of a broader tension between two different models of governing. The first model of governing, politics-policy, is primarily concerned with governing within a sovereign territory. In this model, governments use hierarchy and bureaucracy in order to achieve their goals. They exercise 'power over' citizens and expect obedience from them given their greater sense of duty towards the state and belief in its legitimacy. Thus, politics-policy is about how pre-constituted political agents, individuals, but also classes, gain access to, and recognition in, the political process. The focus is on the demand side of politics, or input politics.

The second model of governing, policy-politics, is primarily concerned with the security of a population. It is focused on doing 'good for the population' by articulating and performing policy in ways that improve their welfare and well-being. It is a model of governing that is output oriented and focused on what citizens can do for themselves. It does not expect citizens to comply out of obedience, rather citizens are motivated to engage because they feel empowered to make a 'real' difference in 'concrete' projects that they care about. It is about how political elites from the public, private, and voluntary sectors network in order to implement policy and how political authorities create the conditions to enable individuals to help them to realise their project identities. The focus is on the supply side of politics or output politics.

Importantly, Bang recognises that politics-policy and policy-politics coexist in an uneasy tension. Thus, he argues that:

> As I see it, the basic dilemma of Western politics today is that although the politics of everyday life is the discourse that enjoys hegemony over the politics of ideas on the front stage, it is simultaneously firmly in the pocket of the interest driven power politics that goes on back stage.

(Bang, 2012: 13)

Thus, Bang recognises that politics-policy wins over policy-politics most of the time. However, he also argues that politics-policy is increasingly confronting its limits as citizens 'rate their concrete and ethical involvement in particular political actions higher than the abstract (...) and ideologically driven form(s) of participation' (Bang, 2009: 104–5). Indeed, for Bang, this tension helps explain the increased cynicism and distrust that citizens feel towards politics and the decoupling that is taking place between citizens, politicians, and administrators.

Illustrating this with reference to the core executive, Bang argues that communication in the politics-policy model is identified with a one-way, top-down, and sovereign form of rule. Conversely, in the policy-politics model:

> The core executive as the central node in the network must rather engage in convincing the other autonomous, but not quite as central, parts that its 'holistic glance' is necessary to coordinate and monitor their activities in a way that enhance their autonomy and thereby their capacity to do what has to be done in a politically effective manner.
>
> (Bang, 2012: 7)

In other words, this is a core executive that would acknowledge and recognise that 'the state and government can only get stronger by making the population stronger, which exactly requires the population's continuous development and empowerment as reflexive individuals' (Bang, 2012: 15).

This is where I would argue that stories and storytelling are likely to play a crucial role in helping to address this decoupling and as an integral component in the policy-politics model. This is particularly the case for politicians who will need to become much more adept at convincing citizens that they cannot achieve their projects without their involvement (Fawcett, 2014). This would start from the recognition that political authority needs to be exercised to help citizens help themselves. Here, I would like to conclude by briefly considering the role that *parrhēsia*, as a particular form of storytelling, may play in helping to develop the core executive's capacities in these areas and how it may also help address some of the problems that have emerged as a result of the decoupling that has taken place between politicians and citizens.

Parrhēsia barely registers in modern theories of government or governance and does not have its own dedicated body of literature (but see Bang, 2015; Dryberg, 2014; Walters, 2014). Most commonly associated with Foucault's lectures on *parrhēsia* in Ancient Greece, Walters (2014: 277) has defined *parrhēsia* as 'the practice whereby individuals choose at great risk to confront rulers or publics with uncomfortable truths'. Foucault (cited in Walters, 2014: 281) himself defined *parrhēsia* as:

> a verbal activity in which a speaker expresses his personal relationship to truth, and risks his life because he recognizes truthtelling as a duty to improve or help other people (as well as himself). In [*parrhēsia*], the speaker uses his freedom and chooses frankness instead of persuasion, truth instead of falsehood or silence, the risk of death instead of life and security, criticism instead of flattery, and moral duty instead of self-interest and moral apathy.

Thus, the key currency for a *parrhēsiast* is courage and it is this which distinguishes *parrhēsia* from other forms of truth-telling such as prophecy, the wisdom of the sage, and *tekhnē* (the know how or expertise of doctors and other technicians). Thus, *parrhēsiasts* act out of duty to another, or to society as a whole, based on what they know from their personal experience. They are willing to take risks knowing that those with power may retaliate against them and they have nothing to gain personally from speaking out. They act out of personal conviction and it is for these same reasons that they deserve to be taken seriously precisely because they risk so much in order to speak out.[12]

Walters cites several contemporary examples of *parrhēsia*, including the victims of violent crime who speak out against political and legal authorities, certain official public inquiries (such as the 9/11 Commission) and the disclosures of whistle-blowers. However, he also argues that we are 'not faced with the eternal recurrence of *parrhēsia* across the ages but with a novel constellation of elements' (Walters, 2014: 291). This can be seen in the particular way in which *parrhēsia* is practised today compared with how it was practised in Ancient Greece. Walters refers to these differences as '*parrhēsiastic* exposure' – 'a concept that is intended to capture aspects of the changed circumstances under which fearless speech can be exercised in mass-mediated, globalised societies' – and illustrates his argument using the case of Noor Behram, a photojournalist who has spent several years photographing and exposing US drone strikes in the region of Waziristan in Pakistan (Walters, 2014: 277).

Three aspects of *parrhēsiastic* exposure are particularly important. First, the geographical and temporal scales over which *parrhēsiastic* activity can occur have been stretched considerably. This means that the public/s to whom *parrhēsiastic* truth is addressed are increasingly diffuse. It also means that *parrhēsia* is no longer physically confined to the agora, the court or the nation, but, rather, takes place through the multiple and changing topographies of the public sphere. So, Behram is not addressing the President of the United States or the US Congress when he publishes his photographs, rather the audience that he is addressing is a 'virtual social object', an indefinite public 'convened by modern modes of publicity' (Walters, 2014: 292). Second, the range of options by which an affronted sovereign may seek retribution have expanded and are increasingly global in reach. For example, Behram confronts risks and dangers that are multiple and complex by photographing communities that have been impacted by drone strikes, including follow-up strikes, angry residents, secretive intelligence agents, and Taliban militants. Finally, *parrhēsia* is unlikely to be performed through pure verbal speech alone, as it may have been in Ancient Greece. Rather, it will often be delivered through 'new' expressive forms and modes of communication that combine words with images and sounds. This means that effective *parrhēsia* also relies on 'all manner of props, mediators, technological prosthetics and social connections' to help secure attention in a public sphere in which attention is in short supply (Walters, 2014: 293). Heroism and courage may therefore be indispensable preconditions for the individual *parrhēsiast*, but promotion of the message and making sure that it can be heard will also require certain enablers, including a degree of technical competency and good connections.

Walters's argument is an important one, but I would argue that the logic of *parrhēsia* can also be reversed. Whilst it can be used to hold a sovereign or political authority to account, it also highlights why politicians and political authorities also need to adopt a more *parrhēsiastic* approach in the way that they communicate, particularly when compared with the other forms of truth-telling briefly outlined above. In other words, if Bang is right and citizens are looking for a form of politics that is more oriented towards the policy-politics model then politicians and administrators will need to respond by articulating and performing policy in ways that show how and why they can help citizens to improve their own welfare and well-being. *Parrhēsiastic* activity would involve politicians and administrators 'telling the truth' about the uncertainty and difficulty of governing, the risks of action and inaction, the constraints on what they can deliver, the interconnectedness between policy problems, the pressures on the nation-state and the limits of their knowledge. This activity may involve some personal danger to them, but not always. More likely, the risk or danger will involve politicians and political authorities confronting publics with uncomfortable truths. However, this will interact with the two other features of *parrhēsiastic* exposure outlined above, particularly the changing topographies of the public sphere and the modern norm that *parrhēsiastic* activity will combine verbal speech with images and sound.

Finally, I do not have the space to fully develop this argument here, but we may also consider what we could call the 'political economy of *parrhēsia*'. Walters does not raise this point specifically, but he does note that:

> The larger point is that when *parrhēsia* takes place under contemporary conditions of mass-mediated publicity, it is subject to and even complicit in the same processes of selection, reduction and reification that shape most other forms of public communication. *Parrhēsia* does not enjoy a status that entirely escapes or transgresses the norms of governmentality and the grammar of the public sphere.
>
> (2014: 298)

Indeed, we may argue that the selection, reduction, and reification of public communication is becoming ever more important in an era of 'communicative abundance' (Keane, 2013). Stories and storytelling are important, but it is also crucial that we understand their differential transmission and uptake. I would argue that this is particularly the case in political contexts where freedom of speech is unevenly distributed and distinguishing between those who are truly engaged in *parrhēsia* and those who are not may not be as easy as it sounds.

Conclusion

The critical encounters in this chapter reflect three different ways in which my work has engaged with decentred theory. Here, I want to briefly summarise my argument, but also offer some different ways in which I think that the research agenda can be further developed, both within and outwith decentred theory.

Traditions play a particularly important role in decentred theory both theoretically and empirically. In this section of the chapter, I drew on my previous work with Marsh and Hall to argue that we need to combine decentred theory's focus on meaning with at least two other forms of path dependency, one, more institutional and the other, more political–economic. Decentred theory would likely reject this argument by arguing that these other forms of path dependency are reified. However, if we were to work from within a decentred approach then a question of common interest is how researchers can access different types of belief, particularly those that are located at different levels of consciousness. This is a question that appears to be central to decentred theory. For example, Bevir and Rhodes (2006: 9) argue that situated agents use their local reasoning 'consciously and subconsciously' to modify their contingent heritage whilst elsewhere they have argued that, 'The flow of politics is speech and other actions.... Actions can be understood only in terms of the conscious, unconscious, and subconscious reasoning of actors' (Bevir, 2011: 191). As such, I would argue that how we go about accessing beliefs that exist at different levels of consciousness is an under-explored argument in decentred theory but one that is worthy of further attention. This is not only because of the central role that it plays in decentred approaches, but also because it may help to better articulate the relationship between a belief and a tradition.[13]

The section on metagovernance engaged with the challenge that decentred theory presents towards how we conceptualise and study 'the state'. I argued that decentred theory has played a crucial role in explaining why stories and storytelling are crucial to the state, but that does not mean that storytelling and narrative are the only means of steering a decentred state. I examined alternative ways in which to steer the state and argued that it is more about achieving an effective balance between these different forms of steering. Here, I would argue that we need more research that examines in further detail when governing arrangements should be built around networks and when they should not.

Finally, I turned to the question of what decentred theory may mean for democracy and participation. Here, I argued that politicians need to become more adept at telling stories that convey to citizens the challenges of what it means to govern in a decentred state. This reverses the logic found in most existing accounts of *parrhēsia* and highlights the crucial role that storytelling as *parrhēsia* could play in helping to re-engage citizens in politics. Here, I would argue that there are potential synergies between decentred theory and alternative theoretical approaches around a research agenda that examines *parrhēsia* as a form of storytelling. There are several reasons why this may prove fruitful. First, it would highlight different modalities of 'truth-telling', as distinct forms of storytelling. Examining how *parrhēsia* relates to these other forms of truth-telling, such as *tekhne*, may present a complementary framework to one centred around different traditions. Second, we could examine how 'truth-telling' is 'performed' (see Wagenaar, 2012). This would involve studying verbal communications alongside images and sounds. Decentred theory has certainly acknowledged other forms and modes of communication beyond speech but I would argue that a better understanding of how beliefs relate to speech, images, and sound is important, including the similarities and differences between them. Finally, I would argue that there is important research to be done in better understanding the 'political economy of *parrhēsia*'. This research would focus on how stories are transmitted from one site to another and why certain stories capture the imagination when others fail.

Notes

1 Interpretivism and critical realism are two self-proclaimed examples of post-positivist approaches. I will not engage in the debate between these two approaches here because this has already been discussed at length elsewhere (e.g. McAnulla, 2006; Bevir and Rhodes, 2006).
2 The key ideas of post-analytic philosophy centre on humanism and historicism. Bevir and Rhodes (2010: 64) trace its origins back to Wittingstein, Quine, and Davidson.
3 This section builds on the arguments presented in Marsh, Hall, and Fawcett (2014).
4 'Radical' is defined here in relation to the other approaches discussed in this section.
5 Bevir and Rhodes (2012: 204–5) have responded to aspects of this criticism elsewhere citing 'limited resources with which to do detailed and thorough historical analysis', but they also argue that this problem has been partly addressed by their more recent genealogies.
6 Bevir and Rhodes direct the same criticisms towards the second wave approaches that I discuss in further detail below.
7 Sørensen and Torfing (2007) identify four different approaches within the literature on metagovernance: interdependence; governability; integration; and governmentality.
8 There are several other aspects to my argument but I do not have the space to discuss all of them here so I have chosen to focus on possibly the most important point that government and governance coexist.
9 Davies and Spicer (2015) identify seven major problems with governance networks: hypocrisy; distrust; marketisation; subjugation; anti-proceduralism; fragmentation; and 'netsploitation'.
10 I do not have the space to examine storytelling in relation to other interpretivist approaches here, but see Rhodes (2011b: 308 fn 4) and Wagenaar (2011).
11 Elsewhere, Bevir and Rhodes refer to narratives, rather than stories or storytelling (e.g. Bevir and Rhodes, 2006: 20).
12 Importantly, *parrhēsia* is about what it means to be a truth-teller and truth-telling as an activity, rather than the problem of what constitutes the 'truth' (Foucault cited in Walters, 2014: 280–1).
13 Other studies have sought to do something similar, e.g. Akram (2013).

References

Akram, S. (2013) 'Fully Conscious and Prone to Habit: The characteristics of agency in the structure and agency dialectic', *Journal for the Theory of Social Behaviour*, 43(1): 45–65.
Baker, K. and Stoker, G. (2013) 'Governance and Nuclear Power: Why governing is easier said than done', *Political Studies*, 61(3): 580–98.
Bang, H. P. (2009) 'Political Community: The blind spot of modern democratic decision-making', *British Politics*, 4(1): 100–16.
Bang, H. P. (2010a) 'Between Democracy and Good Governance: A national–global quest', in M. Böss (ed.), *The Nation-State in Transformation: The governance, growth and cohesion of small states under globalisation*, Aarhus: Aarhus University Press, pp. 340–62.
Bang, H. P. (2010b) 'Between Everyday Makers and Expert Citizens', in J. Fenwick and J. McMillan (eds), *Public Management in the Postmodern Era: Challenges and prospects*, Cheltenham: Edward Elgar, pp. 163–92.

Bang, H. P. (2011) 'The Politics of Threats: Late-modern politics in the shadow of neo-liberalism', *Critical Policy Studies*, 5(4): 434–49.

Bang, H. P. (2012) 'Democracy and the Public Good: Political community and political authority', mimeo.

Bang, H. (2015) *Foucault's Political Challenge*, Basingstoke: Palgrave Macmillan.

Bell, S. (2011) 'Do we Really Need a New "Constructivist Institutionalism" to Explain Institutional Change?', *British Journal of Political Science*, 41(4): 883–906.

Bell, S. and Hindmoor, A. (2009) *Rethinking Governance: The centrality of the state in modern society*, Cambridge: Cambridge University Press.

Bevir, M. (2011) 'Governance as Theory, Practice, and Dilemma' in M. Bevir (ed.), *The Sage Handbook of Governance*, London: Sage, pp. 1–16.

Bevir, M. (2013) *A Theory of Governance*, Berkeley, CA: University of California Press.

Bevir, M. and Rhodes, R. A. W. (2003) *Interpreting British Governance*, London: Routledge.

Bevir, M. and Rhodes, R. A. W. (2006) *Governance Stories*, London: Routledge.

Bevir, M. and Rhodes, R. A. W. (2010) *The State as Cultural Practice*, Oxford: Oxford University Press.

Bevir, M. and Rhodes, R. A. W. (2012) 'Interpretivism and the Analysis of Traditions and Practices', *Critical Policy Studies*, 6(2): 201–8.

Colebatch, H. K. (2009) 'Governance as a Conceptual Development in the Analysis of Policy', *Critical Policy Studies*, 3(1): 58–67.

Crouch, C. (2011) *The Strange Non-death of Neoliberalism*, Cambridge: Polity Press.

Dahlström, C., Peters, B. G., and Pierre, J. (eds) (2011) *Steering from the Centre: Strength-ening political control in western democracies*, Toronto: University of Toronto Press.

Davies, J. S. (2011) *Challenging Governance Theory: From networks to hegemony*, Bristol: Policy Press.

Davies, J. S. (2012) 'Network Governance Theory: A Gramscian critique', *Environment and Planning A*, 44(11): 2687–704.

Davies, J. S. and Spicer, A. (2015) 'Interrogating Networks: Towards an agnostic per-spective on governance research', *Environment and Planning C, Government and policy*, 33(2): 223–38.

Dyrberg, T. B. (2014) *Foucault on the Politics of Parrhesia*, Basingstoke: Palgrave Macmillan.

Evans, M. (2003) *Constitution-Making and the Labour Party*, Basingstoke: Palgrave Macmillan.

Fawcett, P. (2014) 'Can't Live With Them, Can't Live Without Them: Why politicians matter', *Democratic Theory*, 1(2): 67–75.

Greenleaf, W. H. (1983) *The British Political Tradition, Volume 2: The ideological her-itage*, London: Meuthen.

Grote, J. R. (2012) 'Horizontalism, Vertical Integration and Vertices in Governance Net-works', *Stato e Mercato*, 94(1): 103–34.

Hajer, M. (2009) *Authoritative Governance: Policy-making in the age of mediatization*, Oxford: Oxford University Press.

Hay, C. (2006) 'Constructivist Institutionalism', in S. A. Binder, R. A. W. Rhodes, and B. A. Rockman (eds), *The Oxford Handbook of Political Institutions*, Oxford: Oxford University Press, pp. 56–74.

Hay, C. (2011) 'Interpreting Interpretivism, Interpreting Interpretations: The new herme-neutics of public administration', *Public Administration*, 89(1): 167–82.

James, O. (2009) 'Central State', in M. Flinders, A. Gamble, C. Hay, and M. Kenny (eds), *The Oxford Handbook of British Politics*, Oxford: Oxford University Press, pp. 342–64.

Jessop, B. (2004) 'Multi-level Governance and Multi-level Metagovernance: Changes in the European Union as integral moments in the transformation and reorientation of contemporary statehood', in I. Bache and M. Flinders (eds), *Multi-level Governance*, Oxford: Oxford University Press, pp. 49–74.

Jessop, B. (2011) 'Metagovernance' in M. Bevir (ed.), *The Sage Handbook of Governance*, London: Sage, pp. 106–23.

Keane, J. (2013) *Democracy and Media Decadence*, Cambridge: Cambridge University Press.

Kjær, M. (2011) 'Rhodes' Contribution to Governance Theory: Praise, criticism and the future governance debate', *Public Administration*, 89(1): 101–13.

Klijn, E-H. and Edelenbos, J. (2007) 'Meta-governance as Network Management', in E. Sørensen and J. Torfing (eds), *Theories of Democratic Network Governance*, Houndmills: Palgrave, pp. 199–214.

Kooiman, J. (2003) *Governing as Governance*, London: Thousand Oaks, CA: SAGE.

Kooiman, J. and Jentoft, S. (2009) 'Meta-Governance: Values, norms and principles, and the making of hard choices', *Public Administration*, 87(4): 818–36.

Mahoney, J. and Thelen, K. (eds) (2010) *Explaining Institutional Change: Ambiguity, agency and power*, Cambridge: Cambridge University Press.

Marsh, D. (2010) 'Stability and Change: The last dualism', *Critical Policy Studies*, 4(1): 86–101.

Marsh, D. (2011) 'The New Orthodoxy: The differentiated polity model', *Public Administration*, 89(1): 32–48.

Marsh, D. and Hall, M. (2015) 'The British Political Tradition and the Material–Ideational Debate', *British Journal of Politics and International Relations*, online 1 July 2015, DOI: 10.1111/1467-856X.12077: http://onlinelibrary.wiley.com/doi/10.1111/1467-856X.12077/abstract.

Marsh, D., Hall, M., and Fawcett, P. (2014) 'Two Cheers for Interpretivism: Deconstructing the British Political Tradition', *Australian Journal of Public Administration*, 73(3): 340–48.

McAnulla, S. (2006) 'Challenging the New Interpretivist Approach: Towards a critical realist alternative', *British Politics*, 1(1), 113–38.

Meulemann, L. (2008) *Public Management and the Metagovernance of Hierarchies, Networks and Markets*, The Hague: Physica-Verlag Heidelberg.

Rhodes, R. A. W. (2007) 'Understanding Governance: Ten years on', *Organization Studies*, 28(8): 1243–64.

Rhodes R. A. W. (2011a) 'Thinking On: A career in public administration', *Public Administration*, 89(1): 196–212.

Rhodes, R. A. W. (2011b) *Everyday Life in British Government*, Oxford: Oxford University Press.

Rhodes, R. A. W. (2012) 'Theory, Method and British Political Life History', *Political Studies Review*, 10: 161–76.

Rhodes, R. A. W. (2014) '"Genre Blurring" and Public Administration: What can we learn from ethnography?', *Australian Journal of Public Administration*, 73(3): 317–30.

Schmidt, V. (2008) 'Discursive Institutionalism: The explanatory power of ideas and discourse', *Annual Review of Political Science*, 11: 303–26.

Sørensen, E. and Torfing, J. (eds) (2007) *Theories of Democratic Network Governance*, Houndmills: Palgrave Macmillan.

Sørensen, E. and Torfing, J. (2009) 'Making Governance Networks Effective and Democratic Through Metagovernance', *Public Administration*, 87(2): 234–58.

Torfing, J., Peters, B. G., Pierre, J., and Sørensen, E. (2012) *Interactive Governance: Advancing the paradigm*, Oxford: Oxford University Press.

Wagenaar, H. (2011) *Meaning in Action: Interpretation and dialogue in policy analysis*, M. E. Sharpe: New York.

Wagenaar, H. (2012) 'Dwellers on the Threshold of Practice: The interpretivism of Bevir and Rhodes', *Critical Policy Studies*, 6(1): 85–99.

Walters, W. (2014) 'Parrhēsia Today: Drone strikes, fearless speech and the contentious politics of security', *Global Society*, 28(3): 277–99.

3 Interpreting Hillsborough

Andrew Taylor

Introduction

Hillsborough stadium in Sheffield was selected by the Football Association (FA) as a neutral venue for the 1988–89 FA Cup semi-final between Liverpool FC and Nottingham Forest. Football grounds, which were not all-seater, had steel fencing segregating fans and to prevent pitch-invasions. Liverpool fans were allocated to the Leppings Lane stand accessed by seven turnstiles. In response to substantial overcrowding before kick-off, police ordered an exit gate be opened. This led to an influx of spectators into two already crowded pens. After six minutes the game was stopped. A barrier broke and spectators began to fall over each other; panic spread as fans tried to escape the developing crush. Ninety-six people died and 766 were injured in Britain's, and one of the world's, worst stadium disasters.

The dominant narrative was that these fatalities were the result of ticketless, drunken Liverpool fans rushing the gate causing the fatal crush. The bereaved families challenged this narrative, as did an official inquiry in 1990, triggering a process that culminated in the formation of the Hillsborough Independent Panel (HIP) to collect, review and report on the disaster in the light of the assembled evidence. The HIP's September 2012 report rejected the dominant narrative – the standard story – that Liverpool fans were responsible and that the authorities, notably South Yorkshire Police (SYP), attempted to conceal the disaster's real causes. Hillsborough has become part of a wider critique of a scandal-prone SYP and symptomatic of a range of cover-ups involving 'the Establishment'.

Actors explain social life using narratives or stories (Holstein and Gubrium, 2009). What Tilly describes as standard stories have a distinct structure: 'self-motivated actors in delimited time and space, conscious actions that cause most or all of the significant effects' (2002: 28). A story can provide a compelling account of why something happened in the way it did but still fail to 'adequately represent causes and effects as they unfold in social processes' because 'cause–effect relations are indirect, incremental, interactive, unintended, collective, or mediated by the nonhuman environment rather than being direct, willed consequences or individual actions' (Tilly, 2002: 29, 32). The value of interpretivism is its focus on meanings and beliefs, which means that events are best understood as narratives or stories, constructed by actors responding to dilemmas.

However, in 'The Trouble with Stories' (1999; see also 2002), Tilly argues standard stories are incompatible with social–scientific explanations because they over-state the actor's role and do not specify the causal mechanism(s) producing stories. Interpretivism easily navigates the standard story terrain, rejecting a material reality or 'truth' (other than the contingent) because of the insuperable barrier of the double hermeneutic. Interpretivists can account for collective/organisational and individual behaviour as the contingent product of continuous interaction, but interpretivists still must account for how and why webs of meaning produce behaviour and influence meaning. Interaction and reflexivity are critical in developing and sustaining a story, which social scientists must understand in order to explain political phenomena. Interpretivism poses questions about how to analyse preferences, particularly the relationship between *revealed* preferences (behaviour), *stated* preferences (written and verbal) and *actual* (unknowable) preferences. No certain connection can be made between revealed, stated, and actual preferences (Dowding, 2004: 138) but the world would be inexplicable if we assumed no relationship. Stories provide that linkage.

Tilly argues social science should strive to create a *superior story* that, first, includes all major actors; second, accurately represents cause and effect relationships between actors; third, takes into account the wider context of the standard story; and finally, relates specific causes to a wide range of influences that may not be apparent to actors. Superior stories 'do not identify all the relevant cause–effect relations, but they remain consistent with fuller, more adequate causal accounts' (Tilly, 2002: 39–40). The objective is to construct detailed empirical versions of events in which behaviour is connected to influences and processes not immediately visible to the actors generating the story. Social science explanations rely heavily on institutions. Traditions, norms, and values are institutions generated by interaction, motivating and influencing behaviour, expressing what is conceived of as feasible and desirable (North, 1990: 3). These institutions can be hidden or visible, organisational or normative and imply the existence of a power structure that benefits consistently some more than others. Actors advance and defend preferences by word and action but, operating in complex environments composed of other actors with different perspectives, understandings of the same event will inevitably differ. This variability also encompasses the idea of practice within organisations; behaviours that constrain and facilitate actions and which constitute organisational culture (Wagenaar, 2012). Words and actions mean something and have purposive rationality, but the distinction between standard and superior stories is that the latter postulates a structure of inequality of access and influence over stories and how to respond to a dilemma.

Despite the double hermeneutic, meaning is not 'a blank wall, an opaque screen, or an impenetrable thicket', and by 'tunnelling under' this thicket social scientists can explore causal mechanisms, showing how the influence of webs of meaning comes about and how stories are constructed and sustained (Tilly, 2002: 37–8). By concentrating on *contextualisation* (the situations on which particular stories arise) and *generation* (how stories are created, adopted and evolve) we can develop accounts that go further than standard stories by exploring the idea of 'deep politics', which expresses the idea of politics operating at different levels where hidden influences condition the surface (and therefore visible) behaviour of actors.

Putting aside the awful human tragedy, Hillsborough has significant implications for political analysis and, thanks to the evidence assembled by the HIP, provides an opportunity to test interpretivism and the deep politics thesis. SYP determined the narrative, exploiting their authority and legitimacy to secure early and privileged access to the media to articulate the standard story: Liverpool fans (many aggressive, drunk, and ticketless) broke into the stadium, thereby producing the fatal crush. Liverpool supporters were responsible for the death toll. This chapter explores the construction of the Hillsborough standard story and how this was challenged and then replaced by a superior story that captured a far more complex causality and which was a more accurate explanation of events. Why was the standard story preferred and why did replacement take 25 years? A more accurate account was available on the day of the Hillsborough disaster and was subsequently endorsed by a judicial inquiry. A non-interpretivist account would explain this by reference to material interests and the exercise of power, whereas an interpretivist would stress dominant traditions and webs of meaning to understand outcomes. In explaining Hillsborough, I consider whether these approaches are, despite different ontologies, two sides of the same coin.

My argument is that Hillsborough provides a situationally specific case of how a standard story was constructed, promulgated, and sustained that was itself a manifestation of a wider web of meaning (or tradition) relating to policing football crowds that was influenced, in turn, by broader metanarratives on public order and secrecy. When taken together the event, the organisational–institutional response, and metanarrative are, by using 'thick description', shown to be interconnected and reinforcing. There were 'path dependent' elements at work: the concern about football hooliganism, the reputation of some Liverpool fans, and the reflexive organisational response of 'blaming the victim' (Armstrong, 2003; Frosdick and Marsh, 2005), but path dependency does not capture the complexity of Hillsborough, because of the values, norms and meanings that played a central role in the course of events. These values, norms, and meanings are fundamental to understanding Hillsborough and subsequent developments; interpretivism offers a wider understanding than historical institutionalism of the expressive choices made by actors when confronting a dilemma.

This chapter has three sections. The first shows how systemic and systematic bias determined the standard story of Hillsborough. The second considers the existence of 'deep politics' and that narratives are sensitive to power inequalities embedded in the process of articulating and preserving a dominant narrative. This dominance hinges on the coexistence of situational narratives embedded in and influenced by metanarratives. Metanarrative is a narrative about narratives and involves meaning, experience, and knowledge which, combined, condition the understanding and behaviour of groups in their specific context. Metanarrative and situational narrative combine in governmentality that is both prior to agency and influences how actors understand their world and behave (Bevir, 1999, 2011). The third section focuses on two metanarratives – secrecy and public order – and examines how these influenced situational actions at Hillsborough and the resulting concoction of the standard story. The chapter concludes that two types of continuities influence politics: one is specific to context and can change; the second, metanarratives, provides the frameworks in which context is located, and these frameworks are highly resistant to change. Combined, these constitute governmentality: the 'institutions, procedures, analyses, and reflections, calculations and tactics' that underpin rule and the technologies of power (Foucault, 2009: 108–9). Interpretivism offers a range of tools for exploring this complex multi-levelled interaction.

Interpreting Hillsborough

During the afternoon of 15 April, Chief Superintendent Duckenfield, the police commander, told FA representatives that the trigger to the disaster was fans breaking into the stadium. This 'untruthful allegation was broadcast internationally, establishing the immediate portrayal of the unfolding disaster as a further example of soccer-related crowd violence' (HIP, 2012a: para. 2.12.3). This narrative was reinforced further by unnamed police officers, Irvine Patnick (then Conservative MP for Sheffield Hallam), and Paul Middup, secretary of the South Yorkshire Police Federation (SYPF) (Figure 3.1).

Four days after the disaster, the *Sun's* (19 April) front-page headline was 'The Truth' with three sub-heads: 'Some fans picked pockets of victims', 'Some fans urinated on the brave cops', and 'Some fans beat up PC giving kiss of life'. This story, replicated in other media, built on the foundations laid on Saturday and drew heavily on a story filed by White's News Agency on 18 April,

> Angry police hit back yesterday (tues) at Liverpool fans who hampered life saving attempts after the Hillsborough horror.
> They spoke for the first time after being stung by savage criticism of their actions and claims the Merseyside fans were blameless.
> The shocked bobbies revealed how they were kicked and punched as they gave victims the kiss of life.
> And others were horrified to see Liverpool fans urinating on policemen and victims as they fought to haul them out of the killer crush.
>
> (HIP, 2012b)

Recognising the incendiary nature of this story, White's deemed a single source insufficient. Unsolicited confirmation on 17 June (four officers telling the same story separately and unprompted to three journalists, supplemented by Irvine Patnick MP) led to the report's transmission on 18 June and 'we did as much as we could to check the authenticity of the story in the time available and reported faithfully what we were told' (HIP, 2012c). White's interpretation was presented as 'setting the record straight'. Paul Middup told the Police Federation South Yorkshire Joint Branch Board (27 April) that:

> the press and media coverage had been immense. He added he had initially been interviewed on radio – Radio Sheffield – which had been successful

Figure 3.1 The Hillsborough Standard Story

and it had snowballed from there.... He stated he had been proud to put the members' case forward.

(HIP, 2012d: 4–5)

These minutes of a confidential SYPF meeting give a fascinating insight into the causal effects of cultural and organisational biases. Peter Wright, the Chief Constable, told the meeting that the first task was to construct a 'rock-solid story' and 'we are working tremendously hard on the history and saga of Hillsborough. Once we have the history we can then produce the facts'. An unidentified member stressed that 'to avoid any further operational criticism, the pro-forma [to gather information] which had been distributed throughout the Force, must be completed properly, with everyone's experience; otherwise the Inquiry team would not get the proper facts'. The Chief Constable believed 'the Inquiry team could be directed but if we sit back and let them collect the evidence, we would lose it. We have to do it ourselves.' The Chair agreed; 'It was agreed by everyone we had to get the message – togetherness – across the force' (HIP, 2012d: 10–11, 12, 13, 14). The information gathered, reinforced by the altering of police statements, reflected, and thereby confirmed the standard story.

The police found it inconceivable that the judicial inquiry (the Taylor interim report of August 1989) would not find the fans responsible. A cabinet briefing (2 August) for the Prime Minister gives a different story:

- that the main reason for the disaster was the failure of police control;
- Sheffield City Council were dilatory and inefficient in exercising their responsibility for safety at the ground;
- that Sheffield Wednesday were to blame for not acting to ensure that fans could be evenly distributed between the pens on the terraces and at the Leppings Lane end.

Little or no blame was attached to the Liverpool fans (HIP, 2012e: 1).

A minority of fans had been drinking but neither this, nor hooliganism, caused the congestion precipitating the crisis. Fear of hooliganism determined police strategy, which led to an operational focus on public order, and the main cause of the disaster was a loss of police control. This alternative story triggered a counter-attack and in response 'the police had initiated a vilification campaign directed towards Liverpool fans' (HIP, 2010a: para. 1.31).

On 6 September 1989 Peter Shersby MP (the Police Federation's parliamentary spokesman) met Douglas Hurd (the Home Secretary) and Shersby stressed Taylor's adverse effect on police morale (a 'not in the public interest' argument). A meeting at SYP headquarters on 3 October 1989 (which Shersby attended) developed the full rebuttal (HIP, 2012f: 8, 21). This reiterated the original narrative (that the disaster was caused by drunken, ticketless Liverpool fans) and challenged the accuracy and veracity of Taylor (and therefore any alternative narrative), a process described as 'putting the record straight' and 'putting our side of the story'. A meeting, which divided on party lines, at the House of Commons (8 November 1989) arranged by Shersby, listened to Superintendent Bettison present SYP's case prior to a proposed parliamentary debate (HIP, 2012g: 2). A commentary on Taylor in the magazine, *The Police*, condemned the report, reiterating that 'a large section of Liverpool fans who had been drinking to excess, many of whom were ticketless, but all of whom were determined to get into the ground before the kick off' were responsible for the deaths. Conceding the 'vast majority' were not in this category, there was nonetheless 'a large contingent of drink sodden louts whose general behaviour shocked experienced police officers' (Judge, 1989: 26).

The standard story reveals the dynamics of contested stories, of how one narrative, articulated by 'primary definers' (Hall *et al.*, 1978: 183–4) was privileged despite the challenge from, amongst others, the victims' families (for example, Scraton, 2004). The key elements of the police version were repeated and reinforced by the media and viewed through the 'lens of hooliganism' (HIP, 2012a: 1.38 *et seq.*) which framed the official view of football crowds as a public order issue. This interpretation proved resilient (Jemphrey and Berrington, 2000) despite an alternative narrative of overcrowding, poor policing, and stewarding, and an inadequate response by the emergency services. Allegations about the Liverpool fans from official (and therefore authoritative and reliable) sources such as the Police Federation, senior police officers, MPs, and others reinforced the standard story. What is remarkable, and what testifies to the power of institutional inertial bias, is the immunity (*not* invulnerability) of this version to challenge (HIP, 2012a: 2.12.9).

Having passed the Football Spectators Act (1989) in response to the Heysel disaster, a piece of legislation on a par with the Dangerous Dogs Act, the government was moving ahead with a contentious membership scheme but this was abandoned after Taylor's final report. Government was pulled in two directions: evidence confirmed the alternative story of a loss of police control and poor decision making but this was balanced by a reluctance to weaken police morale. Thus:

> The main impact of the report will be on perceptions of the police. It is very critical, and will sap confidence in the police force … Liverpool fans – who <u>have</u> caused trouble in the past – will feel vindicated.… It is a very sorry episode. But there seems no reason to think that report's conclusions are wrong.
>
> (HIP, 2012e: 3, original emphasis)

On the other hand, the Chief Whip believed that once the 'emotion had subsided and the facts about the behaviour of the crowd would have been appreciated, the incident will be seem to stem more from rowdyism than from the police's response' (HIP, 2012h: 2). The Merseyside Police expressed 'a good deal of sympathy' with SYP, and 'the fact that large numbers of Liverpool fans turned up without tickets … was getting lost sight of in attempts to blame the police.' Moreover, Hillsborough was part of a pattern of 'drunken Liverpool fans [causing] disaster' (HIP, 2012i). Douglas Hurd, the Home Secretary, proposed government 'welcome' the report. In reply, Mrs Thatcher wrote, 'What do we mean by "welcoming the broad thrust of the report"? The broad thrust is devastating criticism of the police. Is that for us to <u>welcome</u>?' (HIP, 2012j, original emphasis). The ferocity of her underlining testified to the Prime Minister's concern at Hurd's suggestion.

The Taylor report and the victims' families (http://hfsg.co.uk) rejected this narrative but the alternative could not displace the official version and the government ignored criticism of the police, focusing instead on crowd safety. This reflected the unresponsiveness of deep politics and the resilience of the standard story in the face of external pressure to acknowledge the force of the alternative interpretation. This was hinted at in David Cameron's apology: 'the families have long believed that some of the authorities attempted to create a completely unjust account of events that sought to blame the fans for what happened' (Hansard, 12 October 2012: cols. 283–84). This type of systemic and systematic bias is well documented and understood by political scientists (see Bachrach and Baratz, 1970; Gaventa, 1980).

Ample evidence existed to write a superior story. This alternative was handled not by refutation or rejection but by ignoring it, relying on the obstacles created by procedure, and concentrating on explanation, rather than by establishing responsibility and accountability. This produced the paradox that 'everybody knew' SYP were primarily responsible but no one was to blame, as was demonstrated by the failed private prosecutions of the police by the bereaved families. A comparable case is the trials after 'The Battle of Orgreave' (June 1985) involving NUM pickets and police at a coke works near Sheffield. When police evidence (on oath) against arrested mineworkers was disproved, cases were dropped, the accused acquitted and no action ('not in the public interest') was taken against police officers (Taylor, 2005: 224–6). All that was required to maintain the status quo was inaction, an inaction that sustained the 'double injustice' of 'the failure of the state … and the denigration of the deceased' for 23 years (Hansard, 12 October 2012: cols. 285–6). How can we explain these outcomes?

Interpreting Deep Politics

This section argues that the politics revealed by Hillsborough is multi-levelled. Interpretivism tends to focus on 'surface politics' (directly observable and relatively easy to navigate), to the exclusion of 'deep politics' (Dale Scott, 1996), which deals with meanings, beliefs, and preferences that influence visible behaviour and which is much harder to penetrate. Interpretivists tend to collapse deep politics into a broad concept of tradition, but critics have argued that tradition is conceptually vague and, when used as a portmanteau, conflates different types of tradition (for example, one applying to a specific group influencing the group's context) and renders cause and effect obscure. Deep politics operates in, and through, organisations with interests to advance and defend, actions that condition, but do *not* determine the topology of surface politics. Deep politics points to the significance of institutions, represented here by organisational cultures and traditions – in this case *secrecy* and *public order* – that are extremely resistant to change and which coexist with an 'open' surface polity that projects a different configuration of meaning.

In the standard story, incorrect statements became 'facts', neutralising alternative interpretations. This was despite the existence of an alternative that was sufficiently coherent to induce Jack Straw, the then Home Secretary, to ask Lord Justice Stuart-Smith to explore whether or not there should be a new inquiry into Hillsborough. Stuart-Smith, however, sustained the official interpretation, concluding (Cm. 3878) that insufficient grounds existed to justify re-opening the inquiry. Although presented with evidence of doctored police statements, Stuart-Smith argued these did not materially alter what was already known. However, the opening of SYP police records to Stuart-Smith enabled Andy Burnham (then Secretary of State for Culture, Media, and Sport) to press successfully for the full disclosure of all relevant public and private papers.

HIP (created in January 2010) operated on the principle of maximum disclosure and, using its research and analysis of 400,000 documents, produced a comprehensive and authoritative analytical narrative of events. HIP addressed a different constituency (the victims' families) and constructed its narrative emphasising openness and responsibility. HIP operated outside the rules of the game and challenged a basic component of deep politics: determining what information would be released. Unprecedented disclosure provided the evidence to refute definitively the standard story, exposing the truth in a way that legal and political institutions and processes did not.

The official, standard story depended on football fans as drunken, violent thugs and this influenced the perception of Hillsborough and the response to the dilemma it posed: undermining confidence in the police was not in the public interest. However, it was also in the public interest to establish what had happened. The result was to ignore responsibility and accountability, focusing instead on the safety of football stadia. The alternative (and truthful) narrative was inaudible because there was little institutional architecture to support a narrative of police responsibility. Only after 23 years of external pressure was the 'official' truth debunked by the release of massive amounts of private information that showed deep politics in action. Hillsborough demonstrates the construction of a narrative by those who benefit from the status quo and how their values and beliefs are nested within wider webs of meaning.

Whilst accepting institutions, combining organisation and values, are socially constructed and contingent, they nonetheless persist over time. Actors are constituted by institutions, which provide opportunities for creative agency within the constraints represented by organisational structures and meanings. This reduces the scope for dramatic reconfigurations because organisational continuity is sustained by robust meanings and traditions (and vice versa), both specific to the organisation and part of the context in which an organisation is located, thereby reinforcing day-to-day practices and creating space for situated agency. Individuals act within and through institutions that encapsulate the practices and meanings that influence behaviour, which then influences the organisation. Reflexivity enables situated agency where actors respond to dilemmas utilising long-established meanings and practices. This points to a historicist and decentred approach to studying politics, together with an emphasis on agency in the creation and modification of narratives. The result is both a more focused and nuanced understanding of politics and, in particular, how different levels of political action are influenced by interdependent narratives and metanarratives.

Hillsborough was a power scandal 'in which hidden forms of power are suddenly disclosed in the public domain' (Thompson, 2000: 198), showing how 'private' power was used to subvert and neutralise publicly accepted norms (inclusive, open, accessible) and expectations. Revealing 'hidden' power structures (exclusive, closed, inaccessible) and alternative traditions nested within, but hostile to, the dominant normative tradition, produced public responses of outrage, condemnation, and reproach. This type of politics poses complex analytical problems for interpretivism: first, the desire to cover up actions detrimental to the organisation can be understood as a metanarrative common to all organisations; and second, Hillsborough indicated the existence of power normally hidden from public view but assumed to exist. An interpretivist sees 'hidden power' not as a structure or institution but as a situational narrative embedded in, but contrary to, a visible public tradition. Power cannot therefore be understood as a unitary top-down phenomenon and must include the stories internalised by individuals and groups. Hillsborough shows the clash of two traditions – one hidden, one open – manifested in the violation of due process, rules and procedures governing the exercise of power and generating a dilemma that demanded a response.

Deep politics is the product of organisational micro-practices and competing understandings in the organisation in relation to its interaction with its environment. Non-members are not party to these meanings. Deal and Kennedy (1998) define organisational culture as 'the way things get done around here', which can produce 'groupthink' (Janis, 1972). Groupthink captures the situation where the desire for conformity and harmony produces a particular way of interpreting the world that results in dysfunctionality. Faced by a challenge, the group seeks to minimise conflict and maximise consensus, failing to critically evaluate (or even consider) alternative accounts. Group loyalty and cohesion coalesce around an understanding that squeezes out alternatives, sustained by stereotyping, reinforcing in-group sentiments and confirmation bias with alternatives representing disloyalty and with individuals subject to pressure to conform.

Organisations do not have a single culture, and which one predominates is a manifestation of power. Ravasi and Schultze (2006) interpret organisational culture as shared mental assumptions that guide actor interpretation and action by defining what is appropriate and thinkable behaviour. The fostering of norms such as trust and reciprocity encourage organisational coordination and coherence; organisations are also motivated by the need to avoid blame and members are attuned to external reputation. When failure occurs (which it invariably does) they will engage in blame-avoidance ('we are all in this together'), which is particularly significant in dilemmas involving high political risk or where failure is catastrophically manifest (Moynihan, 2012). This syndrome can be seen in the police's actions during and after Hillsborough and, to some extent, in the government's response. Actors were heavily influenced by the football hooligan paradigm, the post-Heysel reputation of some Liverpool supporters, and the police hierarchy's assumptions that encouraged developing and adhering to the standard story, clustering for mutual support, and blame avoidance. This reflex can be seen clearly at the Special Joint Board Branch Meeting (19 April) (HIP, 2012d), even more strikingly at the post-Taylor meeting on 3 October at South Yorkshire Police HQ (HIP, 2012f), and in the presentation to MPs (HIP, 2012g).

Organisational culture is 'hardened power' but it is not determinist; rather it constrains and facilitates behaviour and outcomes, and it evolves. This is the 'Ship of Theseus' paradox. Imagine a knife possessed by an individual for many years but during this time the knife has had two new blades and three new handles: is it the same knife? Aristotle sought to resolve the paradox by distinguishing *formal cause* (does the design change?) from *final cause* (does the intended purpose change)? Deep politics testifies to continuity in design and purpose, and shows how change can be grafted onto stable structures of meaning. An institution can change whilst remaining the same. The Ship of Theseus paradox influences how actors interpret and respond to dilemmas as well as influencing the conduct of everyday bureaucratic politics. Deep politics is an institution composed of ideas, relationships, predispositions, and organisations that stimulate responses to dilemmas; deep politics is more than an ideational construct; it is a powerful autonomous structure.

Researching the hidden inner-workings of a political process is difficult because of a shortage of hard evidence and the necessity for secrecy. Discussing the 'chilling effect' (the fear that confidential discussions would become public, acting as a disincentive to frankness and honesty) in policy formulation, the Justice Select Committee inquiry on freedom of information noted

> it would, by its nature, be very difficult to find hard objective evidence of it. That is why, on this subject, it is necessary at least to consider anecdotes and impressions, albeit they might lack the academic rigour on which we would ideally like to base conclusions.
>
> (HoC, 2012a: para. 170)

The chilling effect would encourage 'stairwell meetings' to preserve confidentiality and autonomy, an instance of deep politics that is easy to infer but difficult to demonstrate. Evidential and methodological inadequacies mean research can degenerate into conspiracy theory but there is ample evidence that deep politics exists, which enables us to differentiate standard and superior stories. It is possible to distinguish standard and superior stories because of the massive amount of relevant raw material put in the public domain over the last 15 years. Since 1996, there have been some 24 inquiries under the 1921 and 2005 inquiries acts. The reports are of secondary importance, but the raw evidence is critical as a data mine. No definitive account of *any* event is possible, so the political scientist's job is to provide plausible accounts, which rest primarily on observing *and* interpreting behaviour (Dowding, 2004: 140–1). The evidence gathered for these inquiries provides the material for observation, interpretation, and constructing plausible accounts of 'deep' politics influencing 'surface' politics. Deep politics is an attitude of mind, a predisposition to see the world in a particular way and behave accordingly and can therefore be recognised by interpretivists.

What we can loosely call 'organisational culture' is the first element of deep politics. Organisational cultures are specific but embedded within metanarratives. At one level, Hillsborough can be explained as a response by an organisation to events that threatened it and its members. The loss of life, the organisations involved and their response make this an inadequate explanation and suggest a more complex pattern of cause and effect. Now we move to metanarrative.

Secrecy and Order

In their contemporary forms, secrecy and order as metanarratives developed as a response to the interconnected pressure for democracy and the emergence of an urban, industrial working class that spawned technologies of rule (for example, the police) but also narratives and traditions. Secrecy and order are concerned with the exercise and nature of power, and both influenced the specifics of Hillsborough. Secrecy is both something to be achieved and a cultural artefact influencing how actors (individuals and organisations) behave and order is what is permitted in the public sphere; they combine in the idea of the public interest.

Secrecy

For Weber, secrecy was fundamental to bureaucratic power 'and nothing is so fanatically defended by the bureaucracy' (Weber, 1970: 233). Hillsborough sheds light on the state's historical identity, an identity protected by secrecy and concerned with order, creating autonomous institutions resistant to change (Vincent, 1998: 13). Secrecy involves both the denial of information and deciding which information should be released. Hennessy describes secrecy as

> the bonding material which holds the rambling structure of central government together. Secrecy is built into the calcium of a British policymaker's bones.... It is the very essence of the Establishment view of good government.... The rule is that the fewer the people who know, the better, including insiders.
>
> (1989: 346)

This goes wider than the bureaucratic-organisational culture, because it portrays secrecy as a pervasive national–political cultural trait. Similarly, Vincent argues 'It was not so much that British political culture was inherently secretive, but rather *that in the British version of a liberal state, secrecy was inherently a cultural form*' (1998: 314, added emphasis). Secrecy determines the bureaucracy's relationship with the 'outside' and is therefore central to the nature and process of governance. The 'culture of secrecy' is more nuanced than just concealing information. It is deeply embedded in a dense web of values and meanings founded on the possession of secret knowledge, which enhances trust and defines probity amongst those privy to information and which defines the public interest. The key is not the concealment of information 'but the right to determine its release ... to judge what ... [is] good for the nation at large' (Vincent, 1998: 16). The state thus becomes synonymous with the public. The basis of solidarity and control is the possession of information, which is essential for sustaining elite autonomy. This culture was challenged by demands for freedom of information, a demand justified by declining trust in institutions accused of inefficiency and protected from criticism by their control of information.

In 2000, the Labour government passed the Freedom of Information Act (FoIA). Although much watered down, the FoIA was sold as a major modification of the governing tradition, a significant augmentation of democracy that would improve the quality of public debate and policy. In his memoirs, Tony Blair described the FoIA as his biggest regret and indulged in uncharacteristic self-flagellation: 'You idiot. You naïve, foolish, irresponsible nincompoop. There is really no description of stupidity, no matter how vivid, that is adequate. I quake at the imbecility of it' (Blair, 2010: 516–17). He concluded freedom of information was 'not practical.... If you are trying to take a difficult decision and you're weighing up the pros and cons, you have frank conversations.... And if those conversations are ... liable to be highlighted in particular ways, you are going to be very cautious. That's why it's not a sensible thing' (*Guardian*, 1 September 2010).

Historically, this culture has remained inviolate, irrespective of the party in government (for example, Rogers, 1997; Naylor, 2009; Wilkinson, 2009; and Brooke, 2010). Secrecy was vital for governing and:

> However impatient [politicians] might be with the culture of Whitehall, they had no intention of compromising its right to determine when and on what terms it shared its confidential knowledge with the people. The secrecy of keeping secrets remained in place.
>
> (Vincent, 1998: 310)

This can be seen, for example, in the memoirs of various New Labour ministers (Diamond and Richards, 2008: 189–91). Secrecy, both a tradition and code, is justified by the need to sustain the autonomy and integrity of decision making and the discussions on which decisions were based. To avoid a 'chilling-effect' a 'safe space' is required 'within which policy can be formulated and recorded with a degree of confidentiality' (HoC, 2012a: 54). The default setting of this culture is risk-averse and conservative, and if challenged the response, as described in the Butler report, is evasion (HoC, 2004: paras 610–11). Note also Taylor's comments on the evidence of senior police officers. The reflexive response reflects the expectation of privacy, which protects autonomy, as fundamental to good and effective government.

The FoIA delineates a 'safe space' composed of exemptions setting out a public interest test. The most important are sections s.35 (formulation and development of public policy) and s.36 (actions prejudicial to the effective conduct of public policy), and the Information Commissioner has since upheld the sanctity of the 'safe space'. Nonetheless, the Justice Select Committee conceded that the act and the possibility of disclosure could change behaviour because it was now unclear to actors what constituted a safe or unsafe space (HoC, 2012a: para. 166). Hazell *et al.*'s (2010, 2011) relatively sanguine analysis of the FoIA's impact on policy formulation was disputed by civil servants and politicians. Lord (Gus) O'Donnell and Jack Straw's evidence eloquently and forcefully demonstrated the strength of the culture of secrecy and its attendant web of meanings (defined as the power to determine what information should be made public) and that those who best know government should define what remains secret (HoC, 2012b: Ev 47 and Ev 64). Reflecting on this, the Justice Committee concluded, 'We see no reason why former senior ministers and officials in particular would flag this up as a concern if they did not genuinely believe it to be so' (HoC, 2012a: para. 200).

The tradition and culture of secrecy at the heart of policy formation is a story of a powerful web of meaning (albeit not unchallenged) and there is little evidence of the erosion of this culture (HoC, 2012a: para. 187). The implications of this for interpretivism are complex. At one level, this is what one would expect. Some aspects of policy formulation and decision making must remain secret. What matters is who decides what remains secret. And secrecy's centrality to, and utility for, the governing tradition is readily admitted by practitioners and academics. However, secrecy reinforces the power asymmetry at the core of policy formation, despite the multiplicity of actors involved in governance. One of the strengths of interpretivism is its interest in the micro-level and with individuals (for example, O'Donnell, Straw) as the bearers of a governing tradition, which conditions their beliefs and actions; but beliefs can change. Blair's position on freedom of information is in this respect interesting: supporting and acting within one tradition, in one institutional context (Labour in opposition), and developing appropriate preferences (FoI) and legislating; then, because of exposure to the governing tradition, events, organisational cultures, and context (governing), Blair changed his revealed preferences.

Order

From the late-eighteenth/early-nineteenth century, public order, the highest of high politics, has been the central concern of the state. The interaction of liberalism, common law, and statute law rendered defining 'order' difficult (for example, the Public Order Acts 1936 and 1986 responded to specific problems) and this suited governments which, under the guise of 'local control', shifted responsibility to local police forces, albeit subject to central direction when required. Reinforcing this was the narrative of police and people in harmony; police power was reciprocal and part of a wider negotiation between state and society. The police were given considerable freedom to determine what constituted order and how it was to be secured when controlling public spaces. The result was the growing political significance of chief constables and the professionalisation of policing encapsulated in the police's operational independence and autonomy from central and local government, reinforced by uncertain (or even absent) 'constitutional definitions and constraints' (Townsend, 1993: 138). The Police Act (1964) s5(1) came closest to expressing the tradition of 'operational' freedom in the absence of 'political' control which, in part, explains the police's hostile reaction to elected Police and Crime Commissioners.

The concept of order remained deliberately vague, conferring advantages on police and government, but enforcement raised profound difficulties for the police. Closely defining order clashed with both the tradition of the police as the civilian in uniform and with professionalisation that promoted the police's social isolation as well as their operational autonomy. The response to these dilemmas combined myth-making (police and strikers playing football during the General Strike, the ritualised and, by implication, complicit behaviour of police and pickets in the 1970s) with regular moral panics (Teddy boys, mods and rockers, muggers, for example) over a decline in civilised values (Cohen, 2011). The history of crowd safety tragedies, seen through the 'lens of hooliganism', was dominated 'by the emergence and consolidation of a growing emphasis on crowd control' so that from the late 1960s football hooliganism 'became a core public order priority' (HIP 2010a: para. 1.38). This was reflected in the Police Operational Order drawn up for the game: 'Spectators travelling to and arriving in Sheffield were to be tracked, directed, randomly stopped and searched, disembarked and "supervised"' (HIP, 2010a: para. 1.73). Police Officer 'L' believed 'had we had more manpower and been more hostile we could have sorted the matter out, maybe have prevented what happened ... looking back I am sure it was a riot' (HIP, 2012f: 12).

When the image of policing by consent was challenged, this was blamed on, for example, unforeseen events, a lack of resources, or individual failings (a 'bad apple'). Animating this narrative was the notion of the police striking a 'balance' between a right to protest and a right to tranquillity. The balance favoured order, reflecting a view that the police, despite their relative historical freedom from scrutiny, enjoyed a unique insight into the public interest, which was served best by police autonomy. This tradition came under massive strain from the late 1960s but by the mid-1980s an organisational culture stressing police autonomy had developed 'that was radically out of line with the consensual assumptions on which the English police system was founded' (Townsend, 1993: 154).

After the publication of the Scarman report (1981) on public order, an explosion of community policing initiatives sought to revivify and reinforce the 'traditional' notions of policing and police autonomy and flexibility in negotiating public order(s). 'Balance' remained at the heart of the dilemma between different types of public order policing (community policing *versus* 'going in hard'), a dilemma that recurred in the 1980s (the miners' strike), 1990s (poll tax protests), and the 2000s (the Occupy protests and 2011 riots). In an interpretivist understanding of public order, the *foundational* police task is difficult to explore but, thanks to data mines such as the HIP report and archive, it is now more open to analysis. Framed this way, the story of policing and the recurring dilemma is eminently suited to an interpretivist interpretation.

Neither organisationally nor culturally were the police opposed to community policing, which articulates the classic view of 'good' policing. What they fear historically is that openness and integration into networks involving a wide range of actors means a loss of autonomy and control. Metanarratives (order and secrecy) help explain why the official version of Hillsborough was so different from what happened. The police have been under pressure to reform in the interests of effectiveness, efficiency, and accountability, but, despite evidence of the inherent conservatism of police culture, (for example, Waddington, 1999; Barton, 2003; Loftus, 2010) conservatism is not a sufficient explanation for police behaviour. The choice between command and control/bureaucracy or networks/community policing is not an either/or choice but is refracted through the beliefs of officers at all levels and the immediate policing tasks they confront. Command and control is more appropriate for some tasks (e.g. public order), networks for others (e.g. crime prevention), but the police's fundamental concern in both remains to maintain operational autonomy in the control of public spaces, and this means the command and control model remains the primary definer.

For political and operational reasons, as well because of external political pressure, the police will engage with 'community policing' whilst retaining a deep suspicion and dislike of openness, which can expose operational activity to those with an inadequate understanding of policing. Nonetheless, adaptation occurs. The SYP, for example – responding to the dilemmas created by Orgreave and Hillsborough – revised its approach, adopting a more facilitative approach and open attitude towards the media in an effort to restore public confidence and police morale (Waddington, 2011). However, police culture was critical in the response to Hillsborough: avoiding blame and reputational damage, and incredulity that any story other than the police's would be considered legitimate, were characteristic responses. This is shown in Taylor's acerbic comment that 'the quality of [police] evidence was in inverse proportion to their rank ... with some notable exceptions, the senior officers in command were defensive and evasive witnesses'. SYP (literally) closed ranks, refusing 'to concede they were in any respect at fault ... the police case was to blame the fans ... and blame the Club' (Cm765, 1989: paras 279–80, 285).

Effectiveness requires loyalty, discipline, and *esprit de corps*, but these sustain an insider mentality and an interest in protecting the organisation from reputational damage, which could undermine police morale and public confidence. A powerful, resilient culture and socialisation permeates policing, merging self-interest and public duty. The 'canteen culture' characteristic of lower ranks is composed of myths, narratives, rituals, and attitudes that bind (negatively and positively) a group, and an equivalent exists for senior officer culture. This is an example of *normalisation*, which emphasises the value of the group and its norms and their suitability as a guide to conduct, inculcated under the guidance of the group to achieve what is for the group, 'normal' behaviour, reinforced by the 'shame' experienced by members acting outside these norms. Reiner's classic, *Chief Constables* (1991), stressed their determination to protect operational autonomy, even while conceding that the public order crises of the 1980s had put the police under increased scrutiny and changes in policing style would be required. Openness and accountability were unappealing as norms because no viable mechanism for securing them existed without a loss of control and autonomy and, as the Metropolitan Police's *Public Order Review* (1986) put it, ' "there will come a time when they [the police] must decide that some voices count for more than others" ' (quoted in Townsend, 1993: 199). Caless (2011) emphasises the importance of personal patronage by senior officers, as well as networking, political savvy, and technical competence in recruiting successive generations of senior officers. *Policing at the Top* emphasises the depth of suspicion of 'external' bodies (police authorities, HM Inspectorate of Constabulary, Police Complaints Commission, the Home Office, Police and Crime Commissioners) 'interfering' in policing, whilst recognising that such interference was an unpleasant fact of life. Such bodies are seen as the locus of politically motivated amateurism that undermines the effectiveness of professional policing and, therefore, damages the public interest. Policing is, then, a prime example of the power of metanarrative.

The standard story of Hillsborough was influenced by metanarratives (secrecy and order) that structure actions in specific situations and locations (football crowds as a public order issue). Combined, specific situational narratives and metanarratives create governmentality – the mentalities, rationalities, and techniques – through which power is exercised by and over individuals. Power is an aspect of formal hierarchies but also resides in the discourses, narratives, and traditions that are internalised by actors – both individuals and groups – and which guide their behaviour. Metanarrative addresses 'the conduct of conduct', discourses that rationalise and guide the exercise of power by individuals and organisations that have situationally specific manifestations. From an interpretivist perspective, political reality is composed of specific situated narratives but these situational narratives are nested in, and influenced by, metanarratives. This enables a diverse range of situational narratives, with unique functional specifics and traditions to coexist and interact, within wider metanarratives capturing 'networks of power and influence which extend across many different sectors of social and political life' (Thompson, 2000: 199). Hillsborough is a significant illustration of this.

Conclusion

Politics and policymaking are suffused by inequalities and power asymmetries that privilege some actors, interests, and narratives over others. The Hillsborough standard story rested on the perception of football fans as violent, drunken thugs, a deeply embedded narrative that influenced, and was sustained by, inter alia, the press, police, and government; but did the standard story capture Hillsborough? Visible politics is dominated by standard stories that fail to capture the complexity of cause and effect; this requires a complex story.

The dilemma created by Hillsborough was clear: undermining confidence in the police was not in the public interest but it was in the public interest to establish what had happened. The dead fans' supporters articulated an alternative (and truthful) narrative that was largely inaudible to a range of institutions because it was incompatible with the standard story and there was little institutional architecture to support this alternative, thereby confirming systemic and systematic bias. This inertial power meant that it required 23 years of external pressure to debunk the 'official' truth with the release of massive amounts of information from public and private institutions, which shows deep politics in action. This material illuminates the multi-layered nature of political reality and the importance of governmentality for drawing together situational specifics and metanarratives. Meaning (and identity) is expressed in interests, ideas, and language that vary by level but which create autonomous institutions resistant to change. Hillsborough reveals how a narrative was constructed by those who benefit from the status quo, and how that narrative was promulgated in response to the values and beliefs constitutive of the British state (secrecy and order) and the dominant web of meaning in the police. The chapter presents a 'superior story' to explain Hillsborough and broaden and deepen interpretivism (*pace* Tilly) by focusing on context and production and exploring in detail the usually obscure but inferred causal mechanisms generating the standard story.

Using the HIP, I argue for an explicit recognition of meanings, and therefore of politics deeper than standard stories, of strategic cultures that influence cause and effect but which are deeper than the traditions influencing situational behaviour. The politics exemplified by Hillsborough are not easy to study but thanks to the HIP it can be done and the effort is worth it because it moves us away from standard to superior stories that offer more nuanced, richer, and accurate pictures of cause and effect.

References

Armstrong, G. (2003) *Football Hooligans: Knowing the score*, London: Berg Publishers.

Bachrach, P. and Baratz, M. S. (1970) *Power and Poverty: Theory and practice*, New York: Oxford University Press.

Barton, H. (2003) 'Understanding Occupational (sub) Culture – a Precursor to Reform: The case of the police service in England and Wales', *International Journal of Public Sector Management*, 16(5): 346–58.

Bevir, M. (1999) 'Foucault, Power, and Institutions', *Political Studies*, 47(2): 345–59.

Bevir, M. (2011) 'Political Science after Foucault', *History of the Human Sciences*, 24(4): 81–96.

Blair, T. (2010) *A Journey*, London: Hutchinson.

Brooke, H. (2010) *The Silent State: Secrets, surveillance and the myth of British democracy*, London: Heinemann.

Caless, B. (2011) *Policing At The Top: The roles, values and attitudes of chief police officers*, Oxford: Polity Press.

Cm.765 (1989) *The Hillsborough Stadium Disaster: Interim Report*, London: HMSO.

Cm.3878 (1998) *Scrutiny of Evidence Relating to the Hillsborough Football Stadium Disaster*, London: HMSO.

Cohen, S. (2011) *Folk Devils and Moral Panics: The creation of the mods and rockers*, first published 1973, London: Routledge.

Dale Scott, P. (1996) *Deep Politics and the Death of JFK*, Berkeley, CA: University of California Press.

Deal, T. F. and Kennedy, A. A. (1988) *Corporate Cultures: The rites and rituals of corporate life*, Harmondsworth: Penguin.

Diamond, P. and Richards, D. (2008) 'The Case for Theoretical and Methodological Pluralism in British Political Studies: New Labour's political memoirs and the British Political Tradition', *Political Studies Review*, 10(2): 177–94.

Dowding, K. (2004) 'Interpretation, Truth and Investigation', *British Journal of Politics and International Relations*, 6(2): 136–42.

Frosdick, S. and Marsh, P. (2005) *Football Hooliganism*, Cullompton, Devon: Willan Publishing.

Foucault, M. (2009) *Security, Territory, Population*, Houndmills: Palgrave.

Gaventa, J. (1980) *Power and Powerlessness. Quiescence and rebellion in an Appalachian valley*, Oxford: Clarendon Press.

Guardian (2010), 1 September.

Hall, S., Critcher, C., Jefferson, T., Clarke, J., and Roberts, B. (1978) *Policing the Crisis: Mugging, the state, and law and order*, London: Macmillan.

Hazell, R. and Glover, M. (2011) 'The Impact of Freedom of Information on Whitehall', *Public Administration*, 89(4): 1664–81.

Hazell, R., Worthy, B., and Glover, M (2010) *The Impact of the Freedom of Information Act on Central Government in the UK: Does FOI work?*, London: UCL/The Constitution Unit.

Hennessy, P. (1989) *Whitehall*, London: Fontana Press.

HIP (2012a) *Hillsborough: The Independent Panel report*, HC581, London: HMSO, 12 September. Available at http://hillsborough.independent.gov.uk/report/ [accessed 20 September 2012].

HIP (2012b) 'Hillsborough', White's News Agency, 18 April 1989. NGN000000010001. http://hillsborough.independent.gov.uk/browse/by-material/index.html [accessed 20 September 2012].

HIP (2012c) 'White's News Agency to Evening Standard', 12 June 1989. NGN000000070001. http://hillsborough.independent.gov.uk/browse/by-material/index.html [accessed 25 September 2012].

HIP (2012d) Police Federation South Yorkshire Joint Board, 19 April 1989. TPF00000001001. Available at http://hillsborough.independent.gov.uk/browse/by-material/index.html [accessed 25 September 2012].

HIP (2012e) 'Hillsborough: Lord Justice Taylor's Interim Report', Carolyn Sinclair to Prime Minister, 2 August 1989, COO00000113001. Available at http://hillsborough.independent.gov.uk/browse/by-material/index.html [accessed 27 September 2012].

HIP (2012f) 'Meeting at South Yorkshire Police Headquarters, 3 October 1989. SYP000046060001. Available at http://hillsborough.independent.gov.uk/browse/by-material/index.html [accessed 27 September 2012].

HIP (2012g) 'Presentation to Members of Parliament on the Subject of the Hillsborough Disaster, 9 November 1989'. SYP000097010001. Available at http://hillsborough.independent.gov.uk/browse/by-material/index.html [accessed 28 September 2012].

HIP (2012h) 'Football Spectators Bill': Andrew Turnbull to Prime Minister, 18 April 1989. CCO000000820001. Available at http://hillsborough.independent.gov.uk/browse/by-material/index.html [accessed 28 September 2012].

HIP (2012i) 'Merseyside Police Views on Hillsborough', Carolyn Sinclair to Prime Minister, 20 April 1989. COO00000009701. Available at http://hillsborough.independent.gov.uk/browse/by-material/index.html [accessed 28 September 2012].

HIP (2012j) 'Hillsborough', Caroline Slocock to Prime Minister, 2 August 1989. COO0000000114001. Available at http://hillsborough.independent.gov.uk/browse/by-material/index.html [accessed 28 September 2012].

HoC (2004) *Review of Intelligence on Weapons of Mass Destruction*, HC 898, London: TSO.

HoC (2012a) *Post-legislative Scrutiny of the Freedom of Information Act 2000, Volume 1 Report*, HC96-I, London: TSO.

HoC (2012b) *Post-legislative Scrutiny of the Freedom of Information Act 2000, Volume 2 Report*, HC96-II Oral and Written Evidence, London: TSO.

Holstein, J. and Gubrium, J. F. (2009) *Analysing Narrative Reality*, Thousand Oaks, CA: Sage Publications.

Janis, I. L (1972) *Victims of Groupthink*, Boston, MA: Wadsworth.

Jemphrey, A. and Berrington, E. (2000) 'Surviving the Media: Hillsborough, Dunblane and the press', *Journalism Studies*, 1(3): 493–503.

Judge, T. (1989) 'Hillsborough – the Police who Dispute Taylor's Verdict', *The Police* (November), 24 and 26, Hillsborough Independent Panel, SCC000002600001. Available at http://hillsborough.independent.gov.uk/browse/by-material/index.html [accessed 1 October 2012].

Loftus, B. (2010) 'Police Occupational Culture: Classic themes, altered times', *Policing and Society*, 20(1): 1–20.

Moynihan, D. P. (2012) 'Extra-Network Organizational Reputation and Blame Avoidance in Networks: The Hurricane Katrina example', *Governance*, 25(4): 567–88.

Naylor, J. F. (2009) *A Man and an Institution: Sir Maurice Hankey and the custody of Cabinet secrecy*, Cambridge: Cambridge University Press.

North, D. C. (1990) *Institutions, Institutional Change and Economic Performance*, Cambridge: Cambridge University Press.

Ravasi, D. and Schultze, M. (2006) 'Responding to Organizational Identity Threats: Exploring the role of organizational culture', *Academy of Management Journal*, 49(3): 433–58.

Reiner, R. (1991) *Chief Constables*, Oxford: Oxford University Press.

Rogers, A. (1997) *Secrecy and Power in the British State: History of the Official Secrets Act, 1918–1989*, London: Pluto Press.

Scarman, Baron L. S. (1981) *The Scarman Report: The Brixton disorders 10–12 April 1981: report of an inquiry by Lord Scarman*, Harmondsworth: Penguin.

Scraton, P. (2004) 'Death on the Terraces: The contexts and injustices of the 1989 Hillsborough disaster', *Soccer and Society*, 5(2): 183–200.

Sun (1989) 19 April.

Taylor, A. J. (2005) *The National Union of Mineworkers and British Politics. Volume II, 1969–1995*, Aldershot: Ashgate.

Thompson, J. B. (2000) *Political Scandals. Power and visibility in the media age*, Cambridge: Polity Press.

Tilly, C. (1999) 'The Trouble with Stories', in R. Aminzade and B. Pescosolido (eds), *The Social Worlds of Higher Education: Handbook for teaching in a new century*, Thousand Oaks, CA: Pine Forge Press, pp. 256–70.

Tilly, C. (2002) *Stories, Identities, and Political Change*, Lanham, MD: Rowman & Littlefield.

Townsend, C. (1993) *Making the Peace: Public order and public security in modern Britain*, Oxford: Oxford University Press.

Vincent, D. (1998) *The Culture of Secrecy: Britain, 1832–1998*, Oxford: Oxford University Press.

Waddington, D. P. (2011) 'Public Order Policing in South Yorkshire, 1984–2011: The case for a permissive approach to crowd control', *Contemporary Social Science*, 6(3): 309–29.

Waddington, P. A. J. (1999) 'Police (Canteen) Sub-Culture', *British Journal of Criminology*, 39(2): 287–309.

Wagenaar, H. (2012) 'Dwellers on the Threshold of Practice: The interpretivism of Bevir and Rhodes', *Critical Policy Studies*, 6(1): 85–99.

Weber, M. (1970) 'Bureaucracy', in H. H. Gerth and C. Wright-Mills (eds), *From Max Weber: Essays in sociology*, London: Routledge & Kegan Paul, pp. 196–244.

Wilkinson N. J. (2009) *Secrecy and the Media: The official history of the United Kingdom's D-notice system*, London: Routledge.

Part II

High Politics and Political History

4 Executive Governance

An Interpretive Analysis

R. A. W. Rhodes

Human nature does not change ... the skulduggery – and downright lies – by which Pitt contrived to down Fox ... are echoed in the calculated manoeuvrings by which Macmillan repeatedly denied Butler, and by Brown's obsessive briefing against Blair.

(Campbell, 2010: 7)

Introduction: The Story So Far

As Elgie (2011: 64) claims, the ideas of the core executive and resource dependence have become the 'new orthodoxy' in executive studies (see Rhodes, 1995).[1] However, within this orthodoxy, there are spirited arguments around the question of the 'predominant prime minister' (Heffernan, 2003, 2005). In this chapter, I do not offer a critique of existing approaches. I have done that elsewhere (see Rhodes, 2013, 2014a). Rather, I outline and defend an interpretive approach to 'court politics' as an alternative way of studying the executive.

The unit of analysis in core executive studies is neither the prime minister nor the cabinet, but the web of networks at the heart of government charged with coordination and the resolution of conflicts (Rhodes, 1995). The prime minister is a key actor because of his or her access to institutional and personal resources and position at the centre of key networks. He or she has the *potential* to exercise significant power. The fates of Tony Blair, John Howard, and Kevin Rudd, who at various points in time were regarded as 'predominant' prime ministers, remind us that unpredictable forces shape, constrain and, sometimes deliberately, undermine leaders' ability to get their own way. So, we must examine relations between leaders and their colleagues in cabinet, the party room, and other 'followers' who depend on them, but on whom they also depend.

The advantage of this formulation is that it gets away from bald assertions about the fixed nature of executive politics. While one pattern of executive politics may operate at any one time, there can still be fluidity as one pattern is succeeded by another. Take for example, the rapid decline in public support for Kevin Rudd that followed his decision to abandon his commitment to an emissions trading scheme. This policy change created an opportunity for those angered by Rudd's domineering leadership style to harness discontent among ministers and the Labor Caucus. Allegiances, including those of Rudd's former supporters, shifted to his Deputy,

Julia Gillard. Overnight, Rudd was ousted in a party-room vote that, lacking support, he did not contest (see Rhodes and Tiernan, 2014).

The importance of such contingencies raises an obvious question. Which pattern of executive politics prevails? When, how, and why did it change? Focusing on the power of prime minister and cabinet is limiting whereas these questions open the possibility of explaining similarities and differences in the broader politics of the core executive (Elgie, 1997: 23, and citations). Few would have difficulty accepting both that prime ministerial predominance ebbs and flows and that the prime minister is at the heart of the core networks in the core executive (Burch and Halliday, 1996; Bennister, 2007; Heffernan, 2005). Now, we need to move beyond the increasingly stale debate about prime ministerial predominance, which is generating more heat than light (see *Parliamentary Affairs*, 66(3), 2013). The questions that should be of central concern focus on changes in the standing of the prime minister in central networks, and the fluctuating personnel and fortunes of those networks.

The interpretive analysis of court politics necessarily addresses these questions, because it uses the ideas of beliefs, practices, narratives, dilemmas, and traditions (Bevir and Rhodes, 2003, 2006a, 2010) to explore the actions of actors in the core networks. The court, or the core network of the core executive, is the term conventionally used to refer to the interactions between a leader and his immediate entourage. Here, I use the term to focus attention on the beliefs and practices of these governing elites. Bevir and Rhodes (2006a: chapters 1 and 2) describe these elites as 'situated agents'. Situated agents possess a creative ability to adopt beliefs or attempt actions for reasons of their own. However, their webs of belief and actions are located in inherited traditions and practices, which constrain their actions. So, to explore court politics is to explore the opportunities and constraints on the actions of governing elites.

In the rest of this chapter, I argue that marrying this notion of court politics to the historical analysis of high politics opens a challenging new research agenda for executive studies. The tools of historical analysis deployed by the 'Peterhouse School' provide a toolkit for accessing these insights. Next, I provide a brief summary of an interpretive approach to history. I then make the case for drawing on the new political history. I sketch its distinctive features, with examples, and explain its relevance to executive studies.[2] I review, with examples, the existing literature on court politics. Finally, I identify the advantages of using an interpretive approach to study court politics.

Interpretive History[3]

Naturalism refers to the idea that '[t]he human sciences should strive to develop predictive and causal explanations akin to those found in the natural sciences' (Bevir and Kedar, 2008: 503). Known variously as positivism, behaviouralism, or modernist empiricism in the social sciences, it holds two central beliefs:

> First, a conviction that all 'knowledge' ... is capable of being expressed in terms which refer in an immediate way to some reality, or aspects of reality

that can be apprehended through the senses. Second, a faith that the methods and logical form of science as epitomized in classical physics can be applied to the study of social phenomena.

(Giddens, 1993: 136)

Anti-naturalism, on the other hand, argues that human life differs from the rest of nature because 'human action ... is meaningful and historically contingent' (Bevir and Kedar, 2008: 505). The task of the human sciences is an interpretive one in search of meaning. Moreover, the epistemology of the social sciences assumes the knower and the known are independent. The humanities consider the two inseparable, interacting and influencing one another, leading to a 'fusion of horizons' – to shared interpretations (Lincoln and Guba, 1985: 28, 36–8, and Table 1.1).[4]

An interpretive approach in executive studies shifts analysis away from institutions, functions, and roles to the actions and practices of webs of actors. We need to grasp the relevant meanings, the beliefs, and preferences of the people involved to understand actions and practices:[5]

We need to go beyond the bounds of a science based on verification to one which would study the inter-subjective and common meanings embedded in social reality ... this science would be hermeneutical in the sense that ... its most primitive data would be a reading of meanings.

(Taylor, 1971: 45)

An interpretive approach seeks to understand the webs of significance that people spin for themselves. It provides 'thick description' in which the researcher writes his or her construction of the subject's constructions of what the subject is up to (adapted from Geertz, 1993: 9). So, the task is to unpack the disparate and contingent beliefs and practices of individuals through which they construct their world, to identify the recurrent patterns of actions and related beliefs. The resulting narrative is not just a chronological story. Rather, narrative refers to the form of explanation that disentangles beliefs and actions to explain human life. Narratives are the form theories take in the human sciences, and they explain actions by reference to the beliefs and desires of actors. People act for reasons, conscious and unconscious.

Human action is also historically contingent. It is:

characterized by ineluctable contingencies, temporal fluidity and contextual specificity. Hence we cannot explain social phenomena adequately if we fail fully to take into account both their inherent flux and their concrete links to specific contexts.

(Bevir and Kedar, 2008: 506)

The notion of tradition is central to understanding the context of action. It explains why people come to believe what they do. People understand their experiences using theories they have inherited. This social heritage is the necessary background to the beliefs people adopt and the actions they perform. Tradition is a starting point, not a destination. Traditions do not determine the beliefs that people go on to adopt or the actions they go on to perform. It is our ability for agency that makes tradition a more satisfactory concept than rival terms such as structure, paradigm, and episteme. These latter ideas suggest the presence of a social force that determines or limits the beliefs and actions of individuals. Tradition, in contrast, suggests that a social heritage comes to individuals who, through their agency, can adjust and transform this heritage even as they pass it on to others. Individuals use local reasoning consciously and subconsciously to reflect on and modify their contingent heritage; they are *situated agents* (Bevir and Rhodes, 2006a: 4–5, 7–9). An interpretive approach represents a shift of topos from institution to individual beliefs and practices and the traditions in which they are located (on the different approaches to history in political science see Bevir and Rhodes, 2013).

This interpretive philosophical argument encompasses the methods of the social sciences as well as those of the humanities. All kinds of methods are valuable ways of gathering and analysing data. But, when scholars seek to explain the data and patterns in it, they should allow for the intentionality of human action. The intentionality of human action implies there is no 'method' for reaching a correct explanation. Rather, political science is a craft – the craft of recovering meaning by telling plausible tales about data and patterns within it. Practitioners of the new political history are one group of storytellers of particular relevance in executive studies.

High Politics

The main sources in the study of 'High Politics', or, as it is referred to nowadays, the 'New Political History', are fragmentary.[6] There is no defining statement, no manifesto, although Craig (2010) draws together various strands and provides a helpful conspectus. Here, I outline briefly the founding ideas on 'High Politics' before turning to the broader agenda of present-day scholars and their concern with the intellectual context of the game of politics.

The founder of this so-called 'Peterhouse School' of history is Maurice Cowling.[7] For Cowling (1971: 3), the 'High Politics' approach meant studying the intentions and actions of a political leadership network, which consisted of 'fifty or sixty politicians in conscious tension with one another whose accepted authority constituted political leadership'. High politics was 'a matter of rhetoric and manoeuvre' by statesmen (Cowling, 1971: 3–4). He explores the tension between 'situational necessity and the intentions of politicians' using the letters, diaries, and private papers of this network of elite leaders. His people behave 'situationally', but Cowling never deploys such reified notions as institution or class. Such 'structures' are defined by the elite; they choose which ones they will pay attention to. Instead, he asks, 'What influences played upon, what intentions were maintained, what prevision was possible and what success was achieved by the leading actors on the political stage' (Cowling, 1967: 322). He analyses the realpolitik of the governing elite. His approach is characterised by 'relativistic individualism' (Ghosh, 1993: 276, n. 76) and an emphasis on historical contingency:

Between the closed world in which decisions were taken and the external pressures it reflected, the connections were so devious and diverse that no necessity can be predicated of the one in relation to the other. Between the inner political world and society at large on the one hand and between personal and policy objectives on the other, no general connection can be established except whatever can be discovered in each instance about the proportions in which each reacted to the other.

(Cowling, 1967: 340)

There were two recurring criticisms of Cowling's work: that he focused exclusively on the governing elite and that he disregarded interests and ideas. Craig (2010: 456, 462) considers these criticisms 'misleading'; for example Cowling sees rhetoric as expressed belief as part of the toolkit of every politician. Nonetheless, as Williamson (2010: 131, 141) observes, Cowling's 'most noted and notorious contribution to political history' was 'High Politics' and his insistence that political leaders had 'relative autonomy, with substantial independence in taking decisions'. A fine example of this approach is Philip Williamson's biography of Stanley Baldwin. Williamson argues that two approaches are necessary to understand major politicians. First, there is the study of 'High Politics':

in the interpretative, not simple descriptive, sense, where the narrative is not of one politician nor even of one party, but rather of the whole system of political leadership. Here individuals are placed within the full multi-party and multi-policy contexts which properly explain the details of their careers.

(1999: 12–18)

Second, there is biography, in which it is necessary to go beyond chronological narrative to examine 'the nature and practice of political leadership'. Context exists not as political parties, institutions, or public opinion but as the narrative the elite both tells itself and seeks to persuade others to accept. This approach explores, 'the remorseless situational and tactical pressures, the chronic uncertainties, and the short horizons which afflict all political leadership'; and it looks for 'the qualities that really distinguish and explain a politician's effectiveness ... in the longer term consistencies or patterns'. In other words, the study of 'High Politics' necessarily involves the study of statesmanship (Williamson, 1999: 12–18).

Baldwin's reputation suffered 'enduring denigration' as the prime minister who betrayed the nation by putting party before country by delaying rearmament and appeasing Hitler. Critics at the time and during the 1940s demonstrate much ability in blurring the distinction between alleged facts, supposed facts, and agreed facts (see Williamson, 2004, for a thorough rebuttal). Belying his latterday critics, Baldwin was a politician of high standing in his day. He was leader of the opposition, in effect prime minister as Lord President of the Council in the coalition, and prime minister for some 14 years. Williamson explores Baldwin's use of political rhetoric in his speeches and other public political and non-political presentations to identify the foundations of this success. He suggests that 'politicians are what they speak and publish', so he uses the speeches to show how Baldwin persuaded his audiences, shaped opinion and created political allegiance. Baldwin was the first politician to master public broadcasting but he also used photographs and the cinema to present himself attractively. Williamson adds these presentational skills to Baldwin's skills at ministerial coordination, his political judgement, party management, and reputation in parliament to explain his standing between the wars. But, and crucially, the bedrock to this reputation lay in his detachment, his non-political persona, his probity, and his ability to address the anxieties of the average person in a way that harnessed them to the Conservative cause. He eased social reconciliation after the Depression, socialised the Labour party to parliamentary ways and government, and created modern 'One Nation' Conservatism, capturing the political centre and restoring popular respect for politicians. Williamson's book is a skilful blend of history and biography that focuses on the beliefs of the key protagonist as analysed through his personal papers and speeches. It exemplifies, as Pederson (2002: 40–2) suggests, the move away from structural and class-based explanations of politics to politics as 'an enclosed rule bound game' and to the 'intellectual setting' of that game.

The study of 'High Politics' complements and contributes to political studies in two ways. First, it builds on the idealist political thought and constructivist history of, for example, Michael Oakeshott and R. G. Collingwood (see, Craig, 2010: 465–9). It is also consistent with recent work in interpretive political science. As Craig (2010: 474) concludes, 'Cowling adopted positions which find *remarkable resonance* in some of the most recent and reflective accounts of the historical method' (referring to Bevir, 1999; Bevir and Rhodes, 2003, emphasis added). So, the bridges exist, we just need to cross them. There is much irony here; 'The theoretical trends of the past twenty years, with which Maurice Cowling would surely have not been in sympathy, have essentially brought his opponents to his door' (Pederson, 2002: 41).

Second, and of particular importance, the proponents of the 'High Politics' approach redefine the function of history in political science and, in so doing, fill gaps in our toolkit. Thus, Dennis Kavanagh (1991) argues that 'the contribution of history, as the systematic study of the past, to political science has been more as a body of knowledge than as a set of methods' (Kavanagh, 1991: 480). He identifies five uses of history in political science:

> as a source of material or data; as an aid to understanding the links between the present and past; as a body of knowledge within which to test theories and frameworks; as a means of analysing political ideas and texts; and as a source of lessons.
>
> (Kavanagh, 1991: 483)

In effect, he reduces historians to fact grubbers for political scientists. It is scarcely a surprise that historians do not agree. Lawrence and Taylor are only two of the dissenting voices. They reject the historian's role of 'furnishing anecdotal material and suggestive counter evidence for the [models of] political scientists' (1997: 15–16). Rather they argue 'the proper task of the historian should be to render theory problematic ... because many theories simply do not time-travel very well' (1997: 15–16). Archival research using the private papers and speeches of elite actors is an essential tool for uncovering the beliefs and practices of the governing elite and understanding their actions. Cowling and Williamson exemplify the skills that political scientists could use in the service of their own questions and concepts. And political scientists need the help. In short, to turn Kavanagh on his head, history is less a body of knowledge and more a set of methods – tools we can use to explore the beliefs and practices of the court.

Court Politics

The most obvious difference between an interpretive approach and existing approaches to executive studies is the shift of topos from institutions, positions, and functions to individual actors. In the analysis of court politics, the emphasis falls on grasping the relevant meanings by focusing on the beliefs and practices of interdependent core executive actors, the traditions in which they are located, and the games people in relationships of mutual dependence play to resolve dilemmas. This shift captures the intense rivalry between, for example, Tony Blair and Gordon Brown, or Kevin Rudd and Julia Gillard. It also rejects any notion of dominance by any one actor or set of actors. As Norton (2000: 11–67) argues, 'Ministers are like medieval barons in that they preside over their own, sometimes vast, policy territory'. Crucially, 'the ministers fight – or form alliances – with other barons in order to get what they want' and they 'resent interference in their territory by other barons and will fight to defend it'. The analysis of court politics focuses on the beliefs and practices of the political and administrative elite.

Court politics have existed throughout the ages (see Campbell, 2010)[8] and the ideas of high politics and statecraft have already crept into political science, most notably in James Bulpitt's analysis of 'statecraft' and Donald Savoie's notion of 'court government'.[9]

Statecraft

For Bulpitt (1995: 518), 'The Court is ... the formal Chief Executive, plus his/her political friends and advisers'. Members of the court, the political elite, have an 'operating code', which is 'less than a philosophy of government and yet more than a specific collection of policies. It refers to the accepted rules of "statecraft" as employed over time by political elites' (Bulpitt, 1983: 68, n. 23). The statecraft of the court comprises: a set of governing objectives (or 'beliefs'); a governing code (or 'practices'); and a set of political support mechanisms, for example, party management (Bulpitt, 1995: 519). Statecraft 'is about the relationship between ideas and political practice. It is about short term politicking or tactical manoeuvring' (Buller, 1999: 695). It is about gaining and keeping office, creating an image of governing competence and creating government autonomy over 'High Politics'. It is an exercise in realpolitik.

The approach rests on three assumptions. First, Bulpitt (1995: 517) assumes the court will 'behave in a unitary (united) fashion'. Second, he assumes the court possesses a 'relative autonomy' from structural factors (1995: 518). Finally, he assumes the court is rational, that is, will 'develop strategies which will enable them to attempt to pursue consistently their own interests' (1995: 519). There are several problems with this account of Court Politics.

Bulpitt is well served by his several disciples, most notably James Buller, Jonathan Bradbury, and Toby James. The criticisms that follow apply to the statecraft thesis, not just to Bulpitt. His disciples claim him for the realist school of political philosophy. I suggest that a more congenial home would be interpretive political history.

First, a persistent criticism of statecraft 'has been its indifference to empirical refutation' and, indeed, to methods more generally (see Buller, 1999: 704). Bulpitt (1983: 239) concedes the point: 'the supporting data for many of these arguments is much less than perfect'. As Buller (1999: 704) notes 'acquiring knowledge about governing codes is a task beset with analytical problems'. The 'New Political History' addresses these matters much more satisfactorily.

Second, Buller (1999: 699–705) argues that Bulpitt neglects ontological and epistemological questions, which is undoubtedly an accurate observation, and the muddles that ensue can be clearly seen in Bulpitt's assumptions about the court. None of these assumptions are necessary and all betray a lingering modernist empiricism in his thought.

Bulpitt (1995: 517) considered all his assumptions as 'operating assumptions, something to guide the analysis until it becomes unsatisfactory'. He qualified the first assumption straight away, calling the question of who is the principal actor 'a very real problem' (1995: 518). For the analysis of court politics, it is less important to ask when the court is united, than to ask when there are factions, and what the consequences are. The second assumption of relative autonomy reflects Bulpitt's epistemological confusions. The language of neo-Marxist state theory has no place in his analysis of high politics. Finally, and again, by assuming elite actors are rational, Bulpitt reveals his commitment to modernist empiricism. Bevir (2010: 443) concluded that Bulpitt was unusual in combining modernist empiricism with Tory historiography. I suggest statecraft is better recast as an exercise in interpretive history (see below). I reject Bulpitt's fixation on modernist empiricist topics and suggest it will be more profitable to employ the notion of situated agency and ask what traditions shape the Court's beliefs and practices (that is, its statecraft).

Buller (1999: 708) seeks to resolve many of these issues by appealing to critical realism. This turn creates a new set of problems, mainly because critical realism and Bulpitt's work are uneasy bedfellows. As Bevir (2010: 445) suggests:

> Bulpitt's account of the interests of the central elite and the particular behavioural topics on which he focuses reflect his debt to a Tory Tradition. He draws in particular on historians such as Lewis Namier and Jack Plumb, treating their portrait of the eighteenth century court as an ideal

type applicable to the whole of British history. This Tory moment provides him with his distinction between court and country and high and low politics.

There is also a clear overlap with the work of the latter-day Tory historian Maurice Cowling; they share a concern with the political elite, high politics, and realpolitik.

It is hard to see how this mix of Tory historiography and modernist empiricism can be assimilated to either critical realism or, as James (2013) suggests, the new institutionalism. Bulpitt equivocated about the notions of institutions and structure when they were used as a reified, deterministic explanation of elite actors' behaviour:

> It may be convenient to leave the definition of structure at any one time to the designated principal actors; on most occasions they will be able to choose which structural features preoccupy them and in what sequence they will be tackled.

> (Bulpitt, 1995: 518)

This view of structure fits uneasily with the critical realists' claims of 'necessity' and 'emergent properties'. This position simply does not admit of structures that have 'causal powers' (Buller, 1999: 706).

Buller's views on structure overlap with Heffernan's analysis of prime ministerial predominance:

> How do actors exchange resources? They do so under the structures imposed by the political system. Institutional *imperatives decide* the arrangement of relations between, say, the executive, the legislature and the judiciary. They also *determine* intra-executive, legislative and judicial configurations.

> (2005: 610, emphasis added)

Here we have a clear dividing line between existing approaches in executive studies and the interpretive approach favoured here. Both Buller and Heffernan reify and overstate the effect of 'structure'. Structures are best understood as inherited practices that are always open to change (Bevir and Rhodes, 2006b, 2006c). Interpretive theory addresses these matters more satisfactorily with its notion of situated agency. I now turn to discuss the idea of court politics as a specific example of situated agency.

Court Politics

Court politics exists as journalists' reportage and in the auto/biographies, diaries, and memoirs of politicians but is rarely at the heart of academic analyses of present-day government.[10] An important exception is Donald Savoie's (1999, 2008) analysis of 'court government'. He defines the court as 'the prime minister and a small group of carefully selected courtiers'. It also covers the 'shift from formal decision-making processes in cabinet ... to informal processes involving only a handful of actors'. He suggests that:

> Court government provides quick and unencumbered access to the levers of power to make things happen and to pick and choose those political, policy and administrative issues that appeal to prime ministers or that need resolution because the media are demanding immediate answers.
>
> (Savoie, 2008: 231)

It suits the prime ministers and his courtiers:

> because it enables them to get things done, to see results, and to manage the news and the media better than when formal cabinet processes are respected. Written documents can be kept to a minimum, minutes of meetings do not have to be prepared, records of decisions are not necessary, formal processes can be put aside, and only the most essential interdepartmental consultations have to be undertaken.
>
> (Savoie, 2008: 231–2)

However, there are problems. Savoie (2008: 230, 339) argues the key adverse consequences are centralisation and the collapse of accountability: 'the centre has slowly but surely been made deliberately stronger'; and 'the chain of accountability ... has broken down at every level'. He also suggests that 'senior civil servants no longer have the experience, the knowledge, or the institutional memory to speak truth to power' (2008: 25).

This centralisation has been brought about by the 24/7 news cycle and the personalisation of politics; the rise of neo-liberalism and its critique of positive government and bureaucracy; the exigencies of the war on terror and other global trends; increasing demands for domestic policy coordination; and the pluralisation of policy advice and the need to coordinate inputs from multiple sources. The emergence and growing importance of political staff is a response to these pressures.[11]

In Savoie's account, court government and centralisation are virtual synonyms. Court government is not just an analytical category but an attack on the predominant power of the Canadian prime minister and the decline of cabinet government. There are problems with both the analytical and the critical sides of his argument.

First, Savoie's conception of court government is too narrow. I accept there is often an inner sanctum, but participants in high politics are rarely so few. I prefer Cowling's more expansive definition. The number of participants is still limited. But, as well as the core network or inner circle, we can also talk of circles of influence (Hennessy, 2000: 493–500), usage that accords with political folklore. In the more formal language of political science, the court is a set of interlocking, interdependent networks. For example, Burch and Halliday (1996, 2004) suggest that the prime minister is at the core of the core networks supported by enhanced central capacity that increases the power potential of the prime minister. However, 'the enhancement of central capacity within the British system of government reflects contingent factors, including the personalities of strategically placed individuals (notably, but not only, the PM)'. They note that such changes are 'driven by prime ministerial whim' and 'if they so desire, [prime ministers] try to shape the core in their own image. However, the extent to which they can do so 'depends on the motivation and skill of key actors, and on the circumstances in which they find themselves at any given moment in time' (Burch and Halliday, 1996: 17, 20, 106).

The court is a key part of the organisational glue holding the centre together. It coordinates the policy process by filtering and packaging proposals. It contains and manages conflicts between ministerial barons. It acts as the keeper of the government's narrative. It acts as the gatekeeper and broker for internal and external networks. And its power ebbs and flows with that of the prime minister.

Second, Savoie's version of the centralisation thesis pays too little attention to the constraints on the prime minister and his court. These arguments have been well rehearsed elsewhere, so I can be brief (for a review, see Rhodes, 2014a). Baronial ministers persist, and prime ministers are dependent on senior colleagues. It is hard to see how a prime minister can be predominant when his authority is continuously challenged, even undermined, by an ambitious finance minister, whether it is Gordon Brown in Britain or Paul Martin in Canada. No prime minister can intervene continuously in everything. They are defeated by the complexity of government and the massive demands on their time not only from the international arena, but also from the more prosaic need to make speeches, media appearances, manage the party caucus, and attend question time in the House of Commons – the list is endless, the diary is packed. He or she has to be selective. Moreover, intervention may not have the desired effect, and it is important to distinguish between intentions and outcomes. Prime ministers are quickly distracted, so incrementalism characterises the overwhelming bulk of government policymaking, not dramatic interventions by the prime minister.

It helps to distinguish between the electoral, policymaking, and implementation arenas. Prime ministerial predominance is most obvious in media management and electioneering. In the policymaking arena, there is some evidence to support the claim of centralisation on the prime minister's office. However, for Australia and Canada as well as Britain, this claim applies to selected policy areas only, with the equally important provisos that the prime minister's attention is selective and intervention is intermittent. Arguably, the continuous search to improve coordination by central agencies speaks of the failure of such coordination, not its success. The prime minister's influence is most constrained in the policy implementation arena. Here, other senior government figures, ministers and their departments, other agencies, state or provincial governments, and even local governments can be key actors. Prime ministers are nodal actors but they are still one actor among many interdependent ones in the networks that criss-cross central, state, and local government, and beyond.

The simple point is that the court government thesis is analytically distinct from the centralisation thesis. The question of their relationship is a matter of evidence and argument, but it is not a matter of definition. As most proponents of the predominant prime minister thesis concede, Savoie included (personal interview, 22 July 2014), there is much ebb and flow. For every Pierre Trudeau and Jean Chrétien, there is a Kim Campbell and John Turner, for every Margaret Thatcher and Tony Blair there is an Alec Douglas-Home or John Major, for every John Howard and Kevin Rudd there is a William McMahon or Julia Gillard. Parenthetically, avowedly predominant prime ministers do not do well in the reputational rankings of prime ministers (see Strangio *et al.*, 2013: Part III).

Conclusions

The term 'court politics' has several advantages, not least of which is that it suggests many promising lines of research.

First, the term 'blurs genres' (Geertz, 1983: 19) with the New Political History and builds bridges between various approaches to executive government in political science. For example, Bennister (2007: 337) and 't Hart (2014: 75–6) cite with approval Rhodes's work on court politics. The example of the new political history should lead us to purchase a hunting licence to raid the humanities for more insights and tools, whether it is architecture (Goodsell, 1988), film and the visual arts (Borins, 2011), or literature (Waldo, 1968). 'Blurring genres' is about edification; about finding 'new, better, more interesting, more fruitful ways of speaking about' (Rorty, 1980: 360) executive studies.

Second, court politics, when allied to an interpretive approach, has an ontological and epistemological foundation that is missing from earlier uses of the term by, for example, Bulpitt, Cowling, and Savoie.

Third, my approach provides the organising concepts for a systematic analysis of elite actors. I suggest the notions of traditions, beliefs, practices, and dilemmas are effective tools for unpacking the statecraft of elite actors and their networks. Two examples will do. First, in sharp contrast to Bulpitt, the interpretive approach turns attention away from the Tory moment to an exploration of the several 'traditions against the background of which elites construct their worldviews' (Bevir and Rhodes, 2010: 96). There is no assumption of unity, only an exploration of 'whether different sections of the elite ... draw on different traditions to construct different narratives of the world' (Bevir, 2010: 455). Second, the volume of 'private information' reported in the work of biographers such as Anthony Seldon and journalists such as Andrew Rawnsley is impressive, and will bear secondary analysis such as mapping the membership of the Blair and Brown courts. We need to mine all publicly available information, irrespective of discipline or profession.

Fourth, I have shown that the toolkit of political science must include the skills of the historian. Documentary evidence in its many forms is the bedrock for the analysis of court politics. As Williamson shows, the analysis of personal papers, speeches, publications, and film appearances provides data on the beliefs and practices of the governing elite. Of course, we have to wait for documentary material to become available from families and friends as well as official sources. Perhaps we are too concerned to comment on the present day. After all, we have the twentieth century to play with, including the private and official documents of the Thatcher era. Perhaps we underestimate just how much is out there. There is much that political scientists could use in exploring the webs of beliefs, practices, and traditions in the shape-shifting core networks.

Fifth, court politics addresses matters of practical import. The key question is whether court politics support or undermine the search for greater central coordination. Under what circumstances are court politics an effective form of executive governance? For Walter (2010: 9–10), 'court politics' implies small, closed-group decision making. He is concerned about the potential for dysfunction – poor decision making, an inability and unwillingness to engage in 'rigorous reality-testing' and other pathologies, if such decision making should become routine. Rhodes (2011: 275–6) reports a siege mentality, which fosters short-termism, stereotyping, and inward-looking processes of decision making during a political crisis. However, I think it is a mistake to focus on the pathologies of small-group decision making. For example, 't Hart (2014: 76–81) distinguishes usefully between the court as think tank, as sanctuary, as arena, and as ritual. We need to tease out the patterns in court politics and the intended and unintended consequences of those patterns.

Court politics are ubiquitous but are more often described than analysed, judged rather than unpacked:

> In a curious way the triumph of mass democracy has brought politics full circle. Though Parliament is no longer the cockpit, in other respects we have returned to the narrow eighteenth century world of patronage, self-promotion and mutual back-scratching where there is nothing at stake but the achievement and retention of office and the opportunities for personal enrichment that it brings. Politics today is little more than a childish game played out by a small and introverted political class, largely ignored by a cynical and alienated electorate except when it throws up some titillating scandal. It was always a game, of course – that was the fascination which kept players like Fox, Disraeli and Macmillan at the table and the audience riveted by every throw of the dice; but it was once a great game, played by serious minded people for serious causes for high stakes.
>
> (Campbell, 2010: 7)

This chapter does not seek to occupy such moral high ground, merely to suggest that historians provide the essential tools for exploring the interdependent set of networks, beliefs, and practices at the summit of government. I have also argued that an interpretive approach is well suited to recovering the beliefs and practices of the governing elite. The study of the court and high politics poses many challenges around access, secrecy, and publication. Despite the difficulties, it behoves us to try, because court politics matter for effective and accountable government.

Notes

1 I would like to thank Paul 't Hart (Utrecht), Anne Tiernan (Griffith), the participants at the 63rd PSA Annual Conference, City Hall, Cardiff, 25–27 March 2013, the participants at the workshop on 'The Craft of Governing', Griffith University, 9 August 2013, and the referees for their comments and advice on earlier versions of this chapter. The author acknowledges funding support provided for this project by the Australia and New Zealand School of Government.

2 Of course, historical analysis is not the only tool in the toolkit. Elsewhere, I have argued for a greater use of ethnography in executive studies; see Rhodes *et al.* (2007); Rhodes (2011, 2013, 2014b, 2015).

3 For an introduction to the 'interpretive turn' or 'the linguistic turn' in history, see Jenkins (1995, 1997). A personal selection of relevant texts would include Ankersmit (1989), Barthes (1970 [1961]), Collingwood (1993 [1946]), Oakeshott (2004 [1983]), Stedman-Jones (1983), and White (1973).

4 For thoroughgoing philosophical critiques of naturalism, see MacIntyre (1983, 2007), Rorty (1980, 1990), Taylor (1985), Winch (2002), and Wittgenstein (1972).

5 I have space for only a brief summary. For a more detailed account of our interpretive approach, see Bevir and Rhodes (2003, 2006a, 2010).

6 On the new political history, see Bentley and Stevenson (1983), Craig (2010), Green and Tanner (2007), Lawrence and Taylor (1997), Pederson (2002), Stedman-Jones (1983), Vernon (1996), and Williamson (1999).

7 Cowling (1971: 1–12) discusses the character of 'High Politics', and Cowling (1967, 311–40) discusses the sources for identifying the beliefs and practices (or, in his terms, intentions and political actions) of the political elite. His approach is assessed sympathetically in Craig (2010) and Williamson (2010), and more critically in Ghosh (1993).

8 See, for example, the debate about court government in the Tudor period in Elton (1976) and Starkey (1987).

9 On 'statecraft', see Bulpitt (1983, 1986, 1995, 1996). For a useful summary, see Buller and James (2012), and for critical evaluations, see Buller (1999) and Bevir (2010). See also Dennis Kavanagh's obituary of Bulpitt in the *Independent*, 25 May 1999, and the special issue of *Government & Politics* 45(3) 2010. On 'court government', see Savoie (1999, 2008) and also Buckley (2014), Campbell (2010), Dexter (1977) and Rhodes (2011).

10 On the reportage, auto/biographies, memoirs and diaries relevant to court politics, there are too many items for a complete listing here. Recent examples for Australia include Blewett (1999) and Watson (2002). Recent examples for the UK include Beckett and Hencke (2004), Blunkett (2006), Mandelson (2010), Peston (2005), Rawnsley (2001 and 2010), Richards (2010), Seldon *et al.* (2004), Seldon *et al.* (2007) and Seldon and Lodge (2010).

11 See, for example, Buckley (2014: 151–63), Peters *et al.* (2000), Savoie (2008: chapters 4 and 5).

References

Ankersmit, F. R. (1989) 'Historiography and Postmodernism', *History and Theory*, 28(2): 137–53.

Barthes, R. (1970) 'The Discourse of History', in M. Lane (ed.), *Structuralism: A reader*, London: Jonathan Cape, pp. 145–55.

Beckett, F. and Hencke, D. (2004) *The Blairs and their Court*, London: Aurum Press.

Bennister, M. (2007) 'Tony Blair and John Howard: Comparative predominance and institution stretch in the UK and Australia', *British Journal of Politics and International Relations*, 9: 327–45.

Bevir, M. (1999) *The Logic of the History of Ideas*, Cambridge: Cambridge University Press.

Bevir, M. (2010) 'Interpreting Territory and Power', *Government and Opposition*, 45(3): 436–56.

Bevir, M. and Kedar, A. (2008) 'Concept Formation in Political Science: An anti-naturalist critique of qualitative methodology', *Perspectives on Politics*, 6(3): 503–17.

Bevir, M. and Rhodes, R. A. W. (2003) *Interpreting British Governance*, London: Routledge.

Bevir, M. and Rhodes, R. A. W. (2006a) *Governance Stories*, London: Routledge.

Bevir, M. and Rhodes, R. A. W. (2006b) 'Interpretive Approaches to British Government and Politics', *British Politics*, 1(1): 1–29.

Bevir, M. and Rhodes, R. A. W. (2006c) 'Disaggregating Structures as an Agenda for Critical Realism: A reply to McAnulla', *British Politics*, 1(3): 397–403.

Bevir, M. and Rhodes, R. A. W. (2010) *The State as Cultural Practice*, Oxford: Oxford University Press.

Bevir, M. and Rhodes, R. A. W. (2013) 'Three Visions of Context as History', in C. Pollitt (ed.), *Context in Public Policy and Management: The missing link?* Aldershot: Edward Elgar, pp. 55–73.

Blewett, N. (1999) *A Cabinet Diary: a personal record of the first Keating government*, Kent Town, South Australia: Wakefield Press.

Blunkett, D. (2006) *The Blunkett Tapes: My life in the bear pit*, London: Bloomsbury.

Borins, S. F. (2011) *Governing Fables: Learning from public sector narratives*, Charlotte NC: Information Age Publishing.

Buckley, F. H. (2014) *The Once and Future King: The rise of crown government in America*. Jackson, TN: Encounter Books.

Buller, J. (1999) 'A Critical Appraisal of the Statecraft Interpretation', *Public Administration*, 77(4): 691–712.

Buller, J. and James, T. S. (2012) 'Statecraft and the Assessment of National Political Leaders: The case of New Labour and Tony Blair', *British Journal of Politics and International Relations*, 14(4): 534–55.

Bulpitt, J. (1983) *Territory and Power in the United Kingdom: An interpretation*, Manchester: Manchester University Press.

Bulpitt, J. (1986) 'The Discipline of the New Democracy: Mrs Thatcher's domestic statecraft', *Political Studies*, 34: 19–39.

Bulpitt, J. (1995) 'Historical Politics: Macro, in-time, governing regime analysis', in J. Lovenduski and J. Stanyer (eds), *Contemporary Political Studies 1995. Volume II*, Belfast: Political Studies Association.

Bulpitt, J. (1996) 'Historical Politics: Leaders, statecraft and regime in Britain at the accession of Elizabeth II', in I. Hampshire-Monk and J. Stanyer (eds), *Contemporary Political Studies 1996. Volume II*, Oxford: Blackwell: 1093–106.

Burch, M. and Halliday, I. (1996) *The British Cabinet System*, Englewood, Hemel Hempstead: Prentice Hall/Harvester Wheatsheaf.

Burch, M. and Halliday, I. (2004) 'The Blair Government and the Core Executive', *Government and Opposition*, 39(1): 1–21.

Campbell, J. (2010) *Pistols at Dawn: Two hundred years of political rivalry from Pitt and Fox to Blair and Brown*, London: Vintage.

Collingwood, R. G. S. (1993) [1946] *The Idea of History*, Revised edition, edited by Jan van der Dussen, Oxford: Oxford University Press.

Cowling, M. (1967) 1867 *Disraeli, Gladstone and Revolution: The passing of the Second Reform Bill*, Cambridge: Cambridge University Press.

Cowling, M. (1971) *The Impact of Labour 1920–1924*, Cambridge: Cambridge University Press.

Craig, D. (2010) '"High Politics" and the "New Political History"', *The Historical Journal*, 53(2): 453–75.

Dexter, L. A. (1977) 'Court Politics: Presidental staff relations as a special case of a general phenomenon', *Administration and Society*, 9(3): 267–83.

Elgie, R. (1997) 'Models of Executive Politics: A framework for the study of executive power relations in parliamentary and semi-presidential regimes', *Political Studies*, 45(2): 217–31.

Elgie, R. (2011) 'Core Executive Studies Two Decades On', *Public Administration*, 89: 64–77.

Elton, G. R. (1976) 'Presidential Address: Tudor Government, the points of contact III, the court', *Transactions of the Royal Historical Society (Fifth Series) 26 (December)*: 211–28.

Geertz, C. (1983) 'Blurred Genres: The refiguration of social thought', in *Local Knowledge: Further essays in interpretive anthropology*, New York: Basic Books, pp. 19–35.

Geertz, C. (1993) [1973] 'Thick Descriptions: Towards an interpretive theory of culture', in *The Interpretation of Cultures*, London: Fontana, pp. 3–30.

Ghosh, P. (1993) 'Towards the Verdict of History: Mr Cowling's doctrine', in M. Bentley (ed.), *Public and Private Doctrine: Essays in British history presented to Maurice Cowling*, Cambridge: Cambridge University Press: 273–321.

Giddens, A. (1993) *New Rules of Sociological Method. A positive critique of interpretive sociologies*, 2nd edition, Cambridge: Polity Press.

Goodsell, C. T. (1988) *The Social Meaning of Civic Space: Studying political authority through architecture*, Lawrence, KS: University Press of Kansas.

Green, E. H. H. and Tanner, D. M. (2007) 'Introduction', in E. H. H. Green and D. M. Tanner (eds), *The Strange Survival of Liberal England: Political leaders, moral values and the reception of economic debate*, Cambridge: Cambridge University Press, pp. 1–33.

Heffernan, R. (2003) 'Prime ministerial predominance? Core executive politics in the UK', *British Journal of Politics and International Relations*, 5(3): 347–72.

Heffernan, R. (2005) 'Exploring (and Explaining) the British Prime Minister', *British Journal of Politics and International Relations*, 7(4): 605–20.

Hennessy, P. (2000) *The Prime Minister: The office and its holders since 1945*, London: Penguin.

James, T. S. (2013) 'Statecraft Theory, Historical Institutionalism and Institutional Change', Paper presented to the 63rd Political Studies Association Annual International Conference, 25–27 March, 2013, City Hall, Cardiff. Available at: http://papers.ssrn.com/sol3/papers.cfm?abstract_id=2128549 [accessed 5 August 2014].

Jenkins, K. (1995) *On 'What is History?' From Carr and Elton to Rorty and White*, London: Routledge.

Jenkins, K. (ed.) (1997) *The Postmodern History Reader*, London: Routledge.

Kavanagh, D. (1991) 'Why Political Science Needs History', *Political Studies*, 39(3): 479–95.

Lawrence, J. and Taylor, M. (1997) 'Introduction: Electoral sociology and the historians', in J. Lawrence and M. Taylor (eds), *Party, State and Society: Electoral behaviour in Britain since 1820*, Aldershot: Scolar Press, pp. 1–26.

Lincoln, Y. S. and Guba, E. G. (1985) *Naturalistic Inquiry*, Newbury Park, CA: Sage.

MacIntyre A. (1983) 'The Indispensability of Political Theory', in D. Miller and L. Siedentop (eds), *The Nature of Political Theory*, Oxford: Clarendon Press, pp. 17–33.

MacIntyre, A. (2007) *After Virtue: A study in moral theory*, 3rd revised edition, Notre Dame, IN: University of Notre Dame Press.

Mandelson, P. (2010) *The Third Man: Life at the heart of New Labour*, London: Harper.

Norton, P. (2000) 'Barons in a Shrinking Kingdom: Senior ministers in British government', in R. A. W. Rhodes (ed.), *Transforming British Government, Volume 2: Changing roles and relationships*, London: Macmillan: pp. 101–24.

Oakeshott, M. (2004) [1983] *On History and Other Essays*, expanded edition, edited by Luke O'Sullivan, Exeter and Charlottesville VA: Imprint Academic.

Pederson, S. (2002) 'What is Political History Now?', in D. Cannadine (ed.), *What is History Now?* Houndmills, Basingstoke: Palgrave Macmillan, pp. 36–56.

Peston, R. (2005) *Brown's Britain*, London: Short Books.

Peters, B. G., Rhodes, R. A. W., and Wright, V. (eds) (2000) 'Staffing the Summit – the Administration of the Core Executive: Convergent trends and national specificities', in G. Peters, R. A. W. Rhodes, and V. Wright (eds), *Administering the Summit: Administration of the core executive in developed countries*, Basingstoke: Macmillan, pp. 3–22.

Rawnsley, A. (2001) *Servants of the People: The inside story of New Labour*, revised edition, London: Penguin Books.

Rawnsley, A. (2010) *The End of the Party: The rise and fall of New Labour*, London: Viking.

Rhodes, R. A. W. (1995) 'From Prime Ministerial Power to Core Executive', in R. A. W. Rhodes and P. Dunleavy (eds), *Prime Minister, Cabinet and Core Executive*, London: Macmillan, pp. 11–37.

Rhodes, R. A. W. (2011) *Everyday Life in British Government*, Oxford: Oxford University Press.

Rhodes, R. A. W. (2013) 'From Prime Ministerial Leadership to Court Politics', in P. Strangio, P. 't Hart, and J. Walter (eds), *Understanding Prime-Ministerial Performance: Comparative perspectives*, Oxford: Oxford University Press, pp. 318–33.

Rhodes, R. A. W. (2014a) 'From Core Executives to Court Politics', in Glyn Davis and R. A. W. Rhodes (eds), *The Craft of Governing: The contribution of Patrick Weller to Australian political science*, Crows Nest, NSW: Allen & Unwin, pp. 53–72.

Rhodes, R. A. W. (2014b) 'Genre Blurring in Public Administration: What can we learn from the humanities?' *Australian Journal of Public Administration*, 73(4): 317–30.

Rhodes, R. A. W. (2015) 'Ethnography', in M. Bevir and R. A. W. Rhodes (eds), *The Routledge Handbook of Interpretive Political Science*, Abingdon, Oxon: Routledge.

Rhodes, R. A. W. and Tiernan, A. (2014) *Lessons of Governing: A profile of prime ministers' Chiefs of Staff*, Melbourne: Melbourne University Press.

Rhodes, R. A. W., 't Hart, P., and Noordegraaf, M. (eds) (2007), *Observing Government Elites: Up close and personal, Houndmills*, Basingstoke: Palgrave Macmillan.

Richards, S. (2010) *Whatever It Takes: The real story of Gordon Brown and New Labour*, London: Fourth Estate.

Rorty, R. (1980) *Philosophy and the Mirror of Nature*, Oxford: Blackwell.

Rorty, R. (1990) 'Is Natural Science a Natural Kind?' in his *Philosophical Papers, Volumes 1 and 2*, Cambridge: Cambridge University Press.

Savoie, D. (1999) *Governing from the Centre*, Toronto: Toronto University Press.

Savoie, D. (2008) *Court Government and the Collapse of Accountability in Canada and the United Kingdom*, Toronto: University of Toronto Press.

Seldon A. and Lodge, G. (2010) *Brown at 10*, London: Biteback Publishing.

Seldon, A., with Ballinger, C., Collings, D., and Snowden, P. (2004) *Blair*, London: Free.

Seldon, A., with Snowden, P., and Collings, D. (2007) *Blair Unbound*, London: Simon & Schuster.

Starkey, D. (1987) 'Introduction: Court history in perspective', in D. Starkey (ed.), *The English Court: From the Wars of the Roses to the Civil War*, London and New York: Longman, pp. 1–24.

Stedman-Jones, G. (1983) 'Rethinking Chartism', in his *Languages of Class: Studies in English working class history, 1832–1982*, Cambridge: Cambridge University Press, pp. 90–178.

Strangio, P., 't Hart, P., and Walter, J. (eds) (2013) *Understanding Prime-Ministerial Performance: Comparative perspectives*, Oxford: Oxford University Press.

't Hart, P. (2014) *Understanding Political Leadership*, London: Palgrave.

Taylor, C. (1971) 'Interpretation and the Sciences of Man', *Review of Metaphysics*, 25: 3–51.

Taylor, C. (1985) *Philosophical Papers, Volumes 1 and 2*, Cambridge: Cambridge University Press.

Vernon, J. (1996) *Re-reading the Constitution: New essays in the political history of England's nineteenth century*, Cambridge: Cambridge University Press.

Waldo, D. (1968) *The Novelist on Organization and Administration: An inquiry into the relationship between two worlds*, Berkeley, CA: Institute of Governmental Studies, University of California.

Walter, J. (2010) 'Elite Decision Processes: The "court politics" debate', paper presented to the Australian Political Studies Association Annual Conference, University of Melbourne, 27–29 September.

Watson, D. (2002) *Recollections of a Bleeding Heart: A portrait of Paul Keating PM*, New York: Knopf.

White, H. (1973) *Metahistory*, Baltimore: Johns Hopkins Press.

Williamson, P. (1999) *Stanley Baldwin*, Cambridge: Cambridge University Press.

Williamson, P. (2004) 'Baldwin's Reputation: Politics and history, 1937–1967', *Historical Journal* 47(1): 127–68.

Williamson, P. (2010). 'Maurice Cowling and Modern British Political History', in R. Crowcroft, S. J. D. Green, and R. Whiting (eds), *Philosophy, Politics and Religion in British Democracy: Maurice Cowling and conservatism*, London: I. B. Tauris, pp. 108–52.

Winch, P. (2002) *The Idea of a Social Science: And its relation to philosophy*, 2nd edition. London: Routledge.

Wittgenstein, L. (1972) *Philosophical Investigations*, trans. G. Anscombe, Oxford: Basil Blackwell.

5   Political Ideas and 'Real' Politics

David Craig

How important are political ideas for understanding 'real' politics? Among political historians, the whole spectrum of answers has been proposed. At one extreme, it seems, are those who have stressed the centrality of ideas: for instance, that the influence of Locke, Smith, and Bentham can be traced, sooner or later, into the practice of routine politics. At the other extreme, and in resistance to this, are those who see politics in a realist vein: interest and power are, within and between states, the determining factors in political life, with ideas little more than, at best, a rhetorical flourish. Clearly, part of the difficulty resides in what is meant by political *ideas*. Typically, historians of ideas still tend to refer to what might be called upper-case 'I' ideas – the arguments of a relatively restricted canon of sophisticated political theorists. But there are also what we might call lower-case 'i' ideas – the sorts of beliefs held by all manner of everyday actors which constitute their understanding of the political world and which will affect their actions in relation to it (MacIntyre, 1983). There is, of course, no clear-cut distinction between the two, nor any necessary reason to suppose that a canonical thinker was recognised as such in their own time.

A strength of the work of Bevir and Rhodes is that they – separately and collectively – take small 'i' ideas seriously. Because of their commitment to what they call 'situated agency', they recognise the centrality of the beliefs and desires of individual agents even as they locate these within broader traditions. Because of their commitment to anti-essentialism, but in the form of pragmatic realism (Bevir, 2010: 60–1), they do not instantiate a dichotomy between ideas and reality – in Charles Taylor's words 'ideas always come wrapped up in certain forms of practices' (Taylor, 2004: 33). Since *Interpreting British Governance* was published in 2003, they have sought to apply these arguments to the understanding of modern governance. Bevir (2005, 2010) has shown how the arguments and assumptions of different styles of social science – first rational choice and then new institutionalism – have shaped new patterns of governance and brought new ideological *and* practical dilemmas to the fore. His concern is primarily to trace the intellectual traditions underpinning and shaping contemporary practice. Rhodes (2011), meanwhile, has applied an ethnographic approach: by observing the everyday lives of ministers and permanent secretaries in three government departments, he is able to show how the routines and rituals of a wide variety of actors – the role of the diary secretary, for instance, is stressed – make an institution work, in good times and in bad.

No doubt most political scientists will primarily be interested in what this can tell us about governance. Here, though, I want to approach the question of the interpretive approach to politics by a different route, and to begin by stressing the centrality of the history of ideas as a subfield. Bevir's training was as an intellectual historian: his 1989 DPhil explored 'British Socialist Thought, 1880–1900', and in the 1990s he published a number of articles on nineteenth-century social and political thought. Indeed, this interest has never disappeared, as various publications throughout the 2000s show – not least his 2011 *Making of British Socialism*. Dissatisfied with the prevailing methodologies of this sub-field, Bevir also spent the 1990s developing his own philosophical approach, which appeared as *The Logic of the History of Ideas* in 1999. Even though some of the terms and arguments have been refined, the centrality of this book to the subsequent work of Bevir and Rhodes cannot be exaggerated – it sits behind everything. Its title, however, does not do justice to its ambition. Bevir was not just interested in the history of ideas as a way to understand canonical thinkers but in its potential to situate the beliefs and desires of *all* agents in a meaningful context, and to use this to understand their behaviour. Hence, as Melissa Lane noted, his concern was not so much 'large "I" ideas' as 'small "i" ideas' (Lane, 2002: 34).

Both Bevir and Rhodes want to use their interpretive approach as a means of rethinking the practice of political science. In part they do this through philo-sophical engagement with alternative epistemologies and methodologies, but they also stress the importance of disciplinary genealogies. In *Modern Political Science* (Adcock *et al.*, 2007), they and their collaborators examine the historical development of their discipline, showing the different routes taken by Anglo-American political science over the last century, from the eclipse of develop-mental historicism, through empiricist modernism, to the emergence of new institutionalism. The radical historicism outlined in the *Logic* shapes their approach, but they also argue that such histories are important to contemporary political science – they undermine caricatures of past scholarship and recapture lost insights, they can help us refine the concepts in current use and clarify the beliefs we study. Crucially, radical historicism 'undermines the assumptions of the natural, progressive, or disinterested character of the development of polit-ical science and the institutions that it informs and by which it is informed' (Adcock, *et al.*, 2007: 15) and enables us to evaluate alternative approaches. The history of political science is therefore part of the subject of political science.

This chapter aims to contribute to the task of exploring the history of political science, and in particular its relationship to political thought and political history. In an earlier essay (Craig, 2010) I tried to show how an influential style of 'high political' history – the 'Peterhouse School' of Maurice Cowling – could be understood in a more anthropological light, and that, as a result, could be seen as a part of a broad tradition to which Bevir and Rhodes belong. Indeed, Cowling's *Nature and Limits of Political Science* has made fleeting appearances in their work (Bevir and Rhodes, 1999: 233; 2003: 43). Here, I want to look at a strand of development taken by the 'Cambridge School' of the history of political thought. While the influence of Quentin Skinner is well understood, that of John Dunn is rather less so. This is relevant to Bevir's work: while he disagrees with Skinner's methodology, his *Logic* nevertheless emerges out of close engagement with the arguments of the 'Cambridge School'. There is an affinity between them. But while Skinner has largely remained concerned with the history of ideas, Dunn's significance arises from his more direct interest in the way that hermeneutic approaches can be applied to political science and the explanatory challenges they raise. Yet, despite the potential synergies between Bevir and Dunn, the latter has made only the most cursory of appearances in the former's work. In what follows I trace the development of Dunn's thinking – an exercise in intellectual history – to show how his interpretive commitments have posed important questions about the nature of explanation in the social sciences and about the irreducibility of political judgment, and how these underpin a particular style of 'realism' in recent political theory.

John Dunn, Political Thought, and Political Science

Dunn's first book on *The Political Thought of John Locke* was published in 1969, and was quickly championed as a manifesto for a new style of contextualised history of political thought. Certainly, it was written in reaction to two dominant styles of interpretation at that time. On the one hand were the philosophers who tended to view the historical specificity of texts with 'massive indifference' and instead found them stimulating largely according to contemporary concerns – the danger here was anachronism (Dunn, 1996: 19). On the other hand were those historians – especially Marxists – who explained the significance of a text by reference to the social relations of the period, as if the author's expressed intentions were of little concern. But Dunn's interest was not just to restore the historical identity to an argument from the past – indeed this might be seen as a 'trivial' ambition – but to encourage recognition that the philosophical and historical approaches were 'logically indispensable complements' (Dunn, 1969: 208). What, he later explained, he was groping for was something like Quine's holism – an understanding of the internal connections and relations of a person's thinking (Dunn, 1990: 10).

The groping can first be seen in an influential article of the preceding year. Dunn wanted to bring into harmony the two approaches just mentioned, namely a satisfactory philosophical account of an individual's ideas *and* an adequate historical account of them. The objections made to typical histories of philosophy are now familiar. They were histories of 'fictions': rational constructions were squeezed into formal articulations which could not have historically been possible (1980: 15). These histories only focused on one of two necessary things – 'the set of argued propositions in the past which discuss how the political world is and ought to be and what should constitute the criteria for proper action within it' (1980: 20). The defenders of these histories were concerned only with the coherence of a set of propositions, and with commenting on the status of this coherence in relation to contemporary criteria of rationality. Hence, Dunn argued, the central concern was the truth or falsity of what the philosopher being studied had maintained. This style of explanation was therefore 'rational'. Dunn was not opposed to this as such – after all, a part of understanding why, for instance, Plato criticised Thrasymachus' conception of justice will require unearthing the premises which made the arguments seem cogent (1980: 16). His own work on Locke tried to restore as much coherence as possible to what Locke maintained (Dunn, 1969: xi). But, he argued, this was not enough – we also needed an explanation of *why* Locke – or anyone else – maintained what he did. The philosophical histories were bloodless – they were histories with 'breathing, excreting, hating, mocking' left out (Dunn, 1980: 20). Thinking was an activity and its history was a history of people struggling to make sense of their experiences. Hence, the history of thought needed to consider the actions which were being engaged in when statements were made – propositions had a place in the real world and statements were made by real speakers (1980: 20, 21). It was in this regard that Dunn's engagement with Austin's speech-act theory was at its strongest[1] – one cannot always know what someone meant *unless* one knew what someone was doing, as, for example, in understanding cases of irony or parody.[2] In these senses, then, there was a 'causal' approach to the history of thought. That said, Dunn did not want to push this aspect too far – the error of those who saw ideas as simply the expression of social relations. While there might be room to explain *some* aspects of a text as the ideological expression of a group, this could never explain *all* its aspects – the *Republic* might in part have been written as an apologia for the declining Athenian elite, but that could not explain *all* of what Plato wrote.

Dunn's aim was not so much to establish a new school of the history of political thought as to consider the relationship between intellectual and social history – and, as we shall see, his thinking had implications for *both* types of history. He was interested in the philosophy of explanation, and cited Collingwood, Gardiner, Dray, Gallie, Danto, Kuhn, and Gombrich as particular influences. But he was unwilling to declare a side in the 'venerable dispute' between idealist and positivist philosophies of history (1980: 17). He did not think all potentially explanatory questions were of a piece. To ask why Plato criticised Thrasymachus' conception of justice, or why the Roman Empire collapsed, or why the French Revolution happened, were different sorts of questions, which lent themselves to different sorts of answers. In the first case, no set of causal laws could possibly supply an explanation, but in the latter two cases he did not see how answers based on 'reasons' could ever be adequate; 'No explanation of the persistence and change of a complex social system over time can be adequately provided by a story' (1980: 17). Because of Dunn's strong interest in the importance of history *and* sociology in understanding politics (Dunn, 1972: xiii), he could not see any way of abandoning some kind of commitment to causal laws (Dunn 1980: 20n). Rather, one needed accounts that stressed 'reasons' as well as 'causes', and this was particularly the case with the histories of ideas. These needed to explore the history of political arguments, the coherence of a person's ideas, though there was always the danger of imposing anachronistic assessments of rationality (Dunn, 1980: 26–7). Hence, they needed also to consider the history of political arguing, which looked at the explanations of why particular arguments were made at a particular time. This ensured that the history of ideas could be a part of real social history.

These concerns with explanation in the human sciences were to become, if anything, more central in the following ten years. It is worth stressing that in this period Dunn had very little to say about the history of political thought. Since his conclusion – later retracted (Dunn, 1990: 9) – to his book on Locke had been that he could not 'conceive of constructing an analysis of any issue in contemporary political theory around the affirmation or negation of anything which Locke says about political matters' (Dunn, 1969: x), it seems possible that he did not see how historical reconstructions of the thought of philosophers were necessarily terribly illuminating about the present. In any event, he turned instead to empirical political history and social science. In 1972 he published *Modern Revolutions*, a series of case studies of twentieth-century revolutions designed to rebut prevailing social science explanations. We will return to the subject of revolution shortly. He was also pursuing an interest in the development of post-colonial West Africa. This resulted in a co-written study of a province of Ghana (Dunn and Robertson, 1973), based on detailed archival work and wide-ranging interviews, and an edited collection of case studies of individual states (Dunn, 1978). Although by this point Dunn's interests were turning back to political theory, he had in the meantime ample occasion for thinking about problems of explanation in the social sciences.

Practising Social Science

These thoughts culminated in 'Practising history and social science on "realist" assumptions', published in 1978. Dunn by this point showed familiarity with recent post-analytic philosophy, and was aware of the attacks on traditional epistemology by those working in the pragmatist tradition, especially Quine, Davidson, Putnam, and Rorty. While he suggested that the implications of these arguments for social science were not yet fully clear (Dunn, 1980: 3–4, 109), what was apparent was that historicist and rationalist perspectives on cognition had been brought into closer harmony – part of the aim of the 1968 article. Certainly, he argued, any attempt to ground political theory in the analysis of supposedly 'timeless ethical concepts' was doomed to failure (1980: 3). The main aim of the essay was to consider what sort of knowledge of humans was possible, contrasting what might be called the interpretive or hermeneutic approach, which focused on human properties as humans understood them, with the naturalist or positivist approach which 'laundered out' all the anthropocentric properties (1980: 6). He wanted to commit as far as possible to the former approach – which took very seriously human beliefs, and the beliefs embodied in action – but at the same time without abandoning an appreciation of 'a context of social causality' which set limits to what any individual human being could do (1980: 7).

Before exploring these arguments further, it will be useful to consider MacIntyre's work on the philosophy of social science. The essays in *Against the Self-Images of the Age* (1971) and especially a further essay published in 1973 had a substantial influence on Dunn, judging by repeated references to these works. (There are also striking parallels with the arguments of Bevir and Rhodes, for instance in the understanding of institutions.) Although, as Turner (2003) shows, MacIntyre switched over the course of the 1960s from a strong commitment to explanation of meaningful action *solely* in terms of reasons to explanations which stressed both reasons *and* causes, his broader critique of positivist social science – for instance, behaviourism – remained strong. Many of his core themes come together in 'Ideology, Social Science and Revolution' (1973), which offered a sustained attack on the special claims to knowledge offered both by the positivist and by the ideologist. As with his earlier work, it begins with the need to identify an action – as distinct from a movement – by capturing 'the intention embodied in the action and the meaning the agent attaches to what he is doing' (1973: 323). Because of the social character of language, agents cannot characterise their actions in entirely egocentric ways – their descriptions will have some kind of implicit reference to social criteria: 'In order for his action to be what the agent takes it to be, it must be such that others can construe it in the same way' (1973: 324). In addition, since an agent's intentions were inseparable from his beliefs, actions presuppose a wider web of beliefs – for instance, taking a sheep to market presupposes a web of beliefs about economy and husbandry. For other agents to understand such actions requires some measure of shared beliefs, but, because a great deal of divergence of belief can exist within a shared community, agents are oriented to making their actions intelligible, and so our beliefs about our actions always have some reference to what others believe about our actions and about our beliefs. Hence 'the' action cannot be identified independently of the beliefs both of the agent, and of other agents with whom he or she interacts. Drawing on Garfinkel and Goffman, MacIntyre sees agents trying to understand the behaviour of others – including *their* attempts to understand him – within their own evolving scripts or 'theories' (1973: 325). Most of the time agents are largely unaware of the complex and skilful negotiations which social life makes upon them – only in dramatically new or challenging situations do we suddenly become aware of these demands (1973: 327–8).

If this represents the social situation of ordinary agents, it had important epistemological consequences, notably the real challenges in determining the actions of other agents. It might be difficult to know which range of descriptions to apply to behaviour, and even if that was known, which of the possible range had primary status for the agent. Yet the task of imputing intentions to others cannot be evaded because we frame *our* 'intentions, purposes, attitudes, and emotions' in response to those we see in others (1973: 329). So, even though our ascriptions cannot be warranted by the evidence – and mistakes and misunderstandings will creep in – we nevertheless have to make do with them. Another difficulty was that this characterisation of social life compromised an agent's ability to predict the future. In a 'game theoretic' situation, multiple agents were all trying to achieve their aims while recognising that 'no one agent can put a limit on the possibilities that may be opened by the reflections of other agents' (1973: 330). Even regularities, once observed, could be used to mislead. For these and other reasons agents cannot accurately predict the future. These characteristics were central to all social life. The result was that on the one hand humans cannot avoid relying upon the generalisations that help them fix the expectations of others, but that those very generalisations were constantly breaking down: 'we are all being surprised a great deal of the time' (1973: 332; see also MacIntyre, 1971: 243). The rest of the article argued that social scientists – whatever their positivist ambitions – could not transcend the epistemological limits of ordinary agents, but that all agents could try to avoid becoming victims of these limits by becoming more explicitly conscious of them – by recognising the concepts and categories we use in interpreting others and forming our own intentions (MacIntyre, 1973: 336).

These themes are never far from Dunn's essay. He began by defining the core subject matter of human science as 'human acts taken under intentional descriptions, past, present and future, and the causes and consequences of such acts' (Dunn, 1980: 85). Throughout, he was critical of various styles of positivist social science. Like MacIntyre and Taylor, he opposed behaviourism for its untenable claim that intentional categories be eliminated, and argued that even if they could such a science could not serve any humanly useful purpose (1980: 85–6). He was also opposed to those social scientists who claimed that elements of an agent's self-description could be replaced with descriptions supplied by the observer – there were no criteria by which to judge such terms as superior, and in any case, Dunn continued, there were no viable laws of psychology or sociology which could explain motivation (1980: 104). Drawing on MacIntyre (1973), he explained the difficulties of formulating laws in the human sciences. To be sure, one could identify past regularities, but if these were to explain outcomes they needed to take the form of conditional law-like generalisations, and he did not see any way criteria for counterfactual testing could be specified (Dunn, 1980: 100–1; see MacIntyre, 1973: 333–4). Moreover, once regularities had been discovered they then become themselves elements open to manipulation – the theory contaminated the data. Hence, he argued, 'there are probably not any serious candidates for such law-like generalisations of any scope or interest in the more descriptively oriented social sciences' (Dunn, 1980: 101). Rather than concluding that social science was not possible – MacIntyre's argument – a greater degree of cognitive humility was desirable on the part of social scientists.

Dunn's approach was 'strongly', even 'vigorously' hermeneutic (Dunn, 1980: 94, 104).[3] It took the beliefs and desires of agents seriously and argued that the history of such beings cannot deny their possession of intellect and cannot occur behind their backs (1980: 95). Much of the essay was a series of related reflections on how this could be made practicable to the enquirer and what its limits might be. To understand the action of a person would require a full account of the beliefs and desires the agent would have honestly and thoughtfully given of his or her action. There *might* be grounds for supplementing this account – for instance by reference to sociological or psychological considerations – so long as we could know that they were relevant but unmentioned aspects of the agent's actions. Dunn has in mind factors such as denial, self-deception, and rationalisation, as well as ideology and social determination of belief. All these might be relevant aspects of explanation, but only so long as they could be shown within an agent's 'own mapping of his "problem situation"' (1980: 105). Once we have the best description which an agent can offer, we *may* be able to enlighten the agent to himself by showing that his description was inaccurate or misleading, but what we 'cannot do is claim to *know* that we understand him or his action better than he does himself' (1980: 105).[4] The validity of any interpretation of an action will ultimately depend on the 'economy and accuracy' with which it handles 'the full text of the agent's description' (1980: 106).

Dunn countered various criticisms. One complaint might be that his account was highly individualist. He happily accepted this – he was opposed to those social holists who argued that social wholes could be understood without reference to the truth or falsity of any individual action. He also denied those who asserted that his argument committed him to the view that all statements about social wholes could be broken down into statements about individuals – i.e. he did not think his view committed him to methodological individualism. (These arguments are repeatedly stressed by Bevir and Rhodes as well.) This can be seen in his hermeneutic approach to institutions, which, again, draws on MacIntyre.[5] In a favoured quotation, MacIntyre suggested that

> it is an obvious truism that no institution or practice is what it is, or does what it does, independent of what anyone whatsoever thinks or feels about it. For institutions are always partially, even if to differing degrees, constituted by what certain people think or feel about them.
>
> (cited in Dunn, 1980: 89; MacIntyre, 1971: 263)

In practice it might be difficult to specify the boundary between those whose thoughts constituted the institution and those who were external to it – was the British state constituted by all its citizens, or only some of them? And, clearly, it was also partially constituted by citizens of other states; 'There is no such thing as the British state *tout court*', and this problem showed that one of the practical difficulties of social science was the 'gross vagueness' of many of its central terms (Dunn, 1980: 89).[6] Any regularities in the persistence of institutions were the result of the beliefs and actions of agents, and might cease to be regularities once they were uncovered as such (1980: 90, 94). But that did not mean that such regularities could be ignored – they confronted agents, and agents identified them as truths by which to guide their action. There might be 'few, if any' regularities which could not become redundant as a result of future beliefs, but 'one can hardly give a coherent account of the beliefs of an agent without making presumptions about the truth or falsity of any of his beliefs about social reality' (1980: 94). The argument might be individualist, but it need not be voluntarist – men made their own history, but 'some men make far more of their fair share of the history of others' (1980: 94).

A further criticism might be that focusing on the beliefs and desires of agents does not account adequately for either causes or consequences. It might miss out the causal role of material factors which do not have any impact on consciousness, and it might misjudge the material factors which do appear. This was true enough: there was plenty of 'natural, non-intentional causality within human history and around human actions' and so all history could not be explained *solely* at the individual level – there were other entities necessary to populate the human sciences (1980: 85, 100). The sticking points, as we have seen, were attempts to specify psychological or sociological 'causes' which could not be connected in any way to human consciousness. Dunn attached great weight to consequences, especially unintended consequences, and an accurate assessment of them was a central part of his theory of judgment. But they did not raise any problems for a hermeneutic conception of human action because they were external matters of fact. It may be a stylistic feature of historical narrative to describe a set of actions as causing, say, the First World War, but this was not a license to replace the relevant agents' characterisation of their actions (1980: 105).[7]

The other difficulties concerned problems with characterising and describing human consciousness, and with providing criteria for describing meanings. The first problem was best sidestepped: even if one could offer some kind of full verbal transcript of the conscious experience of another person, it would not include experiences that could not be rendered in words, and would likely include all manner of sentences which we could make neither head nor tail of. Better, Dunn argued, to stick with intelligible descriptions of particular agents, as expressed in standard hermeneutic units: texts, speech acts, and individual or collective actions (1980: 98–9). Even this less ambitious task would require enormous simplification to be manageable. The second more radical objection arose from Quine's arguments about the indeterminacy of translation. Because of his commitment to holism, such that the meaning of words depended on their place in the wider context of language, there could be no single manual for translating across languages. These difficulties applied not only to deeply alien cultures – radical translation – but also to those which might be comparatively similar. The difference between early modern and late modern notions of property was a case in point (1980: 96–7). These arguments could be seen to challenge the possibility of an interpretive human science, and Dunn's cautious response provides a good opportunity to summarise his broader themes.

These were sceptical but pragmatic. Dunn placed the beliefs and desires of agents centre stage, but did not deny the difficulties this raised. There were no 'cheap ways' to the knowledge of others and the causes of their actions, but nor was the knowledge acquired more than provisional. The indeterminacy of translation posed real difficulties for the idea that meanings – the core subject matter of the human sciences – could be firmly characterised. But, on the other hand, the very existence of the term 'meaning' was significant: we can and do communicate, we can and do characterise what other agents mean (1980: 108–9). In a passage that echoes MacIntyre's conclusions, Dunn argued that:

> We all hold more or less well-justified beliefs about the beliefs and sentiments and practical situations of others. We all can and indeed *must* attempt to judge methodologically how it is sound to attribute beliefs or feelings to others. Within a common physical world we are all radical interpreters of

one another, assigning beliefs, desires, intentions and meanings simultaneously to one another and trying to make sense of conduct by solving the
resulting simultaneous equations.

(1980: 107)

There were no methods which could provide guarantees against error, but the
absence of such methods did not mean there was nothing true to be said (1980:
109).[8] What was needed – as with MacIntyre – was greater awareness of the way
we interpret ourselves and others, and something that Dunn thought akin to the
principle of charity: 'If we claim to *know* about other men, we must try as best
we can to give them what is their due, their right. This is a simple moral duty,
not a guarantee of epistemological prowess' (1980: 110).

Agency, Revolution, and Explanation

These arguments provided the basis of Dunn's thoughts both about social explanation and political theory, which we shall consider in turn. Throughout the
1970s his empirical work was in part a means of considering the nature of social
explanation. In *Modern Revolutions* he examined eight case studies as a way of
showing the highly variable nature of 'revolution' – the concept was unlikely
ever to be made a sufficiently stable category that could be susceptible to scientific analysis (Dunn, 1972: 226–8, 230, 241–3). In particular, he stressed that,
although revolutions were rarely the *intended* result of actual revolutionaries, he
could not see how an explanation of their course could avoid 'an adequate
account of the character of the wide variety of actions' that comprise them
(1972: 232). The most ambitious attempt to provide a sociology of revolution
came with Skocpol's *States and Social Revolutions* (1979), which Dunn had
positively refereed for Cambridge University Press, as well as offering advice on
drafting the introduction.[9] It was, he believed, in many ways a powerful work
which could also be read as staking bold claims for a new historical sociology.
His lengthy review, however, brought out important areas of disagreement. He
repeated his belief about the difficulty of finding appropriate criteria by which to
define all revolutions, but noted that Skocpol began with theoretical stipulations
which enabled her to focus on three complex instances of social revolution –
France, Russia, and China. As is well known, Skocpol's central innovation was
to move away from the Marxist fixation with crises of production, and instead
place the state centrefold – revolutions were first and foremost crises of states.
As well as the importance of class relations, she stressed the internal extractive
and repressive power of the state and its external economic and military power.
The latter focus on the world economy and the international state system were,
for Dunn, major advances in understanding. Where he differed strongly was with
her relentlessly structural approach which attempted 'to shrink the limits of the
role of agency, human understanding and will, the cognitive and affective states
of human beings' in favour of the 'overwhelming causal constraints imposed by
objective conditions' (Dunn, 1985: 72). In sum, her models of state collapse
refer as little as possible to human intentions or judgments.

Why? Dunn sees three reasons. First, the outcomes of revolutions are not intended by any agent, that is to say, what revolutionaries suppose themselves to be doing and what they are in fact doing overlap little. Second, the actual collapse of an *ancien régime* in any case was not caused by revolutionaries, and third, the real cause – the impact of foreign military and economic pressure – affected the options open to rulers and not revolutionaries. Dunn agrees with the first up to a point, but suggests that the understanding of revolutionaries had *some* causal consequence, and notes that even Skocpol accepts that there were differing options available in the process of reconstruction rather than a material determination of *the* option taken. On the second point, the collapse of a regime could not be understood 'independent of the acts of *any* social actors', and so the intentionality and judgment of state rulers was a relevant consideration. And finally, while the objective factors of revolutionary situations might originally be quite distinct from the practice of actual revolutionaries, by the twentieth century revolution has become an ongoing international phenomenon, and so the wider context of global revolutionaries now played 'a causal role in *creating* objective revolutionary situations' (1985: 75). What was really at stake, Dunn suggested, was the nature and purpose of sociology and explanation – revolutions pose in the starkest terms questions about how much choice humans have over their fate. While it was certainly possible to model the collapse of states from the outside – to see them as structural events beyond control, it was 'absurd' and even 'perverse' to think that the construction of new state powers in a revolution was 'a process external to human will or judgment' (1985: 76). Skocpol evades these hard questions, and adopts the structural terminology of possibilities, obstacles, options, imperatives, and impossibilities – but, as Dunn notes, even many of these terms cannot fully expel the 'flavour of choice' which they suggest (1985: 77).

However illuminating structural approaches to explanation were, they were 'causally inadequate' and, as we shall see, 'politically misleading' (Dunn, 1985: 5). Since the mid-1970s, Dunn had become increasingly interested in the centrality of practical reason, and the counterfactuals it threw up. The key point to which he returned in a number of essays was that political judgment was about making choices and assessing possibilities. This did not deny that there were limits to actions, but it was rather a recognition that, except in brutally determined situations, there was always some kind of choice to be made (Dunn, 1980: 226n); 'The key truth about politics – morally, politically, theoretically – is always that matters could have been different' (Dunn, 1978: 214). In order to understand what was actually the case at any given time, one needed to think about 'what *could*, under other specified circumstances, have been the case' (Dunn, 1979: 106). Thinking counterfactually was the 'central modality of political judgment' – it was to 'revel' in the potential openness of history, but at the same time not to be blind to its 'grubby ràtionality' (Dunn 1978: 215). In the case of *West African States*, for instance, Dunn argued that the most minute and detailed comparison of the structural properties of each would not be sufficient to explain their different political fortunes in the post-colonial period. It simply had to be recognised that 'political initiative, and skill, political lethargy and fecklessness' mattered, that the choices made by powerful players did have causal impact (1978: 212, 216). So, when thinking about the structural analysis of states, one needed to be sure not to confuse what states *can* do with what they *must* do. An ineliminable feature of what they *can* do was human belief about what was possible, and those beliefs 'arise from historical experience and change with it' (Dunn, 1985: 77). The *presumed* causal properties of institutions – and the political strategies based on those presumptions – alter what both rulers and revolutionaries think it is rational to do. In political competition, 'the strategies of one set of competitors are necessarily predicated in some measure on their beliefs about the strategies of others' (1985: 77).[10] This reflexivity meant that revolutions varied over time, and that what might seem fixed structures in one situation, might not be so in the next. So, rather than relying on structures alone to do the explanatory work, one had to examine why 'things are as they are' in light of 'what factors under what circumstances' would have made them different (Dunn, 1984: 2).

The significance of these claims was developed much more fully by Dunn's colleague Geoffrey Hawthorn. His thinking about the role of counterfactuals – partly inspired by Dunn's work – began in 1979, and culminated in *Plausible Worlds* (1991). He started with the paradox that in the human sciences the more we multiply the causes and reasons we give to explain something, that is, the more we appear to be determinate in our explanations, the more we increase the possibilities that things could have been different, and so seem to decrease the power of our explanation. When considering 'causes', most of these turn out to have some measure of contingency, and, in any case, in the human sciences, many explanations turn *not* on causal connections but on practical reasonings. Hence there is enormous potential for counterfactual possibilities. The task of the enquirer, then, is to assess on a case-by-case basis those possibilities which were genuinely impossible and those which were plausible but not chosen (Hawthorn, 1991: 13–15). Some extended case studies made the implications clearer. Take the course of plague and the levels of fertility in early modern Europe – these are typically seen as part of Braudel's *longue durée*, the biological regime of 'restrictions, obstacles, structures' which marked the impossible off from the possible (1991: 28). In fact, however, Hawthorn argues that things could have been different – in towns, at least, political choices might have better controlled the plague, and different choices of French policy towards Spain in the seventeenth century – with implications for taxation of the countryside – might have pressed less hard on rural fertility (1991: 79). Hence, doubts can be thrown on the distinction between structure and agency such that structure is not so much an unchangeable set of affairs, but simply a set of affairs that happened not to have changed much, but which could have been changed (1991: 79). An alternative example considers the politics of the division of Korea after 1945. This might be seen as a classic instance of *événementielle*, a situation where there was a high level of choice among those deciding US foreign policy. In fact, though, while the US could have acted differently in not occupying Korea in 1945, once there they could not have withdrawn without radically revising their reasons for being there (1991: 121). This latter point is key for Hawthorn – assessing plausible possibility requires careful consideration of the counterfactual. It had to start from 'particular agents in particular sets of circumstances as those agents and sets of circumstances actually were', rather than presuming situations or agents to be radically different from what they were (1991: 168). Ultimately, Hawthorn – like Dunn – was sceptical of the generalising claims of the social sciences:

> Practical reasoning is done by particular agents in the light of their particular experiences and the particular circumstances in which they find themselves.... Possible reasonings for them are reasonings for them as them, there and then, reasonings that they can or could have made as those agents *from* where they are.
>
> (1991: 34–5)

To generalise and abstract from this may be habitual in the social sciences, but it is also indeterminate, and, at the extreme, empty (1991: 35). Hawthorn sympathised with Quine's arguments about the underdetermination of theory and indeterminacy of meaning, and doubted that there could ever be cumulative and convergent certainty – the supposed mark of knowledge – in the human sciences.

Being Realistic

Dunn's approach to political theory also emerges from his characterisation of practical reason and social life and was in marked opposition to the styles of political philosophy pursued in the USA. As he repeatedly stated, drawing on MacIntyre (1983) and Taylor (1983), the point of political theory was to understand 'what is really going on in society' (Dunn, 1984: 1; 1985: 1). Unfortunately the historical division of labour within the field of politics had been 'disastrous', split, as it was, between a purely historicist history of political ideas, a political philosophy 'committed to political inconsequence by the self-conscious purity of its methods' and a political science 'ludicrously aping the sciences of nature and uninformed by any coherent conception of political value' (Dunn 1985: 2). Dunn was keen to overcome these divisions and, in doing so, to rethink the way each proceeded. Hence, political theory needed to focus on three tasks. First, it needed to understand what 'political structures, political institutions, and political relations are actually like at present' and consider 'what they prevent and what they bring about'. Second, it needed to have some sense of how we might coherently want society to be, and, third, it ought to tell us what practically can be done to actualise and maintain such a society (Dunn, 1984: 1). Accordingly a core aspect of his political theory is understanding the here and now – and especially the sober assessment of the nature of global economic exchange and the character and power of modern states and the practical limits they impose on possibility (Dunn, 1985: 11). Any conception of politics had to consider 'realistically' how humans 'do in fact see and feel about each other in the settings in which they live and which they understand (and always will understand) so poorly' (1985: 11). It was difficult enough to know ourselves, and understanding others was an even harder task, so knowing how to act, when the consequences of our actions – intended, and all too often unintended – stretched far beyond our intentionality was daunting.

At heart, then, Dunn's is a theory of prudence or judgement – 'not a purely ideal value; it necessarily embodies a conception of how the world could, in historical reality and through real human agency, be changed to meet its requirements' (Dunn, 1985: 11; see Bourke and Geuss, 2009). The aim here is not to assess the validity of such a theory, but rather to draw attention to the way that it emerges out of the characterisation of the practical reason of agents, and the social situations in which they necessarily find themselves. It should now also be clear how this characterisation provides an inspiration for recent advocates of 'realism' in politics. This approach defines itself against various forms of moralism in politics – the 'ethics first' approach most conspicuously associated with Rawls. But advocates such as Dunn, Hawthorn, Williams, and Geuss are *not* simply restating the realism familiar to students of international relations, who dismiss values, principles and ideals as 'mere window dressing' and who believe that 'power and material self-interest are all that matter' (Geuss, 2010: 39). Geuss begins where Weber begins – that anyone who wanted 'tidy solutions' in politics had made a 'bad mistake in being born as a human being' (Geuss, 2010: 40). The real questions to ask were who has the power and motive to act, and what will the consequences be of adopting this, rather than another, course of action. In arguing that political philosophy be realist, Geuss stresses four features. First, it should not begin with what people ought to value and desire but rather with the 'the way the social, economic, political, etc., institutions actually operate in some society at some given time, and what really does move human beings to act in given circumstances' (Geuss, 2008: 9). This does not mean humans lack ideals and aspirations, but that those are only relevant insofar as they affect people's actual behaviour. Second, it must be recognised that politics is about action, motives and contexts and not merely about the truth or falsity of beliefs and propositions (2008: 11–13). Third, politics was always historically located – 'humans interacting in institutional contexts that change over time', meaning that excessive generalisation was unhelpful. Fourth, and as a consequence, Geuss sees politics as more like the exercise of a craft than the application of a theory. It required skill and judgment that did not readily lend itself to being codified. Taken together, this was what 'realism' meant.

By way of conclusion, we can return to the beginning. The father of political history – Thucydides – provides a useful way of commenting on my opening question about the relationship between political ideas and real politics. Although commonly seen as the originator of 'scientific' realism, this is misleading. While he did disdain explanations which placed excess weight on mythology and theology, he nevertheless thought that 'beliefs, attitudes, emotions, valuations, even superstitions' had to be taken 'very seriously indeed' if one wanted to know 'what really moves people to act, and what then happens to them and to others as a consequence of how they act' (Geuss, 2005: 226). In this sense 'ideas' – in the broadest understanding – do matter, but not necessarily in any high-minded way. Hawthorn's recent study of *Thucydides on Politics* (2014) brings this out well. The *History of the Peloponnesian War* managed to covey a strong sense that the people involved did not have a complete sense of what they were doing. Thucydides could do this because, like his contemporaries, he did not separate out motives, intentions, and actions, and was not tempted, like modern philosophers, to privilege the explanatory importance of 'reasoned intention over unreflected motive' (Hawthorn, 2014: 17). Politics was agonistic – intentions were not always reasoned, and even when they were, the premises often were not; rhetoric matters but was rarely simply truthful or reasonable; events have causes, but they are invariably complex, and their effects blend with other effects; people are not bound to act in any one way (2014: 236). These insights remained relevant, Hawthorn suggested, for two reasons. First, irrespective of modern aspirations to global rationality and legality, it remains a world of political actors 'trying more or less imaginatively to achieve what they want to do through the exercise of one or another kind of power'. Whatever their virtues they were limited in mind and body, subject to the foibles of character, the force of habit, and the 'unforeseen and the unforeseeable' (2014: 238). If politics is only ever understood as made up of structural forces, or as driven by rational choices, or as expressions of a political culture, we will miss what any politician knows intuitively. Second, Thucydides challenges us with a 'moment of unillusion'. Ever since Plato, philosophers have turned aside from the messiness of real politics, and have instead conjured up visions of some kind of future in which humans might be fully at home. Thucydides instead encourages the thought that now, as then, we 'are naked in our political condition', and that the most appropriate response is to be 'as realistic as one can be about politics as politics' (2014: 239). Whether this is a congenial conclusion for political *theory*, it surely provides compelling reasons for the serious study of political *history* – not because simple 'lessons' or generalisable 'laws' can be unearthed, but because a greater appreciation of human action in diverse settings may enhance our understanding both of possibility and also of necessity.

Conclusion

Many of the foregoing arguments find ample resonance in the work of Bevir and Rhodes, but it may be useful to highlight four themes. First is the stress on the centrality of history. Dunn repeatedly argues the need for historical understanding, both in terms of the ancestry of the concepts that social scientists and political philosophers use, and also in terms of the actual social, economic, and political development of modern states. He believes that political history, political science, and political theory should be brought into a more fruitful dialogue with each other. Bevir also insists on the centrality of historicism, and argues that even those recent political scientists who have argued that 'history matters' still tend to cleave to modernist commitments to 'determinism, reification and foundationalism' (Bevir, 2010: 268; see also Adcock *et al.*, 2007: 12–17, 284–9). In addition, he and Rhodes stress the importance of the history of disciplines as a means of understanding and evaluating rival approaches. This point can be extended to points of contact across disciplines – indeed, fuller accounts of the historical development of the social and human sciences generally may enable stronger bridges between them to be built.

The second theme is the importance of agency and contingency. Dunn, Bevir, and Rhodes all share a broadly individualistic stress on the integrity of the meanings offered by agents, and a dislike of holistic concepts that seem to bear no relation to those meanings. Bevir's account of situated agency stresses that 'social inheritances' can never fix the beliefs people might come to have nor 'the actions they might *try* to perform' (Bevir, 2010: 267, my emphasis). Dunn would agree – in this respect history is open and things *could* be different from how they are, but he would surely argue that *trying* to do something tells us little about *succeeding* in doing something. The irony that much of Dunn's work considers is that the personal experience of agency is not matched by its social reality.

This opens up the third point: the approach to explanation taken by Dunn, and developed by Hawthorn. In rejecting the strong sense of structural determinism they do not mean to deny that agents face seemingly insuperable obstacles to their intentions. Rather than characterise these as enduring 'structures', it is better to ask counter-factual questions: other things being equal, did the agents have a genuine range of actions they could implement or were they, to all practical purposes, constrained to do what they in fact did? Bevir and Rhodes do not generally talk in these terms, but they might argue that, in order to explain any occurrence, we need to know about the beliefs of particular agents and the deeper traditions to which they belong. This is certainly part of the answer, but in many cases we will also need to know about the beliefs and actions of numerous other agents that may be relevant to the explanation.[11] This may be difficult enough when explaining, say, the decisions of a mundane academic committee, but when explaining a complex occurrence, such as the slide to war in 1914, we need to know about the febrile and fluid responses and counter-responses that characterise diverse agents in a state of high tension, and the extent to which their real options narrowed over time – as demonstrated in Christopher Clark's recent account, *The Sleepwalkers* (Clark, 2012: 361–4).

This leads us to the fourth point, this time normative: the need for political judgment to be realistic. On the one hand, if the beliefs of agents are relatively open, then it becomes much harder for any of us to know – even supposed 'experts' – what someone else is going to say or do. But, on the other hand, the need to act requires some kind of practical knowledge of what is likely to happen, and that may require a measure of realism about what the world is really like – *at least right now* – and therefore prudence in acting in it. Bevir, who places hope in a pluralist and participatory democracy which enables citizens to 'develop voice, enter dialogues, and rule themselves', may find this an unduly pessimistic conclusion (Bevir, 2010: 273). Dunn, however, might reply with the passage from Hobbes's *De Cive* which characterised the opportunity to show 'wisdom, knowledge, and eloquence, in deliberating matters of the greatest difficulty' as the dubious pleasure of seeing 'our wisdom undervalued before our own faces … to hate, and to be hated, by reason of the disagreement of opinions, to lay open our secret Counsells, and advises to all, to no purpose, and without any benefit' (Dunn, 1990: 169).

Notes

1 Although Skinner owed his introduction to Austin's speech-act theory to Dunn, and was to make substantial use of it in his various methodological writings, Dunn himself made no further explicit reference to Austin after this essay.

2 He adds, however, that since we know nothing of Plato's emotional and cognitive states, were we precluded from understanding their meaning? 'Must it not in any case be possible to elicit the correct identification of the meaning from the text itself?' (Dunn, 1980: 23). See Bevir's (1999: 134–9) opposition to the idea that identifying what someone 'was doing' was part of the meaning of an utterance.

3 See also his essay on Charles Taylor, where he suggests Taylor was incautious in advocating a science of interpretation, and that although he, Dunn, would incline on most occasions to the hermeneutic when offered a choice, this was for heuristic reasons, and he would expect to meet objections as they came rather than designing 'some comprehensive piece of pseudo-epistemological apparatus' which could rule out those objections in advance. 'Humanly speaking, the interpretative commitment is a good deal more enticing as a declaration of intention than it is as a claim to achievement' (Dunn, 1990: 183–4).

4 The claim to know more than someone does about their own actions would consist of knowing it 'more deftly, honestly, realistically, dogmatically etc.' (Dunn, 1980: 106). Talking to agents to encourage them to recognise the limits of the accounts they offered about their motivation is akin, Dunn suggests, to psychoanalysis. Compare the account suggested here with Bevir (1999: chapters 4 and 7) which explains how we accommodate distortions such as deception, the unconscious, and irrationality in accounts of beliefs.

5 See also Dunn (1990: 167–70) for a discussion of Roberto Unger's understanding of institutional plasticity.

6 Compare Bevir and Rhodes (2010).

7 See Bevir (1999: 316).

8 See Bevir (1999: 82–5) for criticisms of Skinner's logic of discovery.

9 Skocpol (1979: xvi). Dunn was fulsome in his praise for Skocpol's earlier essays (for example, Dunn, 1980: 320, 338) and contrasted his own 'somewhat crudely nominalist' work on revolutions with her 'very proper structural corrective' (Dunn, 1979: 86).

10 Compare MacIntyre (1973); Craig (2010).

11 And in the case of economic explanations, would the interpretive approach require us to map the beliefs and actions of an astronomically large number of agents?

References

Adcock, R., Bevir, M., and Stimpson, S. C. (eds) (2007) *Modern Political Science: Anglo-American exchanges since 1880*, Princeton, NJ: Princeton University Press.

Bevir, M. (1999) *The Logic of the History of Ideas*, Cambridge: Cambridge University Press.

Bevir, M. (2005) *New Labour: A Critique*, London: Routledge.

Bevir, M. (2010) *Democratic Governance*, Princeton, NJ: Princeton University Press.

Bevir, M. (2011) *The Making of British Socialism*, Princeton, NJ: Princeton University Press.

Bevir, M. and Rhodes, R. A. W. (1999) 'Studying British Government: Reconstructing the research agenda', *British Journal of Politics and International Relations*, 1(2): 215–39.

Bevir, M. and Rhodes, R. A. W. (2003) *Interpreting British Governance*, London: Routledge.

Bevir, M. and Rhodes, R. A. W. (2010) *The State as Cultural Practice*, Oxford: Oxford University Press.

Bourke, R. and Geuss, R., (eds) (2009) *Political Judgment: Essays for John Dunn*, Cambridge: Cambridge University Press.

Clark, C. (2012) *The Sleepwalkers: How Europe went to war in 1914*, London: Allen Lane.

Craig, D. M. (2010) '"High Politics" and the "New Political History"', *Historical Journal* 53(2): 453–74.

Dunn, J. (1969) *The Political Thought of John Locke: An historical account of the argument of the 'Two Treatises of Government'*, Cambridge: Cambridge University Press.

Dunn, J. (1972) *Modern Revolutions: An introduction to the analysis of a political phenomenon*, Cambridge: Cambridge University Press.

Dunn, J. (ed.) (1978) *West African States: Failure and promise, a study in comparative politics*, Cambridge: Cambridge University Press.

Dunn, J. (1979) *Western Political Theory in the Face of the Future*, Cambridge: Cambridge University Press.

Dunn, J. (1980) *Political Obligation in its Historical Context*, Cambridge: Cambridge University Press.

Dunn, J. (1984) *The Politics of Socialism: An essay in political theory*, Cambridge: Cambridge University Press.

Dunn, J. (1985) *Rethinking Modern Political Theory: Essays 1979–83*, Cambridge: Cambridge University Press.

Dunn, J. (1990) *Interpreting Political Responsibility: Essays 1981–1989*, Princeton, NJ: Princeton University Press.

Dunn, J. (1996) T*he History of Political Theory and Other Essays*, Cambridge: Cambridge University Press.

Dunn, J. and Robertson, A. F. (1973) *Dependence and Opportunity: Political change in Ahafo*, Cambridge: Cambridge University Press.

Geuss, R. (2005) *Outside Ethics*, Princeton, NJ: Princeton University Press.

Geuss, R. (2008) *Philosophy and Real Politics*, Princeton, NJ: Princeton University Press.

Geuss, R. (2010) *Politics and the Imagination*, Princeton, NJ: Princeton University Press.

Hawthorn, G. (1991) *Plausible Worlds: Possibility and understanding in history and the social sciences*, Cambridge: Cambridge University Press.

Hawthorn, G. (2014) *Thucydides on Politics: Back to the present*, Cambridge: Cambridge University Press.

Lane, M. (2002) 'Why History of Ideas at All?', *History of European Ideas*, 28(1–2): 33–41.

MacIntyre, A. (1971) *Against the Self-Images of the Age: Essays on ideology and philosophy*, London: Duckworth.

MacIntyre, A. (1973) 'Ideology, Social Science and Revolution', *Comparative Politics*, 5(3): 321–42.

MacIntyre, A. (1983) 'The Indispensability of Political Theory', in D. Miller and L. Siedentop, (eds), *The Nature of Political Theory*, Oxford: Oxford University Press, pp. 17–34.

Rhodes, R. A. W. (2011) *Everyday Life in British Government*, Oxford: Oxford University Press.

Skocpol, T. (1979) *States and Social Revolutions: A comparative analysis of France, Russia, and China*, Cambridge: Cambridge University Press.

Taylor, C. (1983) 'Political Theory and Practice', in C. Lloyd (ed.), *Social Theory and Political Practice*, Oxford: Oxford University Press, pp. 61–86.

Taylor, C. (2004) *Modern Social Imaginaries*, Durham, NC: Duke University Press.

Turner, S. (2003) 'MacIntyre in the Province of the Philosophy of Social Science', in M. C. Murphy (ed.), *Alasdair MacIntyre*, Cambridge: Cambridge University Press, pp. 70–93.

6   The Meanings of Progressive Politics

Interpretivism and its Limits

Emily Robinson

I should start by declaring an interest. My career began in 2003, the year *Interpreting British Governance* was published. I was a researcher for a local government think tank, immersed in the language of governance and policy networks, of breaking down silos and bringing about joined-up governance (an idea so pervasive we took to calling it JUG). Seven years later, at the very end of the New Labour period, while finishing my PhD, I came across Mark Bevir and Rod Rhodes's (2003) book and found it both fascinating and cathartic to see this project historicised and decentred by them.

I was also interested to find that my academic work shared many aspects of their interpretivist approach. At the time I was examining the ways in which party political actors understand themselves to be part of particular traditions, how this both legitimates and constrains their politics, and how they narrate shifts within those traditions – whether as reform, transformation, or betrayal (Robinson, 2012). To use interpretivist language, I was trying to understand the webs of belief within which party political identities are formed, and to examine how individuals respond to the dilemmas that challenge those beliefs. My current research approaches similar questions from a less direct angle. In particular I am looking at how actors from across the political spectrum have defined themselves both as and as not 'progressive', and asking what they have meant by doing so. In interpretive terms, this work could be seen as an attempt to decentre or denaturalise the idea that British politics revolves around a progressive/conservative axis. In this chapter I will be reflecting on both of these projects in order to explore my (still evolving) relationship to interpretivism.

Progressives and Conservatives

The progressive/conservative divide has long been a staple of political positioning and seems to offer a self-evident way of understanding party alignment in Britain. As Nick Clegg (2009: 13) explained before the 2010 General Election, 'the most basic of all dividing lines is that between progressive and conservative thinkers; it's a dividing line built on two different responses to the human condition'. Gordon Brown (2010: 5) echoed these comments, but put them in a rather more binary perspective: 'Left and Right, Labour and Tory, progressive and conservative – these labels represent real and important differences in the

way we understand the world and the society in which we live'. Clegg's definition of progressive politics was based on a temporal orientation (optimism about
the future), Brown's on an ideological one (a commitment to equality and social
justice). But, as the experience of the twentieth century has repeatedly made
clear, there is no necessary connection between the two.

The idea that British politics is organised around progressive and conservative
positions makes rather more sense when it is understood as a hangover from the
nineteenth-century division between liberalism and conservatism. 'Progressive'
in this context expressed the combination of social reform and economic
freedom that characterised liberalism. It was rooted in Enlightenment theories of
history, which tied commercial freedom to political liberty, and saw both as the
drivers of human progress. As the conceptual historian Reinhart Koselleck has
noted, over the course of the nineteenth century, the idea of progress developed
from being an adjunct to other concepts – such as knowledge or art – to being
itself an historical agent. At first this manifested itself in expressions like 'the
progress of time' or 'the progress of history', but by the late nineteenth century
had become simply 'progress itself'. At this point, it became ubiquitous; merely
'a political catchword' used right across the political spectrum. As he added,
'since the nineteenth century, it has become difficult to gain political legitimacy
without being progressive at the same time' (Koselleck, 2002: 230).

This was the very point at which a Lib–Lab 'progressive movement' emerged
in Britain. Its members insisted that, if the Liberal Party wished 'to be regarded
as the progressive party of the future', it would have to embrace an 'enlarged
and enlightened conception of the functions of the State' (*Progressive Review*,
1896: 4). However, this was also the point when mainstream Conservatives
embraced the idea of 'progress itself' – partly due to the influence of Liberal
Unionists who joined with the party from the 1880s. This was not, then, a question of eternally different conservative and progressive mindsets, but of two different visions of progress: one based on economic freedom stimulating
individual achievement, the other on collective action enabling social reform.
The term 'progressive' has since become primarily associated with the latter
cause. This is why 'progressive conservatives' are seen to be on the paternalist
left of their party, rather than the economic right; although in the mid-nineteenth
century, when the term first appeared, it was used to describe Conservative
advocates of free trade.

However, as my research is finding, the idea that 'progressive' means 'left
wing' only became dominant in the late twentieth century. In the 1930s, the label
was used right across the political spectrum. But while we remember the Communist Party's attempt to form a Popular Front of 'progressive forces' against
fascism, and the progressive politics of the centrist Next Five Years Group, the
attempts of Conservatives to establish anti-socialist coalitions under the banner
of 'progressive' politics have faded from historical memory. This latter strategy
resulted in a series of business-oriented Progressive Parties being elected in
municipalities not only in Scotland, where the term retains this meaning, but also
in England (Robinson, 2015). After the war Churchill suggested 'Progressive
Unionists' as a possible label within a merged National Liberal–Conservative

party (Churchill, 1946). And as late as 1983 we find Robin Butler, Thatcher's Principal Private Secretary, suggesting that 'progressive' had the 'right vibes' to describe monetarism, although this was dismissed on the grounds that '*These days* it is almost exclusively associated with the Left' (Cockfield, 1983, my emphasis).

Alliances and Coalitions

The means by which 'progressive' came to be 'almost exclusively associated with the Left' had a lot to do with the prominence of the Edwardian Lib–Lab electoral alliance in academic debates in the 1970s. Peter Clarke's *Lancashire and the New Liberalism* set out to recover the word 'progressive', which he felt had been 'neglected' by historians and been 'forgotten' in the period after the First World War (1971: 397). The term was 'important' to Clarke (1971: 398) 'because it relates to changes in the nature of politics'. For him, this was about the ability of the Liberal Party to respond to the demands of the new working class electorate in the late nineteenth and early twentieth century. He wanted to demonstrate that this process was well under way before the First World War and that the subsequent decline in the Liberal Party's electoral fortunes was not the inevitable result of intellectual paralysis. The key to this was the development of new liberalism in the 1890s, and its 'progressive alliance' with social democracy. Clarke's work was the first of a wave of studies of progressive politics, published between the Liberal revival of the 1960s and the formation of New Labour in 1994 (Clarke, 1978; Freeden, 1978, 1989; Collini, 1979; Blaazer, 1992). It was also the subject of a long-running controversy, particularly with Ross McKibbin, who insisted that Labour was already squeezing out the Liberal Party before the First World War (see Thompson, 1990).

Although the Liberal idea of bringing about a 'realignment of the Left' predates these debates (Jones, 2011: 28–51), its development was more gradual than we might think. As Peter Sloman has explained, 'If the first half of the twentieth century was marked by progressive divergence, the period since the 1950s might be characterized as a slow convergence around social democratic and social liberal ideas' (2014: 47). Since the late 1950s Jo Grimond (1958[?]: 8, 16), leader of the Liberal Party, had been expressing his desire to bring about a '*realignment of parties*' (original emphasis), based around a new 'non-socialist progressive party'. However, this was not to be a party in the Lib–Lab tradition of the Edwardian 'progressive alliance'. Though Grimond wrote of it as a 'new party of the Left' (1958?: 16), he also conceived it as opposing the Butskellite faith in state intervention – exactly the belief around which the Edwardian progressive movement was founded. Indeed, he only abandoned his belief that 'the Conservative Party might really turn into a progressive party' because of their continued reliance on the state and their inability to confront 'the innate conservatism of industry and the Civil Service' (1958?: 9, 20). Grimond explicitly distanced himself from the new liberalism of the early twentieth century, which 'demanded a great deal of action by the State' and put forward a rather different view of 'progressive' liberalism as 'thrusting, progressive, enterprising in outlook' (Grimond, 1959: 22, 182).

Even as late as 1977, when the Liberals had turned more clearly to the left, the Lib–Lab Pact was presented in pragmatic terms, which emphasised the Liberals' equidistance between the two main parties, and the need for a strong centre party: 'Liberals are capable of taming Tory excess as they are of controlling Labour lunacy' (Liberal Party, 1977: 4). It was only in the 1980s that the narrative of re-founding the Lib–Lab 'progressive alliance' and reuniting 'the great streams of social liberalism, divided temporarily in the first half of this century' (Steel, 1987) permeated political culture, shaping the positioning of first the Social Democratic Party (SDP) – Liberal Alliance and later New Labour. One of the key influences seems to have been David Marquand, a Labour MP until 1977, a founder member of the SDP, and the author of two influential texts on the history and contemporary standing of progressive politics (1979, 1991). At this time, the idea of a latent social democratic alliance provided a way of critiquing current Labour politics, while maintaining fidelity to its traditions.

This idea has recently resurfaced with a rather different spin. In 2009 Nick Clegg published a pamphlet for the think tank Demos, in which he set out an argument which drew explicitly on academic debates surrounding the viability of the Lib–Lab progressive alliance and the inevitability (or otherwise) of Labour's rise to power. He referenced the work not only of Peter Clarke, Ross McKibbin, and Duncan Tanner, but also of Alan Sykes, Pat Thane, Bruce Murray, and Matthew Worley. His central argument – 'a claim rooted in history, in values and in policy too' (Clegg, 2009: 80) – was that just as the Liberals had lost their claim to be the progressive party in early-twentieth-century Britain, so Labour had forfeited its right to that mantle today. It was now time for 'a reverse "switch" ', which would lead to 'a new progressive alignment', based on localism, decentralisation and the defence of civil liberties (Clegg, 2009: 11). Although Clegg (2009: 9) made clear that the 'ideologically barren Conservative Party' was no part of his political vision, in the immediate run-up to the General Election he returned to a policy of practical equidistance, promising to speak first to the largest party in the event of a hung parliament. When that happened, it was the turn of others to 'remind' him 'that British Liberals and Social Democrats share the same heritage and aspirations. Our histories are entwined' (Grayson and Lawson, 2010).

The formation of the Conservative–Liberal Democrat coalition was therefore framed with the narrative of the Lib–Lab progressive alliance very much in mind. Despite the shared histories and occasional alliances of the two coalition partners, their new partnership was depicted as a departure from historical precedent. It was described as 'progressive' on these grounds (Cameron, 2010; Clegg, 2010), rather than because it was rooted in a pre-existing tradition of 'progressive' Liberal–Conservative politics. Even when Conservatives had described themselves as 'progressive conservatives' before the election, this was presented as a move away from their own traditions (Cameron, 2009; Osborne, 2009). As Greg Clark and Jeremy Hunt had argued in 2007, 'it might seem paradoxical to claim the label "progressive" for a party of the political right', but it was no longer enough for this term 'simply to be used as an alternative word for left-wing': it was 'time for a reassessment' (2007: 3–4). This was widely seen as a calculated attempt to 'decontaminate' the Conservative brand and to distance the party from Thatcherism through 'a series of counter-intuitive initiatives and [...] unapologetic raids on Labour and Lib Dem territory' (Bale, 2011: 381).

In 2010 all three parties used the term 'progressive' to indicate a position towards the centre or centre-left of the political spectrum. That this seemed a self-evident association can be seen in their rhetoric in the run-up to the election. However, it is not at all clear that voters understood it in the same way. A YouGov survey in 2012 found that citizens tended to consider all Conservative politicians as more progressive than their Labour or Liberal Democrat counter-parts – with Margaret Thatcher coming second only to Boris Johnson (Robinson and Twyman, 2014). Perhaps Robin Butler did interpret the 'vibes' of the term correctly after all. The 'exclusive' identification of progressive politics as left wing does not seem to have travelled very far outside Westminster.

There is clearly a distinction to be drawn here between the existence of a tradition of Lib–Lab politics and the use of the term 'progressive' to describe it. Yet, although my project is concerned primarily with the latter, it also raises questions about the way in which traditions such as this function within contemporary politics. It suggests that, rather than being 'a body of belief widely shared in British society' (Beer, 1965: xiv), they are part of a specialised cultural discourse, understood by political practitioners and analysts but less resonant in the country beyond.

History and Memory

My interest in historicising ideas about the Lib–Lab progressive alliance echoes Bevir's attempts to do the same for both the statist forms of mid-century socialism and New Labour's rejection of them. For him, this is clearly a project with contemporary political purpose. Bevir (2011: ix) described his original aim in writing *The Making of British Socialism* as being 'to recapture the diversity of socialism and thereby find inspiration for a radical democratic and transformative politics'. This was intended to give British socialists 'a new narrative with which to respond to neoliberalism' (2011: ix). Similarly, in *New Labour: A Critique*, he emphasised that 'other traditions of social democracy provide resources with which to develop alternative visions' (2005: 136).

Given these statements, which draw upon the established practice, in both academia and activism, of using the past as a 'radical resource' to critique and unsettle the present, it is surprising to find that Bevir and Rhodes's concept of tradition is rather more limited, rather more functional than this. They seem to see tradition as nothing more than 'the inevitable background to human beliefs and actions' (Bevir and Rhodes, 2004: 160), and as capable of being transmitted only through direct contact between individuals (Bevir, 2010: 231). This seems to me to limit its potential to do the kind of critical and creative work that Bevir himself would like.

Bevir (2010: 232, 235) has written that 'If, for example, historians discovered that Chinese Buddhists and American Indians had held beliefs that resembled those of modern anarchists, they could not talk legitimately of a tradition of anarchism incorporating all these beliefs' and that 'Even if people want to identify themselves with a tradition, they cannot do so by saying that their beliefs and actions share key features with, or address questions raised by, those they see as their predecessors'. But, legitimate or not, both of these things can and do happen. We need only think of the attempts by British communist historians to construct a lineage of English radicalism leading from the Peasants' Revolt, through the Levellers and Chartists to their own Popular Front against fascism. Or of Margaret Thatcher's 'Victorian values', supposedly based on a tradition inherited directly from her father and grandmother and buttressed by an association with the work of certain academic historians (see, for example, Thomas, 1979). Moreover, as I have already suggested, a great deal of contemporary political positioning is based upon exactly such appropriations, themselves also at least partially derived from the findings of academic history. While Bevir recognises such attempts to invent traditions and to claim spurious connections to others, he seems to see this as a misfiring of the 'legitimate' transmission of tradition 'from teacher to pupil to pupil's pupil' (2010: 232), rather than as an integral part of the way tradition functions within our everyday practices and beliefs.

There are two different things going on here. On the one hand are the traditions we subconsciously inherit, and which orient our way of seeing the world, in much the way Bevir and Rhodes describe. On the other, are those we consciously seek out and lay claim to. These are not necessarily mutually exclusive, nor does the latter have to be a calculated act (although we will see below how it can be). One way of thinking through these different forms of tradition might be to see them as analogous to what the French historian Pierre Nora has called communities of memory (*milieux de mémoire*) and sites of memory (*lieux de mémoire*). For him, the latter exist only because the former do not: living memory has been replaced by 'historicized memory'; that is, memory which has ceased to function naturally and has instead become a form of 'prosthetic memory' (Nora, 1996: 10). Nora identified three key characteristics of historicised memory. First, the modern 'obsession with the archive ... in which we attempt to preserve not only all the past but all the present as well' (Nora, 1996: 8). Second, the 'individual duty' to remember, which is associated with the 'psychologization of memory' and which leads us to research the pasts of various groups to which we belong, from professions to ethnicities (Nora, 1996: 10–11). And third, 'alienated memory', mediated through historical knowledge, which distances us from the living past (Nora, 1996: 11–12). I would suggest that all three of these features are apparent in political parties.

Political actors have been particularly assiduous users and creators of historical narratives. A startlingly large number of politicians have, for instance, engaged in historical research, most often biographies of their political forbears. Likewise, party members are 'assiduous producers and consumers of popular histories of the party' (Lawrence, 2000). Even scholarly works are read by party members and subsumed into their understanding of their collective past. Each of the parties has its own semi-official history group, combining witness accounts with academic analysis in meetings that are often standing room only. And although the party archives are not as well used we might expect, individuals are often keen to archive their own papers, to add to the historical record. This is partly a self-interested act. Political actors are, after all, not only aware of their role in history as *what has happened*, they are also intensely aware that they will be part of history as *what is written about what has happened*. Moreover, many also attempt to write the 'first "cut" of history' by publishing 'retrospective justifications of their opinions, decisions and policies, in the form of diaries, memoirs and autobiographies' during the time in which official documents remain closed to scholars (Daddow, 2007: 583). Yet the appetite for history, for reminiscence and for 'historic' memorabilia within political parties requires further explanation.

Nora writes about the desire to connect with the past as a form of personal fulfilment. Likewise, Eric Hobsbawm (1972: 13) has noted the paradoxical 'search for ancestors (Spartacus, More, Winstanley) by modern revolutionaries whose theory, if they are Marxists, assumes their irrelevance.' He adds, 'Clearly the sense of belonging to an age-old tradition of rebellion provides emotional satisfaction, but how and why?' (1972: 14). In order to answer this question, we must grapple with the appeal of the past, its emotional weight.

Tradition and Emotion

We need to understand the power of tradition, not only as 'the ideational background against which individuals come to adopt an initial web of beliefs' (Bevir, 2010: xxxvi), but also as an affective source of identity. That is why activists and academics, Bevir included, repeatedly reach for tradition in their attempts to reformulate the present. It carries its own authority, its own persuasive power. It is itself a way of understanding the world and of orienting one's own position in relation to it – whether as an upholder, reclaimer, challenger, or destroyer.

This is not an attempt to 'recentre' tradition – to return it to an 'aggregate concept' (Bevir and Rhodes, 2003: 2). Indeed, the ways in which we assign authority to tradition are inescapably specific – politically, culturally, and historically. Tradition clearly functions in very different ways within different political communitites. At the crudest level, we might think of it as a bearer of continuity to conservatives and of radical obligation to socialists. While the conservative nostalgic might view the nation in decline and wish to restore elements of the past, radical nostalgics want to right past wrongs. History here has a double obligation: to recover and remember past struggles and martyrs, and to carry forward the outrage necessary to reshape the present and future. However, both of these characterisations leave out the attraction of pastness itself, the exoticism of temporal distance. The conservative sense of history as an almost spiritual presence depends upon the past *as past*, not as a recoverable reality. Likewise, the 'socialist tradition' is about more than a set of ideas including public ownership, redistribution, and collective action. It is about being part of something bigger than this, which connects past, present, and future.

However, this is by no means straightforward and needs to be unpicked with care. For instance, I interviewed a number of members of Battersea Labour Party in 2008, when they were celebrating their centenary. All the members I spoke to were of a similar generation, with similar political backgrounds and beliefs. In Bevir and Rhodes's terms they were certainly part of the same political tradition. However, their views *on* tradition were very different indeed and were subject to ongoing contestation. For some, the idea of being part of an historic struggle was their principal political inspiration; it was how they oriented all of their political views and beliefs. For others, the centenary was a bit of fun, which they thought would be useful in widening their appeal in the local community. For others still, it was a distraction and even a sign of complacency – allowing members to wallow in stories of a proud socialist past at the expense of concentrating on a much more difficult political present, in which the local party was losing its grip on a very small majority (Robinson, 2012).

While there may be political and personal variations to the way we approach tradition, it is also clear that our understanding of its value is historically and culturally specific. Martin L. Davies (2006, 2010) has produced a series of powerful critiques of the way the historical mindset dominates contemporary Western society, a situation he attributes to mid-nineteenth century ideas about history. Similarly, Rhodri Hayward has highlighted the conjunction of new forms of religious narrative, the growth of the historical discipline, and psycho-analysis in nineteenth-century Europe: all three insisted on chronology, on coherent narratives of the past, and on the importance of historical explanation. As he explains, 'the past is now widely seen as the bedrock of our sense of self', while other ways of understanding the relationship between self and society have been pathologised (2007: 1). This does not invalidate Bevir's and Rhodes's argument that tradition is the 'unavoidable' root of all our beliefs and practices (Bevir, 2010: 233), but it does suggest that our ideas about tradition itself and the authority it holds are themselves part of the web of beliefs we inherit and should be considered as such.

The issue of an orientation towards tradition in and of itself is raised in the long interviews quoted in *Interpreting British Governance*, although it is not pulled out. Richard Mottram talks about being socialised into the sense of being part of 'a tradition that went back sort of 300 years', of 'being aware of that tradition' (Bevir and Rhodes, 2003: 181). This tradition may have conveyed the particular values which Bevir and Rhodes analyse – the 'traditional beliefs about the generalist and efficiency' (2003: 190) – but it also seems to have been more than that. It was about 'still working in a building where that tradition was everywhere', of having 'the sort of classic rite of passage for the elite' and the sensibility that comes with that (2003: 180, 182). This awareness of tradition weighs upon the ways in which individuals respond to dilemmas, their propensity to change and the ways in which they justify that. We can read in Sir Robin Mountfield's responses hints about the differences in attitudes to change among individuals, different levels of regret, of nostalgia, of belief in progress: 'It is wrong to look back, as some do, to a golden age in the 60s, but anyway that world has passed [...] we are not in that world any more whether we like it or not' (2003: 185). Even the institution itself was described as holding a temporal orientation: 'Reform is fine but you've got to do it with the grain. There's a great machine here. You can't just change it overnight. You've got to edge it into a new role' (2003: 188).

The narratives presented in this section of *Interpreting British Governance* are not simply accounts of pragmatic responses to a dilemma. Both men were able to adjust to the new ways of working because they made that part of their internal narrative of who they were. Reform was understood as a way of performing their role as elite civil servants, able to keep up with the times, *in the best tradition of those who had gone before*. As Mottram explained, mid-ranking colleagues were held back because 'they didn't see that the purpose was actually to change things'; in contrast, he was proud of having made changes 'which people say were responsive; they were strategic, we seized the chance of a change, we made something of it and we took ministers with us. We didn't sit around all day exchanging pieces of paper' (2003: 189). This orientation towards the future was part and parcel of the tradition into which he was socialised.

Power and Persuasion

In addition to understanding tradition as a barely noticed backdrop, we should also consider it as flamboyant costume, well-practised gesture, or carefully pitched speech. This is about the ability of political actors to use ideas as 'projectiles […], purposefully displacing the context around them' and 'reorienting them towards their situations' (Martin, 2013: 2).

Interpretivism has been criticised for neglecting the question of why particular narratives gain traction, why certain traditions 'stick', and how both come to seem natural and reducible to 'common sense'. It is not enough to note the dominance of the Lib–Lab story of progressive politics – or networked theories of governance – we also have to ask how this happened and what it means. One response to this question can be found in the work of critical realists, who emphasise the extent to which dominant understandings of British political traditions (in their case, the elite, hierarchical, centralising Westminster model) have a privileged status that enables them to constrain other alternatives (see, for example, Marsh, 2008). These authors have stressed that the study of ideas must be supplemented by a hard focus on material reality. However, it is not necessary to leave the realm of the purely ideational to bring power into the equation.

The work of Alan Finlayson and James Martin on political rhetoric is instructive here. Finlayson has suggested that interpretivists do not give enough consideration to this idea of

> politics [as] a creative art in which the political actor seeks to create, out of the materials history has bequeathed, new ways to think about political problems (crises and dilemmas) and to persuade others to see things in these new terms.
>
> (2004: 155)

That is not to say they neglect it entirely. In a reply to Finlayson, Bevir and Rhodes highlighted the centrality of contestation to their work and the ways in which they had delineated the contingency of the various narratives of govern-ance within the traditions they analyse (Bevir and Rhodes, 2004). Yet this point needs to be pressed further. *How* do these struggles and contestations over meaning take place within and between traditions? What are the strategies in play? How are these contests resolved? Are there winners and losers? And what do the outcomes tell us – not only about politics but about the relative status of particular cultural values?

The idea of recovering Lib–Lab progressivism was appealing to social demo-crats in the 1980s and 1990s, not only because it offered a response to the dilem-mas of voter dealignment and Labour's turn to the left, but also – and arguably more importantly – because it did this while also appearing to uphold tradition and retain a 'Labour' identity. The rhetorical power of this strategy lay in the way it enabled social democrats to reclaim rather than reject Labour's past. If we look, for instance, at the debates over the revision of Clause IV, although Tony Blair was keen to depict his opponents as being tied to the past, and hence as sentimental and irrational, he also rooted his own case in an appeal to what he presented as the 'true' tradition of the Labour Party. This narrative reached back before the 1918 commitment to public ownership and drew instead on an older, and therefore seemingly more authentic, tradition of ethical socialism, co-operativism, and social liberalism. As he put it soon afterwards: 'in the rewriting of Clause IV […] far from escaping our traditions, we recaptured them' (Blair, 1995: 4). Tradition here was a rhetorical tool. In the case of the SDP, it was more of an emotional crutch. Although much of their public appeal lay in break-ing with both the past forms of party politics in general and the Labour tradition in particular, the 'Gang of Four' repeatedly framed their decision to leave the party as an act of loyalty to a tradition which had been betrayed by the current Labour leaders. This is not simply a matter of encountering and adapting to a dilemma; it is at once more strategic and more affective than that. It draws on wider questions of authority, legitimacy, and identity.

The centrality of the language of tradition to both sides of the Clause IV debate also tells us something about its cultural value. Blair was challenging a particular political tradition, which carried strong assumptions about inheritance and obligation. Not betraying the past had long been a key part of Labour Party identity. It is no accident that Henry Drucker's famous study of the *Doctrine and Ethos of the Labour Party* (1979) used the chapter heading 'The Uses of the Past' for its discussion of the party's ethos. In the 1970s, when Drucker was writing, it seemed as though this attitude was in danger of being replaced by the social democratic emphasis on being 'up to date' and modern, which had informed Hugh Gaitskell's attempt to rewrite Clause IV of the Labour Party's constitution in 1959–60. However, while Gaitskell's argument was based on a straightforward appeal to forgo tradition and accept the reality of the present situation, 35 years later Blair framed his argument around the idea of recovering an older tradition.

I would suggest that the reason for this difference is due to shifts in wider cul-tural attitudes towards the past and the ideas of heritage and tradition. Since the late 1970s, the idea of 'heritage' as a marker of authenticity had become culturally dominant. This is the period when concerns about losing a connection with the past came to the fore, with the 'heritage panic' of the mid 1970s, leading into furious debates over the politics of a commercialised 'Heritage Industry' in the early 1980s and then the rather depoliticised 'history boom' of the 1990s and 2000s (Mandler, 2002). This is why it was necessary for Blair to describe his project in this way. This is not, of course, to say that Blair was upholding a *socialist* idea of tradition. Where the latter was predicated on a sense of debt, of justice and of being excluded from mainstream national history, Blair tended to use the past in a much more generic way – as a legitimation of the present. The same has been true of Conservatives in recent decades, replacing in their case a more spiritual sense of duty to the past.

However, as we have already noted, even this form of 'tradition-lite' was absent from the formation of the Conservative–Liberal Democrat coalition in 2010. In this cultural context, that seems odd. The coverage of the election and its aftermath was saturated with historical comparisons, but the formation of the coalition was constructed as an extraordinary departure from historical prece-dent. So rather than making arguments of the kind that Churchill – and indeed Thatcher (see Green, 2006: 33) – would have recognised about this marking the reconciliation of two compatible political traditions, the coalition partners pre-sented their union as an heroic and self-sacrificing attempt to set aside significant political differences for the good of the country. This seems to have been due to the fact that it was as one half of the Lib–Lab 'progressive' narrative by which the Liberal Democrats were primarily understood, by commentators as well as by their own supporters. Reviving stories about the mid-twentieth-century Lib-eral–Conservative alliances simply would not have been credible. Perhaps, even more importantly though, this was also the guise under which the Liberal Demo-crats were most useful to a Conservative Party desperate to soften its image.

Methods and Boundaries

Political ideas cannot remain only 'in politics'; they both shape and are shaped by other kinds of ideas. But, as these are not obviously the domain of 'political science', I wonder whether this label serves to limit interpretivism: to prevent it from exploring webs of belief in their entirety, rather than only those sections that relate to the political process.

Other methodologies allow for this kind of analysis more easily. Cultural history, for instance, with its emphasis on mentalities – on beliefs and webs of meaning – has long been a way of studying the sort of questions that Bevir and Rhodes raise. We might think for instance of Robert Darnton's (1984) study of what he called the Great Cat Massacre. Darnton's injunction to scholars to start digging at the point where meaning seems most opaque, where you don't 'get' the joke, was intended, like the ethnography of Clifford Geertz before it (1973), as a way of approaching the unfamiliar mentalities of other cultures – in this case, eighteenth-century France. However, it seems to me just as good a way of defamiliarising – or decentring – the governance narratives of twentieth-century Britain. By picking at the underlying assumptions and asking how and why they make sense to those who hold them – the traditions they have grown out of, the dilemmas they help to address – we start to gain an understanding of the ideas themselves.

These methods have been applied to contemporary British politics outside of the framework of 'interpretive political science'. We might think of the Birmingham Centre for Contemporary Cultural Studies, with its analyses of Thatcherism among much else, or the development of what has been called the New Political History, in the early 1990s. This aimed to rehabilitate political history in the wake of the cultural and linguistic turn, applying these new methods and concerns to questions of politics, power, and representation. Like interpretivists, these scholars have described themselves as anti-foundationalist. They are similarly influenced by post-structuralism but similarly wary of throwing out the idea of agency. The first practitioners of new political history focused on nineteenth-century politics and particularly popular radicalism, seeking to understand 'the meaning of politics to the ordinary man or woman on the proverbial street corner' (Vernon, 1993). This was a corrective to older approaches to political history, which had changed little from E. A. Freeman's (1866: 44) view 'that history is past politics and that politics are present history'. More recent work has extended this approach both forwards to contemporary history (see, for example, Black, 2010; Fielding 2014) and upwards to high politics (O'Hara, 2012). It has examined the beliefs and traditions which orient British political identities (for example, Black, 2002; Schofield, 2013) and the ways in which the state (Gunn and Vernon, 2011; Joyce, 2013), electoral politics (Lawrence, 2009; Beers 2010), and civil society (McCarthy, 2012; Hilton *et al.*, 2013) have been constructed through the narratives and practices of those who operate within them.

For me, the value of this approach is that it is able to locate the ideas of formal politics and policymaking within a much wider cultural frame. It enables us to explore, for instance, the interaction between popular and political ideas about affluence and consumerism (Black and Pemberton, 2004; Hilton, 2009), about perceptions of national decline (Tomlinson, 2000; Ortolano, 2008), or about what it means to be 'progressive'. What does it tell us, for instance, when we see that the trope of the 'progressive business man' was everywhere in interwar Britain, that advertisers plied self-identifying 'progressive' consumers with fast cars, modern fashions, and investment opportunities, or that 'progressive' municipalities were seen to be those that attracted both tourism and enterprise? Perhaps not much in isolation; these uses of the term clearly speak to its forward-looking temporal orientation, in ways that seem unremarkable. When we set them alongside party politics, however, they make the appearance of anti-socialist, pro-business municipal Progressive Parties seem less surprising than might otherwise be the case.

The distinction between interpretivist and positivist political science has been made very clear. The distinction between interpretivism and history, cultural studies, or sociology seems more blurred. What is it that drives interpretivists that sets them apart from these other disciplines? This is not a question that Bevir and Rhodes seem to recognise. Indeed they seem to suggest that there is no difference – on the one hand referring to their own work as 'radical historicism' (Bevir and

Rhodes, 2013), and on the other gathering historians, ethnographers, and philosophers into an interpretive canon, in an attempt to demonstrate the 'distinctiveness, coherence, and value' of their project' (Bevir, 2010: xix). I am therefore left wondering why interpretivism is necessary: what does it offer that is not available in other disciplines?

Conclusion

Politics is all about meanings. It is about the way we tell stories, construct problems, create identities. Showing that all this is historically contingent, a product of the web of beliefs we happen to hold, has radical potential. It shows that things could be other than they are. One of the things that drew me to my current project on the meanings of 'progressive' was the opportunity it offered to denaturalise understandings of party identity, to show that they are dependent on habits of thinking as much as on ideological affinities. By taking a broadly interpretive approach (rooted primarily in new political history), I have been able to unpick the varied and contradictory ways in which people from across the political spectrum have understood themselves to be progressive, and to ask what this means to them, and about the consequences that follow.

None of the arguments I have set out in this chapter should be taken as quarrels with the aims of interpretivism. As should be clear by now, they are very close to my own. My main point of difference is that I would want to extend Bevir and Rhodes's notion of tradition, to show that it operates on an emotional as well as functional level, that this gives it a particular form of authority which can be used strategically by political actors, and finally that this authority is itself both a culturally and historically specific product of a particular set of beliefs and practices.

I also have a reservation about the notion of interpretive political science as a discipline. If it is simply a case of being able to apply the approaches of history, sociology, and cultural studies to subjects more usually confined to political science, then I am a wholehearted supporter (and practitioner). If, however, it is an attempt to erect new disciplinary boundaries, to annexe a gloriously interdisciplinary set of practices into a fixed territory labelled 'interpretive political science', then I remain a cautious observer. The preface to Bevir's (2010: xix) *Interpretive Political Science* laments that although people 'know that numerous books and articles use qualitative methods to study beliefs, actions, and practices', they 'do not necessarily know to call this approach an interpretive one'. My questions are: should they have to, and, what would we gain if they did?

References

Bale, T. (2011) *The Conservative Party: from Thatcher to Cameron*, Cambridge: Polity.
Beer, S. (1965) *Modern British Politics: A study of parties and pressure groups*, London: Faber.
Beers, L. (2010) *Your Britain: Media and the making of the Labour Party*, Cambridge, MA: Harvard University Press.

Bevir, M. (2005) *New Labour: A critique*, London: Routledge.

Bevir, M. (ed.) (2010) *Interpretive Political Science, Volume I: Interpretive theories*, London: Sage.

Bevir, M. (2011) *The Making of British Socialism*, Princeton NJ: Princeton University Press.

Bevir, M. and Rhodes, R. A. W. (2003) *Interpreting British Governance*, London: Routledge.

Bevir, M. and Rhodes, R. A. W. (2004) 'Interpretation as Method, Explanation and Critique: A reply', *British Journal of Politics and International Relations* 6(2): 156–61.

Bevir, M. and Rhodes, R. A. W. (2013) 'Three Visions of Context as History' in C. Pollitt (ed.), *Context in Public Policy and Management: The missing link?* Cheltenham: Edward Elgar, pp. 55–73.

Blaazer, D. (1992) *The Popular Front and the Progressive Tradition: Socialists, liberals, and the quest for unity, 1884–1939*, Cambridge: Cambridge University Press.

Black, L. (2002) *The Political Culture of the Left in 'Affluent' Britain, 1951–64*, Basingstoke: Palgrave Macmillan.

Black, L. (2010), *Redefining British Politics: Culture, consumerism and participation, 1954–70*, Basingstoke: Palgrave Macmillan.

Black, L. and Pemberton, H. (eds) (2004) *An Affluent Society? Britain's post-war 'golden age' reconsidered*, Aldershot: Ashgate.

Blair, T. (1995) 'Let us Face the Future', 1945 Anniversary Lecture, London: Fabian Society.

Brown, G. (2010) *Why the Right is Wrong: The progressive case for Britain's future*, London: Fabian Society.

Cameron, D. (2009) 'Making Progressive Conservatism a Reality', speech to Demos, 22 January.

Cameron, D. (2010) Rose Garden Press Conference, 10 Downing Street, 12 May.

Churchill, W. (1946), 'Letter to Lord Woolton', 3 August. Conservative Party Archive, Bodleian Library, Oxford: CCO 3/1/64 Liberal National Organisation 1944–9.

Clark, G. and Hunt, J. (2007) *Who's Progressive Now?* London: Conservative Party.

Clarke, P. (1971) *Lancashire and the New Liberalism*, Cambridge: Cambridge University Press.

Clarke, P. (1978) *Liberals and Social Democrats*, Cambridge: Cambridge University Press.

Clegg, N. (2009) *The Liberal Moment*, London: Demos.

Clegg, N. (2010) Hugo Young Lecture, London, 23 November. Available at www.theguardian.com/politics/2010/nov/23/nick-clegg-hugo-young-text [accessed 31 July 2014].

Cockfield, A. (1983) 'Letter to Robin Butler', with annotations by Butler and Ferdinand Mount. 2 November. Thatcher MSS, Churchill Archive Centre: THCR 5/1/5/229 Part 1 f66.

Collini, S. (1979) *Liberalism and Sociology*, Cambridge: Cambridge University Press.

Daddow, O. (2007) 'Playing Games with History: Tony Blair's European policy in the press', *British Journal of Politics and International Relations*, 9: 582–98.

Darnton, R. (1984) *The Great Cat Massacre and Other Episodes in French Cultural History*, New York: Basic Books.

Davies, M. L. (2006) *Historics: Why history dominates contemporary society*, London: Routledge.

Davies, M. L. (2010) *Imprisoned by History: Aspects of historicized life*, New York: Routledge.

Drucker, H. M. (1979) *Doctrine and Ethos in the Labour Party*, London: Allen and Unwin.

Fielding, S. (2014) *A State of Play: British politics on screen, stage and page*, London: Bloomsbury.

Finlayson, A. (2004) 'Meaning and Politics: Assessing Bevir and Rhodes', *British Journal of Politics and International Relations*, 6(2): 149–56.

Freeden, M. (1978) *The New Liberalism: An ideology of social reform*, Oxford: Clarendon Press.

Freeden, M. (1989) *Minutes of the Rainbow Circle, 1894–1924*, London: Royal Historical Society.

Freeman, E. A. (1866) *The Methods of Historical Study: Eight lectures read in the University of Oxford in Michaelmas Term 1884*, London: Macmillan and Co.

Geertz, C. (1973) *The Interpretation of Cultures*, New York: Basic Books.

Grayson, R. and Lawson, N. (2010) 'Lab and Lib: A dream team', *Guardian* 9 May, Available at www.theguardian.com/commentisfree/2010/may/09/labour-liberal-democrats-progressive-alliance [accessed 31 July 2014].

Green, E. H. H. (2006) *Thatcher*, London: Hodder Arnold.

Grimond, J. (n.d. 1958?) *The New Liberal Democracy*, London: Liberal Publications Department.

Grimond, J. (1959) *The Liberal Future*, London: Faber and Faber.

Gunn, S. and Vernon, J. (eds) (2011) *The Peculiarities of Liberal Modernity in Imperial Britain*, Berkeley, CA: University of California Press.

Hayward, R. (2007) *Resisting History: Religious transcendence and the invention of the unconscious*, Manchester: Manchester University Press.

Hilton, M. (2009) *Prosperity for All: consumer activism in an era of globalization*, Ithaca, NY: Cornell University Press.

Hilton, M., Crowson, M., Mouhot, J.-F., and McKay, J. (eds) (2013) *A Historical Guide to NGOs in Britain: Charities, civil society and the voluntary sector since 1945*, Basingstoke: Palgrave Macmillan.

Hobsbawm, E. J. (1972) 'The Social Functions of the Past: Some questions', *Past and Present*, 55: 3–17.

Jones, T. (2011) *The Revival of British Liberalism: from Grimond to Clegg*, Basingstoke: Palgrave Macmillan.

Joyce, P. (2013) *The State of Freedom: A social history of the British State since 1800*, Cambridge: Cambridge University Press.

Koselleck, R. (2002) ' "Progress" and "Decline": An appendix to the history of two concepts', in R. Koselleck, *The Practice of Conceptual History: Timing history, spacing concepts*, trans. T. S. Presner, Stanford, CA: Stanford University Press: 218–35.

Progressive Review (1896) 'Introductory', 1(1), October: 1–9.

Lawrence, J. (2000) 'Labour: The myths it has lived by', in D. Tanner, P. Thayne and N. Tiratsoo (eds), *Labour's First Century*, Cambridge: Cambridge University Press: 341–66.

Lawrence, J. (2009) *Electing our Masters: The hustings in British politics from Hogarth to Blair*, Oxford: Oxford University Press.

Liberal Party (1977) 'Putting the Pact Over: A guide for Liberal activists', British Library of Political and Economic Science, Special Collections, Liberal Party Papers, Lib Lab Pact 19/1.

Mandler, P. (2002) *History and National Life*, London: Profile Books.

Marsh, D. (2008) 'Understanding British Government: Analysing competing models', *British Journal of Politics and International Relations*, 10: 251–68.

Martin, J. (2013) 'Situating Speech: A rhetorical approach to political strategy', *Political Studies*, 63(1): 25–42.

Marquand, D. (1979) 'Inquest on a Movement: Labour's defeat and its consequences', *Encounter*, July: 8–17.

Marquand, D. (1991) *The Progressive Dilemma: from Lloyd George to Kinnock*, London: Heinemann.

McCarthy, H. (2012) *The British People and the League of Nations: Democracy, citizenship and internationalism, c.1918–45*, Manchester: Manchester University Press.

Nora, P. (ed.) (1996) *Realms of Memory: Rethinking the French past, vol. I, conflicts and divisions*, English language edn edited by L. D. Kritzman, trans A. Goldhammer, New York: Columbia University Press.

O'Hara, G. (2012) *Governing Post-War Britain: The paradoxes of progress, 1951–1973*, Basingstoke: Macmillan.

Ortolano, G. (2008) *The Two Cultures Controversy: Science, literature and cultural politics in postwar Britain*, Cambridge: Cambridge University Press.

Osborne, G. (2009) 'Progressive Reform in an Age of Austerity', speech to Demos, 11 August. Available at www.demos.co.uk/press_releases/george-osborne-progressive-reform-in-an-age-of-austerity [accessed 31 July 2014].

Robinson, E. (2012) *History, Heritage and Tradition in Contemporary British Politics: Past politics and present histories*, Manchester: Manchester University Press.

Robinson, E. (2015) 'Defining Progressive Politics: Municipal socialism and anti-socialism in contestation, 1889–1939', *Journal of the History of Ideas* 76(4): 609–31.

Robinson, E. and Twyman, J. (2014) 'Speaking at Cross Purposes? The rhetorical problems of "progressive" politics', *Political Studies Review*, 12(1): 51–67.

Schofield, C. (2013) *Enoch Powell and the Making of Postcolonial Britain*, Cambridge: Cambridge University Press.

Sloman, P. (2014) 'Partners in Progress? British Liberals and the Labour Party since 1918', *Political Studies Review*, 12(1): 41–50.

Steel, D. (1987) Speech on the re-opening of the National Liberal Club, Quoted in Catherine Sample, 'NLC begins the new century with £1m refit', *Liberal News*, July: 3.

Thomas, H. (1979) *History, Capitalism and Freedom*, foreword by Margaret Thatcher. London: Centre for Policy Studies.

Thompson, J. A. (1990) 'The Historians and the Decline of the Liberal Party', *Albion*, 22(1): 65–83.

Tomlinson, J. (2000) *The Politics of Decline: Understanding post-war Britain*, Harlow: Longman.

Vernon, J. (1993) *Politics and the People: A study in English political culture, c.1815–1867*, Cambridge: Cambridge University Press.

Part III
Policymaking

7   Extending Interpretivism

Articulating the Practice Dimension in Bevir and Rhodes's Differentiated Polity Model

Hendrik Wagenaar

Introduction

With their interpretive approach, Bevir and Rhodes (BR) have joined a growing chorus of scholars in planning, policy analysis, and political science who argue for an increased role for interpretive methods in political analysis (Wagenaar, 2011).[1] Within this family of interpretive approaches, BR's Interpretive Political Science (IPS) is philosophically sophisticated and grounded in an astute and realistic appraisal of the nature of governing in modern liberal democratic societies. For these reasons, BR's IPS is of considerable significance to anyone in political science, public administration, and planning with an interest in interpretive methods. But while their approach has been welcomed in the community of politics scholars in Britain as a 'useful addition to the tools of political scientists' (Smith, 2008: 143) and a 'major contribution' (Marsh, 2011: 46), it has also attracted considerable criticism. Their main concepts are considered loose and ambiguous, their depiction of mainstream British political science a straw man, and their take on interpretivism narrow and extreme. They pay insufficient attention to power, their ontology is dubious, and, perhaps most damning, their empirical claims are seen as trivial (McAnulla, 2006; Smith, 2008; Marsh, 2011). Although I agree with some of this criticism, I think that parts of it are either overblown or miss the point. I will also argue that some critics of BR have muddied the philosophical waters of interpretivism in politics and the policy sciences. In this essay I will briefly introduce the two authors' approach by describing its philosophical foundations and its main substantive concepts. I will then address the ontological worries of some of BR's critics and why these miss the point, in my opinion. What the critics miss is the central role that practice plays in any form of interpretivist analysis (Wagenaar, 2011). I will then critique the way that BR deploy their central concept of practice and suggest what a more fully articulated theory of practice would look like. Finally, I will spell out some of the implications that a well-conceptualised notion of practice has for research on policy and governance.

Philosophical Background

Rod Rhodes is an influential political scientist who was one of the first scholars to argue, in the early 1990s, that the government was a differentiated and fragmented polity, and who explored the concept of policy networks – which, since then, has become the new orthodoxy in policy analysis (Rhodes, 1997). Mark Bevir is a political theorist whose work shows strong historical leanings (Bevir, 1999). Both of their backgrounds are clearly visible in their articulation of interpretivism.

One of the delights of BR's interpretivism is its philosophical sophistication. Modernist empiricism, with its adherence to the correspondence theory of truth, the fact–value dichotomy, and universalist ideals of knowledge, operates as if a century of by now widely accepted philosophy has simply bypassed it. Smith is probably right that BR are too quick in depicting most of Anglo-Saxon political science as 'modernist empiricist', but the more important observation is that empiricism is not restricted to the relatively small number of political scientists who study rational choice theories. Empiricism with its appeal to 'data', 'methods', its reification of core disciplinary concepts such as 'state, 'institution', or 'power', the taken-for-granted epistemological authority of quantitative forms of analysis (with the ensuing emphasis on reliability and validity), and the claim to (quasi-) causal explanations on the one hand, and its dismissal of qualitative and interpretive methods as 'soft', 'anecdotal', and 'subjective' on the other – is much more pervasive, both in politics and the policy sciences (Bevir and Rhodes, 2010: 43). The core of Bevir and Rhodes's philosophy is antifoundationalism, which they describe as 'any epistemology that rejects appeals to a basic ground or foundation of knowledge in either pure experience or pure reason' (2010: 43). Instead, knowledge is always perspectivist. Whatever we perceive as facts are always facts under a particular description that organises our observations (Fay, 1996: 74). For that reason, knowledge is also provisional; there is no final arbiter (brute facts, pure reason, or the right method) for determining the truth of a statement, and what is considered true today might require revision tomorrow. Although anti-foundationalism is no longer a controversial or outlandish claim in philosophy, as BR rightly point out (2010: 43), it is not always obvious what its implications are for social science research.

Anti-foundationalism often leads to accusations of relativism or an 'anything goes' epistemological position. Marsh, for example, claims that the notion of 'truth' does not apply to interpretations and chides BR for suggesting so (2011: 36). But this shows only that Marsh implicitly adheres to a naïve realist correspondence theory of truth, in which each representation has an exact correspondence somewhere out there in the world (Allen, 1993: 9–10; Wagenaar, 2011: 59). (This is yet another example of the sway that empiricism holds over social scientists of all stripes.) It would go too far to discuss the thorny subject of the philosophy of truth here. Let me just say that after Nietzsche 'Truth' has become 'truth': multifaceted, theoretically loaded, and embedded in historically situated language games and ordinary practices. However, the situation that reality is not the final arbiter of the truth-value of our statements, and that different theoretical propositions may do an equally good job in explaining a particular slice of the world, does not mean that there is no fact to the matter. Theoretical explanations are hooked up with the world, and some better than others. This connection between theoretical proposition and the world does not occur through some unspecified, language-mediated correspondence with brute reality, but through practice, as well as the resistances we encounter when we act upon the world. Truth moves about in a landscape of action. This explains why most people, when provided with the necessary information, are in a relatively good position to judge which statements do a better job in explaining a particular part of reality with which they are familiar. I will return to this important point later.

Although fears of relativism in interpretivism are misguided, I am afraid that BR, with their idealist conception of interpretivism, have not been particularly successful in laying to rest such fears. But before we get there we need a better understanding of the practical implications of BR's anti-foundationalism. They articulate two of them, which they call 'meaning holism' and 'anti-representationalism'. Both hang together. Concepts such as 'state', 'voter', 'unemployment', or 'climate', they argue, are not linear representations of objects 'out there' in the world. Because, as we saw, our observations always appear to us 'under a particular prior description' their meaning or sensefulness, our very ability to recognise them as an observation of something – an office of the state, unemployment statistics, a young offender – hinges on these observations being embedded in a web of concepts. As BR put it:

> Meaning holism implies that our concepts are not simply given to us by the world as it is. Rather, we build them in part by drawing on our prior theories in an attempt to categorize, explain, and narrate our experiences.
>
> (2010: 43–4)

Meaning holism and anti-representationalism imply that we cannot simply read people's beliefs from their position in society. I might be a street-level bureaucrat struggling with too many cases, insufficient means, difficult clients, and overbearing superiors, but that doesn't mean that I will *therefore* use such well known accommodation strategies as favouring deserving and punishing undeserving clients, withholding information, etc. (Lipsky, 1980). I have a measure of freedom here to adapt to circumstances as I interpret them. I might use my discretionary power to arrive at morally informed decisions that balance the client's well-being, the system's integrity, and my standing among my peers (Wagenaar and Hartendorp, 2000; Maynard-Moody and Musheno, 2003; Wagenaar, 2004). Differently put, BR reject the determinism that is common in empiricist political science and argue for an approach to explanation which favours grasping the meaning that actors attach to objects and events and reconstructing the historical path that has led the actors to have those meanings. This is BR's anti-representationalism. This approach flies in the face of much political-science thinking in which big entities external to the individual (economy, institution, state), in a typically unspecified but more or less taken-for-granted way, determine the beliefs, preferences, and actions of that individual. This epistemological trope finds expression in the proverbial regression study in which one reified 'variable' (for example, city size or income level) somehow determines another reified variable (for example, citizen participation) (Oliver, 2000). The point here is not to dismiss the statistical association. Rather, the argument is that it is intellectually more interesting to go *beyond* the statistical association and aim our analytical focus at (1) explaining why small towns often show higher levels of citizen participation, and (2) explaining the large, unaccounted for, error terms in the regression equation – that is, all those cases where, to stay with our example, low income groups in large cities success-fully engage in long-standing participation efforts (Moulaerts *et al.*, 2010; Wagenaar and Specht, 2010). Such explanation will most likely have a narrative form in that it presents the conditional connections between beliefs, preferences, and actions in such a way that the actions become plausible (Bevir and Rhodes, 2010: 78).

Ontology Worries

Like all interpretive approaches, BR's IPS is a mixture of methodological and substantive precepts. This apparent 'fuzziness' has been the target of much criti-cism. Marsh, for example, spends a lot of space wondering if BR present a model or a narrative of decentred governance; in other words, whether decen-tredness is 'out there', in an ontological sense, or that it is a mere representation of a multi-interpretable reality (2011: 36). And McAnulla accuses them of com-mitting the 'epistemic fallacy' of the 'reduction of being to statements about our knowledge of being' (2006: 405). Both detect the absence of a clear commitment to a 'reality independent of narrative or discourse' in BR's work. As Marsh puts it: 'In my view, the problem is that Bevir and Rhodes want it both ways; they talk of narratives and invoke the interpretivist position, but see network govern-ance and the differentiated polity as a more accurate description of how the con-temporary British polity works than the Westminster model' (2011: 37). I skip Marsh's misunderstandings about interpretivism and merely point out that many critics of BR feel uncomfortable with their alleged renunciation of some form of realism (see also Smith, 2008: 151).

While the critics are 'on to something', the significant divide is not that between realism and interpretivism. Issues of ontology, realism, truth, and inter-pretivism pose ever so many philosophical minefields that go far beyond the confines of this chapter. So let me boil these endless debates down to another, in this context more productive, distinction, that between representationalism and interventionism. It is here that we find the largest inconsistency in BR's work. Although BR claim that their interpretivism is non-representationalist, their work shows differently. By foregrounding 'narrative' and 'webs of belief', and by defining their key concept of 'tradition' in these terms, they situate themselves in a solid representationalist position, and with that an idealist one. Let me explain. In general we make two types of statements about the world: simple declarative statements such as 'I sit at my desk', and complex, more speculative ones, such as 'The British polity is organised according to self-organising networks'. Both types of statement claim to be a faithful likeness of the world. But, while no one would challenge the first declarative sentence, many take issue with the second complex statement. There is an intuitive mimetic truth to the matter in the declarative sentence which wholly eludes the complex theoretical statement. In the second case we can think of other complex theoretical statements that do an equally good job in describing the British polity; 'equally good', that is, in terms of prediction, explanation, simplicity, and productiveness (Hacking, 1983: 143). And although one theory might be better than another in some respect, we do not have ultimate criteria outside the alternative theories to decide the 'true' or 'right' one. Or, more precisely, each theory is able to mobilise snippets of reality to bolster its alleged validity. But this only goes to show that social reality is almost infinitely tolerant of any theoretical proposition. Theoretical propositions are only very loosely coupled to 'reality', and what exigent coupling there is, is mostly effectuated by declarative statements, or assemblages of declarative statements, that are hidden in the theoretical statements. This is anti-foundationalism in different words, and in this form it afflicts all social science theories, from the most empiricist to the most interpretive.

If anti-foundationalism is universal in the social sciences, is there a way to salvage reality? Yes, and it can be found in interventionism. When we intervene, when we act in and upon the world, inevitably we bump into resistances. When we act we let ourselves be guided by experience, knowledge, routines, intuition, and hunches. Usually that is enough, but sometimes not, and the world resists. That is when reality hits us. There are, thus, two types of reality. One, metaphysical reality, is a by-product of a fixation of our representation. It is a second-order concept that we need in order to make authoritative statements about the mimetic truth of our theories. It is a reassuring metaphysical fantasy. The second, experiential reality, emerges when we act upon the world. It is direct, initially preverbal, and the source of our practical understanding of the world (Wagenaar and Cook, 2003). Most theories in the social sciences are a mixture of both metaphysical and experiential reality, and it is this that prevents them from sliding into idealism altogether (Hacking, 1983: 37). Let me rephrase that last sentence in a way that brings out one of the conditions of possibility of social science: most social science research includes unacknowledged elements of practice which tie it into experiential reality to a sufficient extent to prevent it from becoming pure metaphysics.

BR's work claims to be all about practice. On the face of it, that should put them in an ideal position to ground their work in unadulterated experiential reality. So, where does the ontological uneasiness of their critics come from? Let us take BR's central concept of decentredness. Decentredness, as we have seen, is couched in terms of meaning and action. It is about 'the ability of individuals to create and act on meanings' (Bevir and Rhodes, 2010: 73). So far, so good. But while BR emphasise the meaning aspect of this description, and the element of contingency that decentredness introduces into governance, they pay relatively little attention to the practice aspect. In fact, practice plays an ambiguous role in BR's conceptual machinery. On the one hand it is mentioned, usually in passing, on almost every page of their work. It is even in the title of their last work, *The State as Cultural Practice*. On the other hand it is barely defined. The only definition I could find is the following: 'A practice is a set of actions, often a set of actions that exhibit a pattern, perhaps even a pattern that remains relatively stable across time' (2010: 75). Differently put: practice is (stable) action. This is a thin-to-the-point-of-emaciation conceptualisation of practice. Whoever introduces the concept of practice, knowingly or unknowingly, introduces a performative idiom, a philosophy of intervening, into his arguments. He will then have to integrate the implications of this idiom and this philosophy into his theory and methodological and analytical prescriptions. I will return to this shortly.

But there is another problem with BR's conception of practice. The above definition of practice is immediately followed by the following passage:

> Practices often give us grounds for postulating beliefs, for we can ascribe beliefs to people only in interpreting their actions. Nonetheless practices cannot explain actions because people act for reasons of their own. People sometimes act on their belief about a practice, but, when they do, we still explain their action by reference to their beliefs about the practice, and, of course, these beliefs need to be accurate.
>
> (2010: 75)

Perhaps I am alone in thinking that this passage lacks the customary clarity of BR's writing, but what I get from it is an opposition, a dualism, between belief and action. In fact, in their zeal to promote their decentredness and avoid even the slightest suggestion of determinism, BR explicitly oppose the role of practice, and privilege beliefs, in grasping how actors move about in their world:

> Clearly practices ... constrain the effects, and so the effectiveness, of an action. But practices do not constrain the beliefs people might come to hold and so the actions they might attempt to perform.
>
> (2010: 76)

However, the point of a performative philosophy is precisely to integrate belief and action to the point where they form one organic activity system for the purpose of moving about effectively in the world (Dewey, 1991 [1938]; Engeström, 1996). BR's insistence on keeping belief and action separate and, in addition, on privileging belief as the major driver of change and adaptation to changing circumstances in the form of dilemmas, inserts a deep inconsistency into their work – an inconsistency that, to my mind, becomes manifest in their own empirical work, which fills the second half of their books. To explain more fully what I mean, it is necessary to insert an exposition of what a practice approach to social and political research amounts to.

Practice and Agency in a Performative Account of Governance

At the heart of a practice approach to social and political research is the recognition that realities emerge from our practical engagement with the world in an ongoing stream of commonplace, task-oriented, local practices (Snook, 2002: 182; Wagenaar and Cook, 2003). We use the plural 'realities' to highlight the deep pluralism – political, ideational, ontological – of the world that we inhabit and that is co-produced through our continuous engaging with our material and social environment through practice (Latour, 1987; Pickering, 1995; Wagenaar and Cook, 2003). Taking a performative approach thus requires a shift from a focus on the representation of knowledge to the insight that knowledge is an aspect, or artefact, of practices, explicable in *its* terms (Cook and Wagenaar, 2012: 16). Arguably, practice theory has had its most significant impact in the sociology of scientific knowledge (Pickering, 1995), organisation theory (Whittington, 2006; Orlikowski, 2007; Nicolini, 2013) and international relations (Adler and Pouliot, 2011). Politics and the policy sciences have been relatively slow in recognising the importance of practice theory (for an early example, see Wagenaar and Cook, 2003).

It is far from easy to summarise the gist of what a practice account, as applied to politics and governance, entails. Practice is an amorphous concept with roots in different philosophical traditions and scholarly disciplines (Wagenaar and Cook, 2003; Nicolini, 2012). Without touching upon too much specificity, and inspired above all by classical pragmatism and some of its contemporary elaborations, I choose to summarise a practice account in three premises. The first, at the same time the most obvious and farthest reaching, is the primacy of interventionism. This is the insight that reality – that is the environment that we live and move about in and that rubs and brushes up against us from all sides, and that we overwhelmingly experience as 'out there', largely independent from ourselves – is a product of our ongoing practical engagement with the world (Schatzki, 1996; Hildebrand, 2003; Dewey, 2008 [1925]; Cook and Wagenaar, 2012; Nicolini, 2012). The second premise concerns temporal emergence. This is the insight that the constraints and affordances of the outer world come to us only through our experience of them in emergent time. The significance of temporal emergence is that two key elements of a practice account, which are necessarily connected to each other in the sense that they bring each other into being – time and experience – are folded into it. The third premise regards the interpenetration of the human and the material in the way we act on, and understand, the world (Pickering 1995; Pickering and Guzick 2008; Bennett, 2010).

The first key insight of a practice account is that we grasp the world by intervening in it. By intervening I mean any activity that more or less purposely aspires to change an aspect of the world (Wagenaar, 2011: 60). The notion of intervening suggests a fundamental orientation towards reality that the pragmatists call 'the practical starting point' (Hildebrand, 2003: 185). The practical starting point must be seen in opposition to the 'theoretical starting point', the widely institutionalised attitude that, as the right way to grasp reality consists of analysing knowledge, reality itself must have a linguistic or conceptual nature (Hildebrand, 2003: 186; see also Cook and Wagenaar, 2012). The practical starting point on the other hand acknowledges that we grasp the world – practically and cognitively – through our experience of it. That is, we do not begin with a theory or a linguistic frame, but through some less defined, more immediate, experience of the world in which we are immersed (Hacking, 1983: 37; Jay, 2005).

However, intervening, as the pragmatist philosophers realised, inevitably provokes resistance. Empirical reality has a way of subverting our best-laid plans and ideas once we act upon it. From an interventionist perspective, the world presents itself as a bundle of affordances and constraints. Our grasp of the world, in a practical, cognitive and emotional sense, as well as in the ontological sense that the world appears to us as a by and large stable, coherent place out there, is produced by our grappling with these affordances and constraints in an actionable manner. Or as Hacking puts it succinctly: '(I) think that reality has more to do with what we do in the world than with what we think about it' (1983: 17). The importance of resistance as an ontological aspect of a practice account is that it embodies three key elements of the practical starting point: 1) our purposes with the world as they follow from our needs, desires, valuations, and affects – intentionality, in other words; 2) the way that the agency of the world subverts our purposes once we act on them; and 3) our understanding of the world – practical, intellectual, and emotional – that emerges from our probing the patterns of affordances and constraints for the purpose of designing accommodations to resistances that the world has thrown up in response to our acting in it. It is in this sense that we do indeed enact realities.

Although acting and intervening is at the heart of the practice approach, we should not make the mistake of thinking that action is its basic unit of analysis. Practice is more than action; it is a conglomerate of acting, actors, the objects involved in the acting, instruments, beliefs, intentions, rules of the game, routines, and the relations between them. Not only do these elements define each other, they also emerge dialectically, in the course of engaging in a practice (Cook and Wagenaar, 2012). For example, in the Netherlands the generally recognised problem of frequent offenders emerges out of the interaction of certain individuals who display unrestrained, often aggressive behaviour, are addicted to alcohol or drugs, without work or income, are intellectually challenged and treatment-resistant, a service system that is functionally dispersed and fragmented, and certain financing rules that discourage any activity that is not client-oriented (such as bringing about service coordination) (Wagenaar *et al.*, 2015). The 'object' of this activity system, the frequent offender, is thus not an object *sui generis* (defined in this case by a psychiatric diagnosis of severe personality disorder) but, at least partly, the product of the way that social services are organised in the Netherlands. For example, the urgency of the problem of frequent offenders, its emotional tenor among service providers, expressed itself as a generalised feeling of helplessness mixed with vexation among professionals. Providers felt that the system failed the offender, but also that the offender played the system. However, one of the main problems in the system was the inability of the criminal justice system and the social service system to collaborate. Each was caught in its operating procedures and organisational mission, resulting in endless, tense case meetings and unsatisfactory, ineffective interventions (Wagenaar *et al.*, 2015). In a kind of perverse feedback loop the outcome of the system, social services to persons in need, laid bare the deep contradictions in the service system.

We can derive two insights about the analysis of practice from this example that are important to our discussion of BR's interpretivism. First, the object of analysis is not just one activity system but a dense, interrelated, web of activity systems. This insight shows similarities to the decentred governance system of BR, but its grounding in practice reveals a significant difference. In BR's ideational approach actions are fuelled by traditions (2010: 78), but in an activity system it is the object (material or otherwise) of activity that drives the system. The object (in my example, frequent offenders) provides the motives for the actors, organises their activities, and gives coherence, meaning, and continuity to the system (even when it is fragmented) (Engeström, 2000). Some critics have questioned the central role of traditions in BR's work and complained that the concept, for all its vagueness and notional qualities, is asked to do too much (Smith, 2008). The alternative of conceptualising decentred governance networks as activity systems that are organised around one or more objects of intervention is a conceptually and empirically more satisfying solution. Instead of positing traditions as a priori ideational frameworks that self-evidently although contingently shape actors' beliefs and actions, a practice approach regards tradition as something that is reproduced and sustained through the active engagement and participation of a community of actors (Nicolini, 2013: 78). This means that we cannot assume the a priori existence of a particular tradition. In fact, an actionable understanding of tradition would direct the analytical gaze – as in the frequent offender example – to the doings and sayings of actors as they engage with and try to make sense of concrete challenges. It is likely that these actors are influenced by larger systems of beliefs, values, and affective states, but how much weight or meaning these have in particular situations in relation to the demands of the situation at hand always remains an empirical question. What this means for empirical research I will discuss in the final section of this chapter.

The second insight is that a practice, in the sense discussed so far, is inherently fragmented, conflictual and, thus, unstable. As Nicolini puts it:

> For one thing, the object is not visible in its entirety to any one of the participants. At the same time, because it is composed of heterogeneous entities that are embedded in different practices and discourses, the object is inherently multiple and may hold together orientations, interests and interpretations that are potentially contradictory. This means that the socio-material community performed by the object is unlikely to be an integrated whole in which parts move in harmony, and will look more like a community without unity where contradictions and conflicts abound.
>
> (2013: 112)

The heterogeneous, conflicted character of activity systems makes the concept of dilemma as the driver of change unnecessary, and in fact misleading. Actors who are engaged with activity systems constantly encounter what Dewey calls 'situations', states of affairs that defy easy accommodation according to routine operating procedures and therefore require some form of intervention by an actor. This can be a client who attacks another client in a treatment setting, a provider experiencing difficulty with finding a treatment facility for his client, or actors in a case meeting who are unable to agree on a suitable course of treatment

(Wagenaar *et al.*, 2015). Usually such resistances of the system do not result in change but at best in a pragmatic form of accommodation. The therapist of the aggressive client might terminate treatment and count on other providers in the system to pick up the slack, for example (Wagenaar *et al.*, 2015). While this is hardly ideal from the perspective of the client and comes with considerable cost to society, this negative fallout is sufficiently dispersed to keep the system going. If such problems persist, or the costs to the participants come to be seen as too high, some participants of the activity system, for example a manager or a local councillor, might reflect on and interpret the problem and look for a solution, for example, allocating funds to some researchers to find a solution. The structural clash of legal rules and treatment principles that resulted in the repeated failure in the case meetings to find workable treatment options for frequent offenders was such a situation (Wagenaar et al., 2015). Differently put, we do not need the concepts of tradition or dilemma as some kind of external shock to the system to explain why people change their practices; dilemma, contradiction, fragmentation, and instability are built-in elements of practices as activity systems, and actors engage in pragmatic solutions to either sustain the system or design least-cost changes.[2] Practices display a certain coherence and stability precisely because they are intrinsically disparate and unstable, so that actors, in the course of acting on the situation at hand, need to work hard at keeping the activity system together. But to fully appreciate this insight we need to turn to the second element of the practice approach, temporal emergence.

Acting in and on the world takes place in emergent time (Wagenaar, 2011: 284–9). One of the enduring aspects of the theoretical starting point, as exemplified in almost all social science research or policy analysis, is its rear-view mirror attitude towards time.[3] The theoretical starting point is retroactive; it explains how actors think and decide *ex post facto*. Despite the evocation of the term practice, BR's interpretivism is retroactive, explaining events after the fact. However, in a performative account people live under the imperative to look forward, to act on the situation at hand. Engaging in practice, such as grappling with a banking crisis or dealing with frequent offenders, means to harness uncertainty, complexity, and the limits of predictability when actions extend in time. This is an obvious but deep requirement. Once all the information on how a particular decision has run its course is in, we can more or less exhaustively explain or give an account of how that decision was made. Much policy analysis, for example, is of this kind. But actors live in a world where the outcome of decisions is generally *not* immediately or completely known, where problem formulations are unclear and fundamentally contested, where no one can oversee the implications of alternative courses of action, where, in short, the answer to the question 'What to do?' is shrouded in the fog of time.

However, emergent time is not simply the admonishment to look forward. In a performative account, time is neither retroactive time, nor the arrangement of pre-existing elements in linear time. Instead, emergent time is *becoming* through an ongoing engagement with the world. As the example in the preceding paragraphs showed, the object of action, the meaning it has for practitioners, their intentions and goals, the resistances practitioners encounter, and the solutions they effectuate all emerge together, in an ongoing process of negotiating the situation at hand. In fact, the emergent quality of practice is closely associated with the conflicts and disturbances that are ever present to the activity system. The intrinsic instability of the system acts as the escapement in a pendulum clock, both moving and regulating the movement of the system. In this continuous movement, past achievements, current interpretations, and future projections are folded into each other.

Time, action, and object are mediated in practice through 'experience', another key concept in the practice account. Practice is animated by experience (Cook and Wagenaar, 2012). Our notion of time, our sense that our life is stretched out on a line that extends the present into the past and into the future, is a by-product of the unfolding of action and the experience of change and novelty that accompanies it (Wagenaar, 2011: 287). Our actions are therefore not in time, they *are* time. In this emergent sense, experience is time. However, experience is a notoriously slippery concept (Jay, 2005). I summarise a large philosophical debate here by taking the position that experience is not a private affective state, but instead straddles the interface of private subjectivity and public language and action (Jay, 2005). Experience is simultaneously immediate, ineffable, *and* shaped by cultural templates. Experience is *transactional* in that it extends beyond the boundaries of the individual. Transactional experience denotes a relational connection of experience. It connects individual experience with the larger world by encompassing the latter into the former (Dewey, 1980 [1916]). Emergent time is, thus, generative. It tells us that realities are artefacts of temporal emergence, simultaneously stable and provisional, obdurate and temporary, emerging in an 'eternally unfolding present' (Cook and Wagenaar, 2012: 21).

Finally, resistance, as we saw, is not confined to human actors but characterises *both* the human and the non-human. Sociologists of science argue that there are certain advantages to thinking of resistances in terms of agency (Pickering, 1995: 6).[4] The advantage is that it allows us to unpack the interactive give and take between people and the world when the first acts upon the latter. The third key insight then is that in a practice account of policymaking the world of governance is seen as 'a field of powers, capacities and performances' (Pickering, 1995: 7) and extends to humans, non-human organisms, and things. As Wagenaar (2012: 92) puts it, 'The term agency denotes a world in which various agents are continuously doing things; things that bear upon us, that have an impact, and with which we as humans have to grapple and to cope'. Agency, thus, is what makes the world 'talk back' whenever we intervene (Schön and Rein, 1994). Agency is a 'creative presence of organic beings, technological devices and discursive codes' (Franklin, 2008: 28). In ordinary terms, each system is to a greater or lesser extent impervious to our intentions. That is what the law of unintended consequences in public policy is about. That is what I have in mind when I assert that activity systems are inherently contradictory and unstable. We can implement a treatment protocol or send a policy proposal into the world, but we have little control over the human, artefactual, and sometimes natural, agency that receives and absorbs the treatment or policy and spits it back at us in an unforeseen way. Backtalk is brutal, immediate and consequential, operating through natural and artefactual agency, even though it is subsequently mediated through the interpretive powers of human agency.

When we ask the question, 'What is it that we do – in a practice sense – when we act in a goal-directed or intentional manner in a world that is filled with agency?' the answer is that 'we try to *capture* agency' (Pickering, 1995: 23; Wagenaar 2012: 93). Pickering (1995) calls this the dialectic of resistance and accommodation. He defines *resistance* as 'the failure to achieve an intended capture of agency in practice' and *accommodation* as

> an active human strategy of response to resistance, which can include revisions to goals and intentions as well to the material form of the machine in question and to the human frame of gestures and social relations that surround it.
>
> (Pickering, 1995: 22)

From a practice perspective, then, a policy practice, such as dealing with frequent offenders or moving a law through parliament, requires that

> we extend our intentions and understandings into this indeterminate world without being able to predict how its agency will effectuate itself and impact us. Knowledge of the world is important, but is only a partial and incomplete guide to our stabs into the future.
>
> (Wagenaar 2012: 93)

Pickering, in discussing the practice of science, is clear about the implications of this and explains, in somewhat overblown language,

> There is not a thread in the present that we can hang on to which determines the outcome of cultural extension. We just have to find out, in practice ... how the next capture of material agency is to be made and what it will look like.
>
> (1995: 24)

This tempers the capacity for cognitive knowledge, analytical representations, and narrative renditions to accurately inform the likely impacts of policy initiatives.

To sum up: the concept of practice has considerably more inner complexity to it than BR have allowed in their work. Despite the fact that practice theory is not a unified field, I have argued that the primacy of action, temporal emergence, and the interpenetration of the human and material worlds through the effects of agency and resistance, are the minimal and necessary elements of any practice theory. Taken together these elements suggest a theoretical and methodological program that honours the anti-foundationalism and interpretivism that BR rightly emphasise but avoids the idealism and retroactive quality of their approach. Clarity about the nature of practice has direct consequences for the way we teach, learn, and engage in research in the social sciences. In the final section of this chapter, I will briefly outline the methodological implications of a practice approach to politics and governance.

The State as Cultural Extension

If I were to summarise the central problem of BR's interpretivism, then I would say that they present a performative conception of political science in a largely representative idiom. This epistemological ambivalence results, to my mind, in a disconnection between the sophistication of their (interpretive) theory and its practical application. BR argue for research that is anti-foundational in conception, and historicist and interpretive in approach. But when they put their theory into practice, their research is simply not dynamic and fine-grained enough to capture the dance of agency and the dialectic of resistance and accommodation. This tendency is most pronounced in their work on 'living traditions' (2010: 157; similar work is discussed in Bevir and Rhodes, 2003; 2006). 'Traditions', BR argue, 'are selective legacies passed down from generation to generation, and adapted to present-day use' (2010: 157). And further on; '(P)ractitioners reach for historical notions of governance and call into play antecedent notions to enable them better to manage or understand their present-day circumstances' (2010: 157–58). This sounds reasonable enough. However, how do we identify traditions in action? BR simply latch on to traditions as they are discussed in political science handbooks – Tory, Liberal, Whig, Westminster, Labour, etc. Again, this sounds reasonable enough, as these labels are generally recognised. But do they also describe what is going on in the fine-grained ethnography of political behaviour? Do we not run the risk, in adapting widely used labels for political traditions, of imposing them on a wide range of behaviour that might very well emerge from wholly different traditions?[5] Let us look at an example that throws doubt on the wholesale adoption of existent traditions.

First, take the three types of democratic participation that BR discuss at the end of their book: participatory democracy, collaborative forms of governance, and dialogic policymaking (2010: 210). Like the earlier traditions, we do not have any difficulty in recognising these as distinct modes of democratic governance. But is this how the everyday world of urban governance is organised? In my study on neighbourhood regeneration in The Hague, we saw all three forms of democratic governance – and some others too – in play *simultaneously*, with actors rapidly cycling through different modes of hierarchy, governance, and collaboration, as the situation demanded. Citizens called upon the city council to back them up, and a high-ranking civil servant used formal budgetary procedure to speed up an overly long deliberation process that threatened to get mired in endless talk. All very confusing, falling outside our preconceived categories, and suggesting an emerging form of democratic governance that is improvisatory, results oriented, very much concerned with democratic legitimation, and often dependent upon the timely intervention of a public entrepreneur (Wagenaar and Duiveman, 2011). The study confirms one of my recurring experiences in fine-grained, practice-oriented, interpretive research – namely, that it tends to explode one's preconceived categories.[6]

Fine-grained, ethnographic research is only one side of the coin in practice-oriented research, however. It is crucial in capturing the ordinary stuff of the everyday working life of actors: the sayings and doings, the timing and tempo, the practical, mundane concerns of actors, the interactive choreographies that shape work, the tools and instruments that make work possible, the normativity of routines, and the instances where deviation from the norm is called for and the boundaries of legitimate practices are tested (Nicolini, 2013: 220). Nicolini call this part of the research process 'zooming in'. But for a full picture of a practice it is equally important to engage in 'zooming out' (Nicolini, 2013: 230). By zooming out we follow the trail of connections, through time and geographical space, of a practice with other practices. We try to grasp how the local practice is constituted by other adjacent or overarching practices. We analyse how the local practice contributes to the reproduction of social or political arrangements. We want to trace how practices 'act at a distance and produce effects in different places and distant times', and reversely how phenomena in different places and times manifest themselves through the local practice (Nicolini, 2013: 235). For example, in trying to make sense of the welter of improvisatory work of participatory governance in The Hague, we looked elsewhere for similar examples. What worked best for us in the end, we concluded, were notions of civic capacity that were developed in urban studies to explain the joint efforts of marginal groups, societal actors, and officials to address stubborn problems.

To sum up, BR's theory of governance is an important contribution to interpretivist social and political science. Mainstream political scientists will see its main theses as a provocation; but I am confident that over the years more and more political scientists will come to see the usefulness of their approach. However, although they purport to formulate a theory of how social actors, embedded in the sweep of emergent time, adapt to an ever-changing environment in the face of a resistant, intractable world, in the end they shy away from a consistent performative account of political analysis. Both in their theoretical formulations and their empirical examples, they are ambivalently poised between a representational and a performative account of governance – 'dwellers on the threshold of practice' as I called it in an earlier piece (Wagenaar, 2012). In this chapter I have tried to articulate that final step towards what I have called a practice approach to political analysis. In a practice approach, the question is not about which representations (theories, models) of political life are the most 'true' (or, in practical reality, supported by purportedly unassailable method). Rather, the more interesting and relevant question is, and I follow Andrew Pickering, a major practice theorist, here; 'How are connections between knowledge and the world made, and of what do those connections, *as made in practice*, consist?' (1995: 182; my emphasis). In the realm of the state, or governance, this means tracking down, methodically and in precise detail, the everyday work of actors, their sayings and doings, their practical concerns, the tools and objects of their trade, and the mediating work they do, and the meanings and affects that shape that work. But equally importantly, we need to situate that mundane work in a larger web of practices that extends through time and space, and trace how local practices thus embedded contribute to sustain or subvert larger configurations of politics and power. Although BR have made an important contribution to such a decentred analysis, so far we have not seen nearly enough of such analysis in their interpretive political science.

Notes

1 An earlier version of this chapter was published as Wagenaar, H. (2012), 'Dwellers on the Threshold of Practice: Ambivalence and inconsistency in the interpretivism of Bevir and Rhodes', *Critical Policy Studies*, 6(1): 85–99; it is used here with the kind permission of the editors of Critical Policy Studies.
2 Conversely, actors also engage in change without urgent pressures to the system, simply because some policy entrepreneur formulates a policy doctrine that promises major improvements.
3 This term was suggested by Noam Cook. Interestingly, the retroactive nature of political science and policy analysis applies both to traditional empiricist as well as 'postmodern' interpretive analysis (Wagenaar, 2011: 295).
4 The idea is hardly new and has been articulated, as Cook (2008) points out, in sociotechnical systems theory during and after the Second World War. As he says:

> (T)he key idea was, for a given task, to see both devices and people as a functioning unit, and to apply this perspective to the conception, design, application and assessment of what was then taken to be a socio-technical system.
>
> (2006: 3)

Scholars working in the Actor–Network Theory tradition push this observation into a rare metaphysical realm, however, by giving equal treatment to human and non-human actors in analysing the composition of the world. They argue the world is semiotically 'assembled' in ever-shifting relation between people (and their symbolic renderings of the world) and materiality (Callon, 1986; Latour, 1987). The difference with sociotechnical systems theory is that, in its urge to dispel any anthropocentric connotations, Actor–Network Theory poses a complete symmetry or interchangeability between the human and material realm. I believe that this is an untenable position as human agents are appreciably different from material agents in that they exhibit intentionality (see also Pickering, 1995: 15).
5 See also Wagenaar (2011: 100) for a further elaboration of this point.
6 In their 2003 book, BR are critical of the famous study on 'everyday makers' by Bang and Sørensen (1999). They argue that ethnographic analysis alone fails to capture the force of tradition, either at a historical moment in time or in a particular culture. Interpretive analysis of governance should also include historical and comparative analysis. Bang and Sørensen's micro-analysis of Nørrebro prevents them from seeing the activist reputation – call it tradition – of this district, even within a society that is itself famous for its tradition of high levels of citizen participation and consensual modes of conflict resolution in local governance networks. I do not disagree, but Bang and Sørensen did exactly what BR exhort us to do: connect individual behaviours with the larger context of beliefs in which this behaviour is embedded. What BR fail to see is that Bang and Sørensen's careful ethnographic research allows them to challenge traditional disciplinary categories. The Everyday Makers seem to be oblivious to the reach of local officers and city administrators. They operate outside political belief systems. Yet, they are a force in Copenhagen city politics. Politics, as a conceptual category, took on a new meaning, as an integral part of everyday life (Wagenaar, 2011: 100).

References

Adler, E. and Pouliot, V. (2011) 'International Practices', *International Theory*, 3(1): 1–36.

Allen, B. (1993) *Truth in Philosophy*, Cambridge, MA: Harvard University Press.

Bang, H. P. and Sørensen, E. (1999) 'The Everyday Maker: A new challenge to democratic governance,' *Administrative Theory and Praxis*, 21(3): 325–41.

Bennett, J. (2010) *Vibrant Matter: A political ecology of things*, Durham, NC: Duke University Press.

Bevir, M. (1999) *The Logic of the History of Ideas*, Cambridge, UK: Cambridge University Press.

Bevir, M. and Rhodes, R. A. W. (2003) *Interpreting British Governance*, London: Routledge.

Bevir, M. and Rhodes, R. A. W. (2006) *Governance Stories*, London: Routledge.

Bevir, M. and Rhodes, R. A. W. (2010) *The State as Cultural Practice*, Oxford: Oxford University Press.

Callon, M. (1986) 'Some Elements of a Sociology of Translation: Domestication of the scallops and the fishermen of St Brieuc Bay' in J. Law (ed.), *Power, Action and Belief: A new sociology of knowledge?*, London: Routledge & Kegan Paul, pp. 196–233

Cook, S. D. N. (2008) 'Design and Responsibility: The interdependence of natural, artifactual, and human systems', in P. E. Vermaas, P. Kroes, A. Light, and S. A. Moore (eds), *Philosophy and Design: From engineering to architecture*, Dordrecht: Springer, pp. 259–27.

Cook, S. D. N. and H. Wagenaar (2012) 'Navigating the Eternally Unfolding Present: Toward an epistemology of practice', *The American Review of Public Administration* 42(1): 3–38.

Dewey, J. (1991) Experience and Education. In J. A. Boydston (ed), *The Later Works of John Dewey, Volume 13 1938-39*, Carbondale, IL: Southern Illinois University Press, pp. 1–62.

Dewey, J. (1980 [1916]) *The Middle Works of John Dewey, Volume 9, 1899–1924: Democracy and education, 1916*, edited by J. A. Boydston, Carbondale, IL: Southern Illinois University Press.

Dewey, J. (2008) *The Later Works of John Dewey, Volume 2*, 1925–1953, edited by J. A. Boydston, Carbondale, IL: Southern Illinois University Press.

Engeström, Y. (1996) 'Developmental Studies of Work as a Testbench of Activity Theory: The case of primary-care medical work', in S. Chaiklin and J. Lave (eds), *Understanding Practice: Perspectives on activity and context*, Cambridge, UK: Cambridge University Press, pp. 64–104.

Engeström, Y. (2000) 'Activity Theory as a Framework for Analysing and Redesigning Work', *Ergonomics*, 43(7): 960–74.

Fay, B. (1996) *Contemporary Philosophy of Social Science: A multicultural approach*, Oxford: Blackwell.

Franklin, A. (2008) 'A Choreography of Fire: A posthumanist account of Australians and eucalypts', in A. Pickering and K. Guzik (eds), *The Mangle in Practice: Science, society, and becoming*, Durham, SC: Duke University Press.

Hacking, I. (1983) *Representing and Intervening: Introductory topics in the philosophy of natural science*, Cambridge: Cambridge University Press.

Hildebrand, D. L. (2003) *Beyond Realism and Antirealism: John Dewey and the neopragmatists*. Nashville, TN: Vanderbilt University Press.

Jay, M. (2005) *Songs of Experience: Modern American and European variations on a universal theme*, Berkeley, CA: University of California Press.

Latour, B. (1987) *Science in Action: How to follow scientists and engineers through society*. Cambridge, MA: Harvard University Press.

Lipsky, M. (1980) S*treet Level Bureaucracy: Dilemmas of the individual in public services*, New York: Russell Sage Foundation.

Marsh, D. (2011) 'The New Orthodoxy: The differentiated polity model', *Public Administration*, 89(1): 32–48.

Maynard-Moody, S. and Musheno, M. (2003) *Cops, Teachers, Counselors: Stories from the front lines of public service*, Ann Arbor, MI: University of Michigan Press.

McAnulla, S. (2006) 'Critical Realism, Social Structure and Political Analysis: A reply to Bevir and Rhodes', *British Politics*, 1(3): 404–12.

Moulaert, F., Swyngedouw, E., Martinelli, F., and Gonzalez, S. (eds) (2010) *Can Neighbourhoods Save the City? Community development and social innovation*, London: Routledge.

Nicolini, D. (2013) *Practice Theory, Work and Organization: An introduction*, Oxford: Oxford University Press.

Oliver, J. E. (2000) 'City Size and Civic Involvement in Metropolitan America'. *The American Political Science Review*, 94(2): 361–73.

Orlikowski, W. J. (2007) 'Sociomaterial Practices: Exploring technology at work', *Organization Studies*, 28(9): 1435–48.

Pickering, A., (1995) *The Mangle of Practice: Time, agency and science*, Chicago, IL: The University Of Chicago Press.

Pickering, A. and Guzik, K. (eds) (2008) *The Mangle in Practice: Science, society and becoming*, Durham, SC: Duke University Press.

Rhodes, R. (1997) *Understanding Governance: Policy networks, governance, reflexivity and accountability*, Buckingham, UK: Open University Press.

Schatzki, T. R. (1996) *Social Practices: A Wittgensteinian approach to human activity and the social*, Cambridge: Cambridge University Press.

Schön, D. A. and Rein, M. (1994) *Frame Reflection: Toward the resolution of intractable policy controversies*, New York: Basic Books.

Smith, M. J. (2008) 'Re-centring British Government: Beliefs, traditions and dilemmas in political science', *Political Studies Review*, 6(2): 143–54.

Wagenaar, H. (2004) 'Knowing the Rules: Administrative work as practice', *Public Administration Review*, 64 (November/December): 643–56.

Wagenaar, H. (2011) *Meaning in Action: Interpretation and dialogue in policy analysis*, Armonk, NY: Routledge .

Wagenaar, H. (2012) 'Dwellers on the Threshold of Practice: The interpretivism of Bevir and Rhodes', *Critical Policy Studies*, 6(1): 85–99.

Wagenaar, H. and Cook, S. D. N. (2003) 'Understanding Policy Practices: Action, dialectic and deliberation in policy analysis', in M. Hajer and H. Wagenaar (eds), *Deliberative Policy Analysis: Understanding governance in the network society*, Cambridge: Cambridge University Press, pp. 139–71.

Wagenaar, H. and Duiveman, R. (2011) 'De Kwaliteit van een Stadswijk: Good Governance door stedelijke daadkracht' [Trans. The Quality of Neighborhood; Good governance through civic capacity], in F. Hendriks and G. Drosterij (eds), *De zucht naar goed bestuur in de stad: Lessen uit een weerbarstige werkelijkheid*, The Hague: Boom/ Lemma, 63–78.

Wagenaar, H. and Hartendorp, R. (2000) 'Oedipus in the Welfare Office', in H. Wagenaar (ed.), *Government Institutions: Effects, changes and normative foundations*, Dordrecht: Kluwer Academic Press, pp. 147–77.

150   *H. Wagenaar*

Wagenaar, H. and Specht, M. (2010) *Geëngageerd Bewonerschap. Bewonersparticipatie in Drie Europese Steden.* [Engaged Residents: Citizen participation in three European cities], The Hague: Nicis Institute.

Wagenaar, H., Vos, J., Balder, C., van Hemert, B. (2015) 'Overcoming Conflicting Logics of Care and Justice: Collaborative innovation in dealing with habitual offenders in the Netherlands', in A. Agger, B. Damgaard, A. Hagedorn Krogh, E. Sørensen (eds), *Collaborative Governance and Public Innovation in Northern Europe.* Bentham Science. Available: http://ebooks.benthamscience.com/book/9781681080130/chapter/130082/.

Whittington, R. (2006) 'Completing the Practice Turn in Strategy Research', *Organization Studies*, 27(5): 613–34.

8 The Inadequacy of Interpretivism

Explaining Britain's Failure to 'Number the People'

Perri 6 and Christine Bellamy

This chapter takes issue with two sentences in Bevir's and Rhodes's recent work which crystallise the central claims of interpretivism. They declare that '[a]ny variable other than the beliefs and desires of a relevant actor can do explanatory work only if it is unpacked as beliefs and desires' and 'we reject the idea that other causal logics apply to human beliefs and actions' (Bevir and Rhodes, 2010: 68; see also Bevir, 1999). While we agree with Bevir and Rhodes that interpreting beliefs and ideas is an important, even central, task of social science, we argue that, by itself, it offers an insufficient and unsatisfying explanatory strategy. Rather, we use a case study to show that beliefs and desires cannot be satisfactorily explained *without* looking beyond them to the circumstances which make them intelligible, and that there is more in the causal links between thought and action than reasons and justifications.

Bevir and Rhodes charge those who disagree with their claims with modernism, institutionalism, structuralism, and foundationalism. We have proudly proclaimed that we hold these positions (for example, Bellamy *et al.*, 2008; 6, 2011, 2014a), and have offered explicit methodological arguments in their defence (6 and Bellamy, 2012). We therefore take grave offence at Bevir's and Rhodes's assertions (2010, for example) that we hold them unthinkingly, from 'lingering' adherence to out of date methodologies or because we are 'bewitched' by metaphors. We especially have refuted (6 and Bellamy, 2012) the accusation that these positions are necessarily 'positivist', even of a 'lukewarm' kind (Bevir and Rhodes, 2003: 45). Like many scholars working on British government (Bellamy, 2011), we use a realist approach. Positivism and realism are distinct philosophical positions, and each has respectable credentials. Bevir and Rhodes should not be allowed to elide them, even for polemical effect. Moreover, realism is not to be conflated with 'critical realism', the only form that Bevir and Rhodes discuss, despite the fact that realism, in various forms, is probably the mainstream position in the philosophy of the social sciences.

We have justified our realist methodology elsewhere, and rebutted the various anti-realist arguments put forward in the philosophy of social sciences (6 and Bellamy, 2012), and there is no need to do either of these things again here. Rather, our purpose is to draw on realist methodology to explore what counts as a credible explanation of civil servants' policymaking work, by considering an empirical case in the history of British public administration, namely, the decisions in the 1960s secretly to draft and then to bury a green (i.e. consultation) paper proposing a single identifying number for each person in the UK, to facilitate linkage of personal records. Our aim is to show how the interpretation of desires and beliefs can be harnessed to a more powerful and satisfying explanatory strategy than is offered by Bevir and Rhodes.

The Inadequacy of Interpretivist Explanation: A Realist Critique

Pointing to politicians' beliefs and desires – for example, their adherence to specific economic doctrines or their interpretation of polling evidence about which policies would find most electoral support – can certainly contribute to explaining their attitudes, say, to the use of quantitative easing in response to economic recession. So, too, can their affiliations to broad 'traditions' of ideas, such as neo-liberalism. But such explanations are hardly ever complete. Many types of factor encourage or constrain particular beliefs and desires, and help to explain people's actions or decisions. Most obvious are external events, such as half-expected currency crises in the eurozone or worse-than-expected unemployment statistics. Then there are contextual constraints, such as those imposed by limited fiscal resources. Realists may agree with interpretivists that beliefs and desires specify the significance of particular events and constraints, and that statistics are calculated using concepts which result from processes of social construction. But, more fundamentally, they want to know, too, why, from the vast mess of potential beliefs and desires, people settle for, or disagree about, the ones that they do. To answer this important question, we reject methodological *individualism* to assert the importance of *social* relations, especially those of an informal kind, and of the ways in which they are institutionalised, in explaining people's beliefs and desires. Elsewhere, we have shown that the causal effects of social institutions lie not so much in directly determining the content of beliefs and desires as in encouraging particular 'styles of thought', by which we mean a tendency to adopt particular ways, rather than others, of looking at the world (6, 2011, 2014a; see also Douglas, 1986). In the case presented here, divergent, but institutionally framed, *styles* of judgement led policymakers to adopt very different ways of classifying problems and of assessing opportunities, imperatives, and constraints.

Bevir's and Rhodes's accounts of life in the British civil service are less free from structuralist explanation than they claim. Their version of interpretivism acknowledges the influence of other people on a person's beliefs and desires, both informally and by overt persuasion, by recognising 'intersubjective' sources of beliefs and desires (for example, 2003, 2006). But it is unclear whether their framing of 'intersubjectivity' is sufficiently capacious to recognise how the cultivation of social relationships, whether among acquaintances or among members of well-established informal 'clubs', professions, or occupational groups, encourage particular kinds of belief or desire. They speak of the 'common beliefs' of civil servants, and their explanation of how people acquire occupational norms – the 'framework of the acceptable' (2006: chapter 7) –

appears to acknowledge socialisation processes. They also write about the 'features' and 'failings' of the 'patterns of rule' within which civil servants work, and even bring themselves to write about 'the state', although their caveat that it is a 'family resemblance category' (2010: 93) implies that it somehow does not count as a social institution. Bevir and Rhodes (2010: 81–100) accept that 'structure' is a useful metaphor for the patterning of social life, but claim that 'emergent structures are better understood as practices'. They also acknowledge that 'practices – or at least the actions of others – can constrain the effects, and so the effectiveness of an action' (Bevir and Rhodes, 2010: 76), but nevertheless insist that 'practices do not constrain the beliefs people might come to hold and so the actions they might attempt to perform' (Bevir and Rhodes, 2010: 76). And they explain that 'traditions' change and may even be reinvented when they are confronted by 'major challenges' and 'cease to work' (2010: 160), and that the resulting dilemmas often reflect changes in 'material circumstances' (2003: 41). It would be tempting, in the spirit of Bevir's and Rhodes's strictures on other political scientists, to accuse them of an unthinking realism, if they were not so anxious to hedge it with so many 'get-out' qualifications. Instead, as Smith points out (2008), their denial of the causal effects of social structure and other constraints, and their insistence that such factors must always be reduced to beliefs and desires (see Bevir and Rhodes, 2006a), leads their attempts at explanation – even of the 'humanistic' kind they seek – to collapse into a tautological mire, in which beliefs and desires form both the beginning and the end, the purpose and the means of social scientific explanation.

Bevir's and Rhodes's insistent, yet hedged-about denial of institutional explanations stems from their methodologically individualistic claim that taking social structures seriously amounts to their 'reification', and that using social institutions to explain beliefs, desires, and traditions involves a 'deterministic' logic:

> Mechanisms and processes ... are treated as having objective content divorced from specific times and places ... [I]institutionalists' ... explanations ... rely on the abstract logic of the mechanism or process ... [which is] not historical because their operation is reduced to an abstract logic. It is not contingent on the particular beliefs and actions of people at a particular time.
>
> (2010: 77)

This is a parody of the institutionalist position: it tilts at a straw man. First, it elides the social scientific search for causal explanation with the use of research designs that privilege parsimony and generality over other design criteria. But, as we have shown elsewhere (6 and Bellamy, 2012), most scholars who seek to go beyond establishing associations between explanatory and outcome variables to understanding the causal mechanisms linking them, tend to favour case-based designs specifically concerned with how exactly these mechanisms work. Second, a recent survey shows that, despite Bevir's and Rhodes's frequent claim that the study of British government is bedevilled by tendencies to abstraction, the most commonly used design for empirical research is a case-based one which places a great deal of emphasis on local, idiosyncratic circumstances to explain changing governmental practices or policies (Bellamy, 2011). Indeed, our criticism of this work lies in its unwillingness on such grounds to advance general theoretical claims. The challenge is to engage in useful, discriminating and explanatory abstraction, not to eschew it. This brings us to our third objection to Bevir's and Rhodes's parody of institutionalism – namely, their disingenuous refusal to acknowledge that their own version of interpretivist explanation depends, just as much as structuralist explanations, on an 'abstract logic'. 'Beliefs' and 'desires' are no less abstract than 'social structures', and are not ontologically privileged above them. The explanatory relationship of beliefs to actions is neither less nor more 'deterministic' than that of social relations to (for example) thought styles. It is dogma of the purest kind to insist that beliefs and intentions are to be taken seriously in social scientific explanation but institutionalised social relations are not.

Bevir's and Rhodes's dogma seems plausible only because it is bolstered by another 'straw man' assertion: that the 'modernist empiricism' used by other political scientists, and specifically their willingness to ascribe causal effects to factors or structures beyond people's subjective mental and intersubjective social lives, amounts to 'positivism', to the claim that external structures and factors lead by 'abstract logic' directly to actions, and thus to outcomes, without passing through actors' minds (see Bevir and Rhodes, 2006b). This is a fundamental misreading: most empirical political science in the UK is realist, not positivist. Realists hold, with interpretivists, that events, imperatives, and constraints do not, in this sense, have independent agency, and, moreover, that they can rarely, if ever, be the subject of 'positive' knowledge. We cannot observe a constraint or interview an institution, any more than we can measure a 'web of belief'. So we interview people to find out how they are affected by an institution or comply with, resist or cope with an event or constraint, or we undertake detailed ethnographic observations of their practices or search archival sources for clues about how they categorise imperatives, problems, and opportunities. We agree that this is, essentially, an interpretive process, and that interpretation is thus a necessary element in social scientific inquiry (6 and Bellamy, 2012). But it is not a sufficient one. Realists reject the interpretivist claim that we cannot know about anything beyond people's subjective beliefs and desires, along with the positivist claim that we cannot know about anything we cannot directly measure or observe. Rather, just as pollsters use data obtained from sampling to make *statistical inferences* about the voting intentions of whole electorates, realists use the patterns discovered in such evidence to make *explanatory inferences* about the causal significance of external events and factors, and to build theories about the ways in which the structuring of social life influences how actors respond to them in forming intentions and decisions. By contrast, Bevir's and Rhodes's approach prompts, but cannot address, the most interesting questions about social life. For example, what factors constrain and encourage new beliefs and desires, in what kinds of social context? Are 'webs of belief' articulated and modified in the same ways under different 'patterns of rule' or in the context of other social practices? In holding that traditions are invented or modified when old ones are challenged, Bevir and Rhodes identify an important change mechanism. Yet their restricted methodology inhibits them from systematically building satisfying theories to describe and explain how it works. By denying that mental life is ever to be explained by reference to material constraints and events and to the mediation of social institutions, interpretivism provides a poor account of what is valuable in interpretation, and, moreover, offers a restricted and unsatisfying strategy for case-based research.

To illustrate our argument, we present a study of fraught attempts over two decades by British civil servants to build an acceptable case for a single identifying number for each individual, so that personal data in government's administrative files could be linked. A green paper, provisionally entitled *People and Numbers* was eventually drafted in 1969, but Prime Minister Harold Wilson judged it too sensitive to publish. As many officials suspected at the time, blocking that initiative was to have important repercussions in British public administration throughout succeeding decades. The absence of a unique, reliable personal identifier constrained applications of information technology in health and social security; it raised barriers to joined-up government more generally; and it seriously restricted the scope of official statistics about social mobility, neighbourhood deprivation and migration. Nevertheless, academic histories of the British 'information state' and identity cards have hardly noticed this episode (but see Agar, 2003: 353–5), although Philip Redfern, chief statistician at the Department of Education and Science (DES) in the 1960s, has alluded to it (for example, 1989, 1990, 2004) and H. O. Dovey (1986), a former Treasury official, wrote briefly on the 1950s background. In the 1950s and 1960s, a population numbering scheme seemed to offer important opportunities and benefits. This initiative failed because it presented considerable difficulties and risks. Officials disagreed about the nature and significance of both benefits and risks. As well as its intrinsic interest, this case therefore offers a rich opportunity to explore how key actors came to adopt very different positions on this sensitive issue. It will show, too, that we cannot achieve a satisfactory explanation of these positions without invoking factors and constraints which cannot sensibly be reduced to individuals' beliefs and desires. Bevir and Rhodes might expect that structuralist critics would seek to explain them by reference to departmental interests of a more-or-less enduring kind, but we show that officials from the same departments sometimes interpreted these interests differently, and that their interpretations were sometimes unstable. Nor can they be satisfactorily explained by Bevir's and Rhodes's concepts of 'rationalities', 'narratives', or 'traditions'. Rather, we argue that a satisfying explanation needs to take account of the informal institutions which ordered these officials' positions by cultivating distinct and divergent 'thought styles'.

In presenting this case in the history of the 'information state' we need, first, to point out that any reference in the 1950s and early 1960s to a formed concept of, let alone a coherent normative set of beliefs about, 'data protection' would be anachronistic. The concept of 'privacy' was in use, especially in the legal system where there was a statutory right to private life not invaded, for example, by the press. The courts also recognised a common law of 'confidentiality'. But neither notion had yet led to established principles capable of regulating the processing of personal data by corporations or government. Some public services – especially personal and business taxation, social insurance, and health – had developed departmental or professional rules to protect the confidentiality of personal records. But the narratives sustaining them spoke mainly to instrumental needs to establish the trust necessary to ensure popular compliance with bureaucratic or professional routines (which was widely assumed in Whitehall to be somewhat fragile) rather than to ethical imperatives, let alone to broader traditions of political ideas. We will see from this case that, by the mid- to late 1960s, the landscape was beginning to change, in that official discussion of common numbers was forced to acknowledge an increasingly influential political and media narrative about the dangers of databanks and dossiers. This narrative was founded, in part, in ideas generated outside the UK (see Westin, 1967) and was promoted domestically by a high profile campaign launched in 1968 by the National Council for Civil Liberties (NCCL). But papers in The National Archives (TNA) show that, although officials were forced to recognise its growing political power, most did not substantively engage with it on an ideational level, but sought only to dull the impact of press and pressure group activity upon their policy options.

We begin with the context in which aspirations for common identifying numbers arose.

The Common Number Proposal, 1949–53[1]

The origins of our case can be conveniently traced to 1949, to the recommendations of an inter-departmental committee under Sir Nicholas de Villiers which examined how government might manage without the wartime national register (NR) which was fast becoming unacceptable in peacetime. The committee concluded that the NR's functions were necessary to good public administration, but that most could be performed, albeit less well, by national insurance (NI) records. These records covered the population of most interest to agencies which needed to identify or trace people, namely, the working-age male population. Because employers annually renewed employees' NI cards, they also held more-or-less up-to-date addresses.

The recommendation reflected the Treasury's view that the new welfare state's burgeoning administrative functions would generate costly proliferations of large-scale records systems unless departments were compelled to rationalise them. In particular, Treasury officials were resisting Ministry of Health (MH) plans to create a central register of patients on general practitioners' lists. If one were needed (which they doubted), it should be combined with that for NI. All British personal records systems depend on identifying numbers, because common names recur frequently and people often change spellings or use diminutives or alternatives. A common NI/NHS register would therefore require a common NI/NHS number. But there were three difficulties. First, these records covered different populations. NHS records covered everyone from cradle to grave. But children, and (in the early 1950s) most retired people and married women had no NI number. Second, NI and NHS numbers had different purposes.

NHS numbers (which were the same as the NR number) were issued when births were registered, and included alphabetical codes for date and place of registration, to facilitate the General Register Office's (GRO's) compilation of population statistics. The NI number was shared with employers, and, in accord with Ministry of NI confidentiality rules, did not carry personal information, coded or otherwise. It had also been designed to be as short as possible, to reduce labour costs and transcription errors in annually updating some 30 million contribution accounts. The third problem was that doctors' lists inherited from pre-NHS days were in a poor condition. Many entries had no number at all. A significant proportion was redundant or duplicated, because patients were not deleted when they died or joined another list. Therefore, the number of patients nominally on doctors' lists inflated steadily: this mattered because doctors were paid *per capita*. There was no systematic way of updating addresses. In 1953, an experiment at Ministry of NI's Records Branch in Newcastle found that, in consequence, in a high proportion of cases, it was impossible to match a person's NHS record to his NI record, making a merger of the two systems difficult and costly. The MH continued to insist, from experience of administering health insurance before 1948, that the only way to check inflation in doctors' lists was to require all changes to be transacted through a central patient register. After protracted discussions, the Treasury eventually agreed that the former national register at Southport be converted into a NHS central register (NHSCR), to be run by the GRO on behalf of the MH. Except for regular queries in Parliament about the apparent anomaly of maintaining both Newcastle and Southport, the matter rested there, though no one believed it had gone away.

Merging NI/NHS numbers: The Issue Resurrected, 1963–65[2]

In March 1964, Miss G. M. Jones, Assistant Secretary in charge of statistics at (what had become) the Ministry of Pensions and National Insurance (MPNI) discovered from contacts in the MH that the numbers issue was reviving. Jones was also aware of growing interest among medical researchers in techniques for linking medical and administrative records, as their focus shifted from controlling infectious diseases to understanding social, environmental, and occupational causes of degenerative diseases. She was not surprised when the Occupational Health Committee of the Medical Research Council (MRC) formally asked MH to consider a common number scheme, to facilitate research into occupational causes of morbidity by linking NHS and NI records. In April 1964, Dr Richard Benjamin, MH's Chief Statistician, invited other departments, including MPNI, to discuss the MRC's request.

In the previous month, Francis Rooke-Matthews, the assistant secretary in charge of the NHS Central Register at the GRO, had warned MH that the current series of NHS numbers would soon run out. This, Jones believed, created an opportunity for MPNI to negotiate an acceptable NHS/NI common number. She therefore called a meeting of MPNI's Organisation and Methods (O&M) and Automatic Data Processing (ADP) specialists, and also invited senior managers from Newcastle. They emphasised the practical constraints on the format of a common number, by insisting that the automation of NI administration, then being planned, would be prohibitively expensive if the number was composed of more than eight characters, or included more than two alphabetical ones. But they believed that this format could accommodate the GRO's statistical requirements. Jones and Rooke-Matthews duly reported this conclusion to Benjamin's meeting. And, after much detailed numerical analysis – involving such arcane issues as how to make combinations of characters memorable and to avoid numbers that can be mistaken for letters, especially ones that suggest rude words – they produced a format providing codes for year, quarter, and district (but not sub-district) of birth, within MPNI's constraints. Jones also accepted the emphatic advice of colleagues responsible for NI policy (reinforced by the Newcastle experiment in 1953) that MPNI should not accept any conversion plan which assumed that people could accurately quote their NHS number and be reliably matched to their records by this means alone. This, they believed, ruled out a once-for-all conversion to a new number. They favoured, instead, a gradual conversion by which new numbers would be issued to successive population cohorts at birth or at 15 years. Colleagues at Newcastle protested, however, about the impact on their automation plans, warning that the conversion process would cost about £50,000 a year, mainly for extra clerical support to deal with mismatching errors. They were also concerned about disrupting the Inland Revenue's preparations for automating the pay as you earn (PAYE) income tax scheme, which was to use NI numbers.

Unlike officials responsible for statistics in other departments, Jones did not work in a separate technical branch, but in the policy branch concerned with national insurance. MPNI was a strongly hierarchical and integrated department, in which senior officials shared an over-riding focus on maintaining the integrity of their large-scale clerical operations. These factors enabled her quickly to establish an agreed line to take in inter-departmental negotiations, and she maintained it consistently and unflaggingly over the next few years.

By contrast, MH's responsibilities were more diverse, and internal opinions on common numbers divided. In November 1963, the Permanent Secretary commissioned a review of MH's case against a common NI/NHS number in the light of new automation technologies. He was informed that the issue had already been revivified by a Treasury O&M study, which was revealing continuing inflation in doctors' lists, resulting, the Treasury argued, from the inefficiency of the Executive Councils (ECs) that administered them locally. Senior officials, especially A. R. W. Bavin, Under Secretary in charge of ECs, initially took the view that the core issue was the future of ECs, and that the Treasury should be discouraged from linking it to the wider issue of numbers and registers. But, as interest in common numbers grew during 1964, they felt unable to stand aside from inter-departmental discussions. Their main goal was to retain the NHS Central Register, without which, their own analysis indicated, the inflation of patient numbers in doctors' lists would probably be some 300,000 more than the 89,000 officially estimated in 1964. They recognised, too, that this goal was becoming harder to defend, because of substantial capital investment being made in MPNI's Newcastle site. But they also came, reluctantly, to recognise that it might be more effectively secured by showing interest in a common number, than by giving in to Treasury's continuing insistence that an NHS central register would be redundant if the ECs were efficient. They also believed, however, that it would be difficult to justify a common number on efficiency grounds, and that resonances with the wartime national register made it politically sensitive. For these reasons – and despite Benjamin's initiative on medical record linkage – they were unwilling to lead inter-departmental discussions, and were content to let them develop slowly, to Benjamin's frustration. Unlike Jones, Benjamin worked in a separate Statistics Branch and was only marginally involved in departmental policy discussions. But he was the main line of formal communication from MRC to MH. He therefore pressed record linkage and common numbers enthusiastically, railing against delays imposed by Rooke-Matthews's and Jones's work, and complaining bitterly that the GRO's statistical requirements were imposing unreasonable constraints. The medical statistician in Benjamin's branch M. A. Heasman and the Ministry's Chief Medical Officer's staff also pressed the advantages of record linkage, though with gentle warnings that bounds should be set on what records could be linked: 'As a private citizen, I should wonder where it will end' (Heasman to Bavin, 9 Nov. 64, MH153/361).

Advice from the GRO was also ambivalent. In the 1960s, the GRO was a subsidiary department of MH, and the Registrar-General Michael Reed was responsible to the Minister of Health. Reed had been a generalist administrator in MH, not a career statistician. His views on this subject were more lukewarm than those of his predecessors, two of whom had strongly advocated peacetime national registration (Mallet, 1917, 1929; Agar, 2003; Higgs, 2004; Elliot, 2006; Sir Sylvanus Vivian's official *History of National Registration*, which made a case, remains unpublished). Some of Reed's subordinates believed that he should push for the restitution of the NR, on the ground that it would lead to efficiencies in NHS administration of at least £10 million a year. But the manager of the GRO's Southport installation was sceptical. He pointed out that this calculation assumed that patients would be able to quote their NHS number reliably, and queried whether MH officials could enforce its use as a condition of receiving treatment. In July 1964, Rooke-Matthews also warned senior MH officials that the MPNI would refuse to apply a common number to family allowances and pensions, which then used different numbers. Moreover, the Scottish Registrar-General would not use it, because the birth codes would not fit the districts used in Scotland to register births. Reed viewed these as show-stopping constraints. He dismissed the case for common numbers as 'allowing a desire for tidiness to get out of hand' and advised Bavin that its advocates had failed to produce a case that would convince the Treasury. He and Bavin agreed that a once-for-all conversion to common numbers would require a prohibitively expensive special population enumeration, but failed to agree a common line on the wider issue. Bavin was therefore left to prepare a proposal for an inter-departmental study without involving Reed.

Bavin submitted his proposal to the Treasury in spring 1965, and was much relieved when Treasury O&M branch offered to lead it. But it was overtaken by events. The previous summer (1964), a report by the Central Statistical Office

(CSO) on educational statistics had endorsed a recommendation of the 1963 Robbins Report on higher education that a single record – and therefore a unique identifying number – be used throughout each person's educational career, to aid measurement of social mobility. During the winter of 1964–65, W. H. G. Harvey, head of automatic data processing at the DES, was commissioned to examine its feasibility. DES was also pressed by the Local Authorities Management Services and Computer Committee and the Institute of Municipal Treasurers and Accountants for a national numbering scheme, to support administrative automation in local government. So Harvey, too, urged the GRO and the Treasury to consider a common national number. In parallel, the CSO was asked by the new official Committee on Social Statistics to study record linkage, including the introduction of common numbers, in response to a recommendation of the Heyworth Committee on Social Studies for better co-ordination in social statistics (DES, 1965). The new Prime Minister Harold Wilson was also anxious about the weakness of social statistics as a foundation for his government's social policy. In May 1965, uncomfortably aware of its political difficulties and potential costs, the Treasury willingly ceded the common number issue to the CSO's more enthusiastic leadership.

In this phase of the case, we observe actors grappling with important administrative, financial and technical constraints, including those stemming from the incompatible purposes of the population numbering systems already used in government; the restricted facilities for processing and storing data associated with early office automation systems; spillover effects from the prospective automation of PAYE taxation; the different structure of registration districts in England and Scotland; and perverse effects of arrangements for remunerating GPs. All these must be understood in the context of growing financial burdens associated with the administration of the welfare state. There were objective bases for each of these constraints, which are not simply reducible to individuals' beliefs. As civil servants with formal responsibilities for official statistics, Benjamin, Jones, and Reed might be expected to have shared a common professional view of them, and their formal departmental and professional duties certainly defined which aspects they addressed. But there were clear differences in the ways in which they assessed them, and their degree of integration in, and control by, their respective departments mattered more than their shared technical interests in influencing their judgments. This social dynamic became more obvious in the next phase, when the issue was more clearly classified as one about official statistics.

Common Numbers: The CSO Review, 1965–67

In March 1965 the new inter-departmental Committee on Social Statistics began a study of common numbers, led from the CSO by one of its chief statisticians Harold Bishop who circulated a paper. After much intra- and inter-departmental correspondence, MH, MPNI, and the GRO all reaffirmed their positions, though none was comfortable about escalating the issue into a pan-government one. At MH, Benjamin worried, rightly, that it would become bogged down in inter-departmental disagreements. Staff in the Chief Medical Officer's office warned their senior policy colleagues that, whereas NI and NHS systems shared similar confidentiality rules, a common number that facilitated record linkage with a wider set of departments would raise major ethical issues for medics. Senior MH officials even considered briefly whether to pursue a common NI/NHS number independently of the CSO initiative. But eventually in January 1966 they settled for a defensive submission to Bishop, emphasising the critical importance of the NHS number and NHS Central Register not only in controlling doctors' lists but also for many NHS-wide administrative and financial purposes. MPNI, too, closed ranks. Jones's submission identified threats to departmental confidentiality rules in the casual elision, in Bishop's paper, of common numbers with record linkage, and warned him against working on such a 'powerful tool' as record linkage without first consulting ministers. She also complained strongly that the paper neglected the previous two years' work on a joint NI/NHS number. Jones mobilised support from Inland Revenue, GRO, and MH for her submission, and commissioned detailed explanations of the operation of the NI system, especially at Newcastle, to underline the administrative constraints on which the Jones/Rooke-Matthews numbering format had been based. She also arranged for Bishop's group to visit Newcastle in December 1965.

To the consternation of Jones, Rooke-Matthews, and the Newcastle management, the DES's representative, Philip Redfern, its chief statistician, used the visit vigorously to assert the case for an entirely new, synthetic number, on statistical rather than administrative grounds. Redfern was to become a leading advocate of a population register throughout the next four decades (for example, 1987, 1989, 2004). He argued strongly throughout the 1960s that a common number scheme should not be influenced by existing administrative systems, but should be based, rather, on a fresh enumeration of the population. Such radical purism, and his determination to refuse all compromise and to press his demands on departments which had important constraints and had already invested in extensive work, exhibits a thought style that could develop only in someone weakly integrated in departmental and inter-departmental policy discussions, and indeed the files show only infrequent discussions between him and DES's policy branches.

In May 1966, after extensive technical work and inter-departmental negotiations, Bishop informed Redfern that DES must use the NHS number, or the joint NI/NHS number, or else develop its own synthetic number: he had found no support among other departments for an entirely new common number. These three options were developed in Bishop's paper on *Departmental Needs for a Numbering System* which he circulated for successive rounds of comment in summer 1966 and early 1967. Later drafts reduced them to two options: Procedure P, which would allocate existing NI numbers to all children at 15, and Procedure Q which would allocate a new NI/NHS number to children at a much earlier age, by deriving the necessary codes from their birth certificates. After consulting Rooke-Matthews, Jones rejected Procedure Q because of the known difficulty of linking a person's birth registration number to their NI record and also rejected the use of a coded date of birth on confidentiality grounds. She commissioned an internal O&M study on implementing Procedure P. Harvey, DES's ADP specialist, by contrast, favoured Procedure Q on the obvious grounds that it would capture more children, more swiftly. But Harvey further argued that the resultant population index could replace the electoral roll, provided that a statutory duty was imposed on the whole population to notify changes of address. Redfern backed Harvey, arguing for a single national register of basic personal data for use by all government departments, and, rejecting both options P and Q, called again for a full, open-minded, 'scientific' investigation of all possible numbering schemes to secure the best, long-term solution. He also subsequently called for fresh examination of confidentiality rules, unconstrained by current rules. The GRO's response was guarded. Internal minutes conceded that a case could probably be made for a common number with limited application to NI and the NHS as a reasonable modification of existing practice, but that a new numbering system, for more or less universal use across public services, raised political issues that should be referred to ministers.

By the summer of 1967, then, Whitehall's discussion of common numbers had polarised. One cluster of officials, especially Jones, Bishop and the GRO's staff, prioritised the need to grapple with practical problems of accommodating (what they perceived as) strong technical, administrative, and financial constraints. Jones and Reed were also concerned about the political sensitivity of the issue, and some medical statisticians were worried about medical ethics. These people were therefore sceptical about the value of a common number and prioritised the management of operational and political risks. But Redfern, as a statistical radical, entertained no risks but those of failing to introduce the best possible scheme. Again we see that, while most of the leading players in this case had formal responsibilities for statistics and shared some aspects of a common technical 'rationality' (in Bevir's and Rhodes's sense of that word), there were different 'thought styles' at work. By early 1967, however, the debate moved on again, and the political aspects became more salient. Increasingly for civil servants, the issue became mired in very different judgements about how best to manage conflicting political concerns.

Common Numbers and a UK Population Register:
The Green Paper That Wasn't, 1967–69

The issue of common numbers was originally escalated to ministerial level because of growing anxieties about deficiencies in official social statistics (for example, House of Commons, 1966). In early 1967, at Harold Wilson's personal instigation, Professor Claus Moser was appointed to head the CSO, with a brief to create a government statistical service. Moser was an academic statistician, who had acted as statistical consultant to the Robbins Committee. He was a Whitehall 'irregular' without strong department loyalty or administrative experience, but had direct official access to ministers and shared friendships with some of them, including Richard Crossman. Unlike his predecessor Sir Harry Campion, who had struggled to progress the cause of social statistics beyond the official level, Moser also had support from a ministerial committee, the Statistics Policy Committee. Wilson himself attended its first meeting in April 1967. It featured a preview of the Jackson Committee's report on the government statistical service, which advocated a central statistics agency, the use of computerised databanks and more integrated data flows. Confidentiality was discussed but briefly. Although Moser subsequently offered to undertake a review of confidentiality practices, he several times deferred it as being less urgent than other statistical reforms, and, like Redfern, regarded it as an opportunity to loosen, rather than strengthen, departments' confidentiality rules. At least initially, Moser's appointment tilted discussions on common numbers toward greater scepticism about administrative and confidentiality constraints.

In July 1967, Bishop submitted his report on common numbers to Moser, with a note on unresolved issues. The report majored on benefits from linking administrative data, especially to meet the needs of educational statistics, but also to improve population statistics more widely by overcoming the limitations of census data and allowing statisticians to drill down into smaller geographical areas. Although Bishop emphasised that no numbering system could be universally applied across government, the report identified most large-scale administrative systems in government – the registration of birth, marriages, and deaths, the census, the NHS, NI, PAYE, education, and, possibly, driving licences – as potential users of common numbers. Technical work by Bishop, Jones and Rooke-Matthews on numbering formats and conversion schemes was relegated to appendices. Moreover, discussion of confidentiality appeared as an afterthought, with a statement that it might be unnecessary to test public opinion if common numbers were treated as 'a natural extension' of NI and NHS arrangements. While this draft was out for departmental comments, an interdepartmental group, including Bishop, Rooke-Matthews, and Harvey, attended an international symposium in Jerusalem on population registers and returned eager to spread the news that that the UK risked falling badly behind in this important development. On Moser's initiative, subsequent drafts of Bishop's paper included a proposal for a peacetime population register, and a formal proposal for a feasibility study was approved by the official-level Committee on Social Statistics in December 1967. In the traditions of his office, Reed was much more attracted by a population register than by common numbers and record linkage, but he and Rooke-Matthews were concerned about the NHS central register (which GRO managed) being converted into a de facto national register without formal political cover. Reed therefore insisted that the proposal be submitted to ministers. Jones's report to her colleagues of the meeting fretted about the practical difficulties of applying a common number to so many public services and of updating a population register, and noted that discussion of confidentiality was deferred.

Moser seems not to have regarded the issue as an urgent one. But, by early 1968, DES faced considerable pressure from the new Universities Central Council on Admissions, further education colleges and the General Certificate of Education examinations board for a common number for their proposed computer systems. Jones's proposal to issue NI numbers at 15, which Redfern had rejected, would have provided numbers for this population. Harvey was indeed in discussions with the (now) Ministry of Social Security, while Redfern consulted MH about using the NHS number. But Redfern and Harvey were reluctant to adopt a costly interim solution pending (what Redfern, as a consistent statistical radical, still regarded as) the inevitable introduction of a national number, and Redfern complained bitterly to Moser that the educational world alone seemed to understand the issue's urgency. Moser then put the issue formally on ice, while Redfern submitted an urgent proposal for inter-departmental work on a government-wide interim solution. But Moser became aware that Reed, and the new Director of Statistics at MH Wolf Rudoe, were worried that plans developed by MH to computerise EC administration of doctors' lists ignored both the NHS Central Register and medical record linkage. The Ministry of Transport inquired about using the NI number for their new central driver and vehicle licensing centre (the future Driver and Vehicle Licensing Agency), and the Home Office inquired how their work on modernising electoral registration would be affected by a common number. In May 1968, Moser therefore decided to take the issue off its ice, instructing his staff to help Reed draft a proposal to ministers. It went to the Statistics Policy Committee on 23 July signed by Moser, Reed, and the Scottish Registrar-General Jim Ford, but only after Kenneth Robinson, Minister of Health, and Crossman, who was taking charge of the soon-to-be-merged Department of Health and Social Security, had leaned on Willy Ross, the Scottish Secretary, who baulked at its political and staffing implications. The Committee agreed that the project would improve statistics but expressed concern about its political implications. In October 1968, the Cabinet's Home Affairs Committee decided to test public reaction by publishing a green paper. After discussions with ministers, Reed agreed to draft it.

Reed's task was unenviable. Of all the officials most directly involved, he was among the most sceptical, and, by 1968, the political sensitivities surrounding this issue could no longer be regarded as stemming only from unfocused unease about re-establishing something like the much-maligned national register. There was now a sustained and high-profile campaign focusing on the risks to privacy associated with just the kind of initiative the green paper would propose. In late 1966, the recommendation for a national data centre by a US Federal Government task force on official statistics (the Kaysen Report) elicited a strong privacy backlash, leading to much-publicised Congressional hearings during 1967. In the UK, extensive press coverage of threats to privacy from computerised databanks, fuelled subsequently by the NCCL campaign, was generating a string of private members bills and parliamentary questions. And Reed, unlike most of his colleagues, had some grasp of the substantive privacy issue. For example, in early 1967, he had insisted on calling an inter-departmental meeting to discuss the MRC's proposal for record linkage, following which he informed MRC that its proposal to establish permanent files, linking the medical records of the whole population, would not only be impractically expensive but would also contravene professional, statutory, and departmental confidentiality rules. Only ad hoc linkage for purposes specially approved at ministerial level should be permitted. Reed and Ford now pressed Moser to recognise that common numbers and record linkage raised political issues that were not simply figments of the overwrought imaginations of the press and NCCL, and advised him that the critical issue – which might require legislation – was whether information belonged to the government or department. Moser's reaction was that a population register was a bigger threat, because it allowed individuals to be traced. Record linkage for statistical purposes dealt only with aggregates, and his long-awaited confidentiality review would deal with confidentiality rules by removing many of them.

Reed's first draft of the green paper in April 1969 reflected Moser's approach: it dealt with the technical case, hardly mentioning confidentiality. Most people who read it thought it unpersuasive and disingenuous, and feared it would inflame rather than reassure public opinion. Reed's second draft, entitled *People and Numbers*, dealt explicitly with confidentiality but retained the focus on technical benefits. Predictably, Redfern complained that this draft was too diffident, that the privacy issues were well understood, and that the most urgent need was to understand the technical barriers to better population statistics. But the CSO's comments on it indicated a change of approach. Moser now asked that it foreground an inquiry into legal, technical, and administrative methods of protecting privacy. He and Bishop advocated sharper distinctions between record linkage for statistical and administrative purposes, and between common numbers and a population register. The latter, in particular, should be played down.

Moser's change of direction reflected his relative freedom from departmental baggage and his sensitivity to advice from the centre of government. During the spring of 1969, he and Reed met with Jean Nunn, Under Secretary at the Cabinet Office, and A. A. Creamer from the Civil Service Department. They were advised not to duck difficult issues – including the fact that a population register would include addresses – and to refrain from claiming that record linkage would be used only for statistical, and not for administrative, purposes. The green paper must show above all that the government was alive to the awkward problems. In June 1969, Nunn met permanent secretaries to discuss Reed's final draft. They agreed that it satisfied none of its audiences and risked inflaming public opinion, but failed to agree an approach to redrafting. Nunn eventually persuaded them to agree that a proposal for a technical study should be submitted to the relevant cabinet committee, along with one for a separate study of privacy protection, and complained to Sir Burke Trend, Cabinet Secretary, that the common number issue was taking flak because of a policy vacuum on the wider privacy issue.

An amended draft was circulated in early July 1969. Officials invited ministers to consider a parliamentary statement rather than a green paper, so that external interests, especially the NCCL, could be consulted at an early date. This suggestion also split opinion. Most statisticians and management services specialists (Moser, Bishop, Redfern, and Creamer) favoured a green paper because it would allow the technical issues to be fully explained. Most generalist administrators favoured a planted parliamentary question. On Crossman's authority, Moser's technical group began work during summer 1969, in advance of discussion at cabinet committee. However, in November, Wilson abruptly forbade further work on the issue, after Trend warned him that Home Secretary Calla-ghan would be forced to concede a public inquiry into privacy (the future Younger Committee) in response to Lord Windlesham's privacy bill. Trend sub-sequently agreed that Moser's technical study could continue, but this, too, was pulled in February 1970 when Wilson was forced to make another parliamentary statement. Trend wanted to exclude the public sector from the inquiry, to main-tain government's freedom to rationalise its increasingly complex records, and feared embarrassment if Moser's study became public knowledge.

In this period, then, we find key officials responding to ministerial ambitions for improving social statistics, while bringing increasingly divergent styles of thought to bear on handling the political sensitivities. Reed, Ford, and Jones regarded confidentiality as a substantive constraint on record linkage. Redfern, as a statistical purist, regarded the confidentiality problem as a largely spurious one, based on ignorance of statistical method, and of much lesser urgency than overcoming technical barriers to a grand scheme. Moser needed record linkage to deliver his statistical reforms, and initially adopted a similarly cavalier approach. But when Cabinet Office pressure led him, and his organisational location permitted him, to seek consensus, Redfern reproached him with exces-sive accommodation to unreasonable political sensitivities, just as Benjamin had earlier accused his colleagues in MH's policy branches of giving in to the GRO's unreasonable demands. By contrast with Jones, who occupied a similar role in the Ministry of Social Security but was actively involved in accommodating her department's administrative and financial constraints, Redfern showed hardly any concern with the costs and implementation of a scheme, even in education. And, although Registrar-General Reed renewed his predecessors' hopes for a population register, his generalist background and his continuing answerability to generalists at MH led him to acknowledge the administrative and technical problems with both common numbers and record linkage, and to seek political cover for a population register. Thus, we find four different thought styles at work among people who shared a technical interest in improving social statis-tics. They do not map directly onto formal roles or departmental interests, but follow the informal institutional location of these civil servants and weak or strong integration in, and weak or strong control by, their primary social institu-tional setting.

Conclusion

A Bevir–Rhodes account of this case would appeal to webs of beliefs and desires, which are reworked in response to subjective dilemmas, where those dilemmas are themselves the products of conflicts in beliefs. This account would yield a limited explanation of the politics of population numbers and registers in the 1950s and 1960s.

'Traditions', 'narratives', and 'webs of belief' do not help. For reasons pre-sented above, it is difficult to regard official beliefs about confidentiality, and especially data privacy, as reaching a threshold by which they might be con-sidered to form an articulated 'web' until after our period, let alone one related to a wider 'tradition' of ideas about relations between state and people. Most officials, such as Jones, who took confidentiality seriously in the 1960s, regarded it as a procedural concept made manifest in formal rules that constrained action, rather than as one capable of making wider normative sense of government's stewardship of personal data. A substantive, developed concept of 'privacy' is rarely explicit in the files, although it is sometimes implicit in such homespun comments as those of Dr Heasman we quoted above. Only Reed was beginning – tentatively – to raise questions in ways that, in the 1970s, were woven into a widely accepted set of data protection principles founded in a narrative about data privacy. And by the time that this was done, most of the relevant empirical claims about opportunities, difficulties and risks were firmly established, partly through the process described in this case.

Nor will Bevir's and Rhodes's notion of 'rationalities' explain the case. For Bevir and Rhodes (2010: 96–7), a 'rationality' is the technical framing of a situation – for example, one shared among an occupational group. Moser, Benjamin, Jones, Redfern, Rooke-Matthews, and Reed all carried formal responsibilities for official statistics, yet they were not driven exclusively by technical imperatives, and their attitude to common numbers varied from the gung-ho (Benjamin and Redfern), through the constructively measured (Jones) to the deeply sceptical (Reed).

Bevir and Rhodes would probably expect structuralists to emphasise 'departmental interests', but we believe this, too, is not an irreducible explanation. Budget maximisation theory, for example, might predict that the Ministry of National Insurance (later MPNI) would welcome the conversion of their NI records into a de facto national register, and that Reed would follow his predecessors as Registrar-General in strongly advocating a national register to be administered by the GRO. But we saw that, with few exceptions, official attitudes in both departments varied from the cautious to the strongly resistant, because officials weighed perceived threats to their operations more heavily than opportunities to grow bureaucratic empires. By contrast, Redfern's overoptimistic insistence on a 'scientific' solution led him to scorn Bishop's option P, which would have met DES's immediate needs for a number to administer public examinations and university admissions. Thus, the interesting question is not whether officials pursued departmental interests, but why they interpreted them as they did.

We conclude, therefore, that a Bevir-Rhodes approach to this case would fail to recognise three key factors that shaped perceptions and decisions, beyond individuals' beliefs and desires. First, we emphasise practical *constraints* stemming from the operational, technical, and financial conditions of British public administration in the 1960s. There were objective bases for each of these constraints, but they were not palpable to observation, and, like social researchers, officials had to make judgements about them from available evidence. Our argument is not that officials construed constraints with unyielding accuracy or that they necessarily all weighted them wisely. Nor do we argue that they were inherently impossible to overcome, or that they offered actors only the choices they made. Rather, we have shown that civil servants disagreed about such things.

Some constraints – such as confidentiality rules – were highly salient for some officials, but dismissed by others. Likewise, Bavin, Reed, and Jones were all exercised by the financial costs and operational problems involved in converting to a common number, but they never agreed how big they were or which procedures would minimise them, while Redfern was uninterested in them. Nevertheless, their judgments about these constraints were derived from inferences that were intelligible in the situations they occupied.

Second, people's location in *informal institutions* of social organisation – within their departments, in relation to their professions (statisticians, generalist policy-oriented civil servants) and previous career (the academic Moser, the ex-generalist Reed) – profoundly shaped their judgements about the salience, weighting, and significance of constraints, their willingness or otherwise to contemplate fallback positions, and their time horizons for decisions. For example, as an 'irregular' brought in from academic life by senior politicians to undertake particular reforms – which would doubtless enhance his wider professional reputation – Moser occupied a position in informal institutional ordering which was weakly socially integrated into any department, and weakly regulated by civil service structures: in short, he occupied a zone of individualistic institutional ordering. As we should expect, Moser was prepared to operate much more flexibly, first postponing and then addressing confidentiality issues by shifting the arguments for his feasibility study, aided, perhaps, by the slightly improving budgetary situation in summer 1968. By contrast, for other key officials, the whole process took place against the backdrop of the strongly articulated informal institutions of the higher civil service in the 1960s. Strong social integration combined with strong social regulation shaped the situation of generalist administrators, such as Bavin, and those less strongly tied to their technical profession, such as Jones. As we should expect, Jones proceeded by seeking to integrate colleagues' concerns into a departmental line that gave due weight to each but made none over-riding, and then pressed the line consistently and firmly. Her thought style was as cognitively integrated and constrained as her institutional position. By contrast, Redfern operated at some remove from the DES's policy branches, but he identified strongly with his technical profession and was left largely alone, except for his relations with Harvey, the ADP specialist, to champion a particular type of statistical ambition. As we should expect, his bunkered position led him to act like a sectarian, in calling for a comprehensive fresh start, in refusing to countenance fallback positions, and in becoming deeply reproachful when his dismissive attitude to constraints was not shared by others. By contrast again, we can observe the effects of informal ordering in the situation occupied by Reed. As a former generalist, he was not a member of the statistical profession, and as Registrar-General, occupied a weak power base vis-à-vis the great departments of state. As the civil servant responsible for what remained of the national register (now the NHSCR), he seems to have felt especially vulnerable to the NCCL and press campaigns. He came under ministerial instruction to draft a green paper, and was constrained by Moser to present the argument in a particular way, but was also strongly constrained by conflicting departmental claims and by the policy vacuum on the wider privacy issue. He exhibited the kind of sceptical, coping approach we should expect, as he worked through drafts, seeking, not very successfully, to make a coherent narrative from imperatives and constraints that he had little institutional power to force together.

We have seen that these informal institutions of social organisation did not cultivate among these actors (what might pass as) an explicit narrative or articulated set of beliefs about data privacy. However, the papers prepared by the CSO and MRC, and also the early drafts of the green paper, offered the kind of heroic narrative about the benefits of a population register and about (what we now call) data sharing and 'big data' that has since become all-too familiar to students of technological hubris. Indeed, its ambitions closely resemble those of recent reforms. But the most interesting questions are not about the content of this narrative, but about civil servants' styles of judgement: why did some actors commit enthusiastically to it, while others emphasised risks, and why did they arrive at such different judgements about opportunities and constraints? What matters about Redfern's approach is not so much his belief in the advantages of common numbers, which was shared, for example, with Jones, or in the lesser importance of confidentiality, which was similar to Moser's, but the sectarian intransigence with which he pursued his belief. He was as much aware of the technical, administrative, financial, and political constraints as his colleagues. But the explanation of his very different weighting of them is not primarily to be found either in an ideological tradition or narrative or in the interests of the DES, but in his location in the informal institutions of the civil service. And likewise, *mutatis mutandis*, for the other actors whose positions are described above.

These three forces – objective constraints, informal institutions, and the styles of thought (as opposed to worldviews, traditions, or narratives) used in the perception of those constraints – form a triangle of causal relations which are not simply epiphenomena of individuals' beliefs and desires, and which, together, provide a more convincing explanation of the policymaking process than can Bevir's and Rhodes's approach. Is this explanatory strategy modernist, foundationalist, institutionalist, and structuralist? Of course it is. But without intellectual machinery of this kind, we cannot satisfactorily understand this case. Elsewhere, we have developed the theoretical basis for our argument from the classic work in foundationalist modernism of Durkheim and Douglas (Bellamy *et al.*, 2008; Bellamy, 2011; 6, 2011, 2014a, 2014b). In this chapter, we have sought to show that it is precisely because this kind of explanation takes seriously ('reifies'?) some foundational social structures that it can capture the powerful ways in which beliefs and desires, and thus the decisions to which they lead, are shaped. In short, the two central claims in Bevir's and Rhodes's version of interpretivism, with which we began this chapter, provide poor guidance about what is valuable in interpreting actors' beliefs or what counts as a convincing explanation of them.

Notes

1 The sources for this section are files in TNA: CAB21/4354, MH 35/139, MH/153/361, PIN28/42, T222/154, T222/436–439, T222/700, T227/391.
2 The sources for the remaining sections are TNA: CAB139/560–3, CAB130/427, CAB139/566–7, CAB139/582–3, CAB 164/392, ED265/3, FD1/8307, MH135/139, MH153/360–1, PIN19/475, PIN28/42, PIN47/145, PREM13/3257, RG22/54, RG26/474, RG28/306, T227/4240.

References

6, P. (2011) *Explaining Political Judgement*, Cambridge: Cambridge University Press.
6, P. (2014a) 'Explaining Decision-making in Government: The neo-Durkheimian institutional framework', *Public Administration*, 92(3): 87–103.
6, P. (2014b) 'Unintended, Unanticipated or Unexpected Consequences of Policy and Surprises for Government: Understanding how bias and process shape causation – comparing British governments, 1959–74', *Public Administration*, 92(3): 673–91.
6, P. and Bellamy, C. A. (2012) *Principles of Methodology: Research design in social science*, London: Sage.
Agar, J. (2003) *The Government Machine: A revolutionary history of the computer*, Cambridge, MA: MIT Press.
Bellamy, C. A. (2011) 'The Whitehall Programme and After: Researching government in time of governance', *Public Administration*, 89(1): 78–92.
Bellamy, C. A., 6, P., Raab, C. D., Warren, A., and Heeney, C. (2008) 'Information-sharing and Confidentiality in Social Policy: Regulating multi-agency working', *Public Administration*, 86(3): 737–59.
Bevir, M. (1999) *The Logic of the History of Ideas*, Cambridge: Cambridge University Press.
Bevir, M. and Rhodes, R. A. W. (2003) *Interpreting British Governance*, London: Routledge.
Bevir, M and Rhodes, R. A. W. (2006a) 'Disaggregating Structures as an Agenda for Critical Realism', *British Politics*, 1(3): 397–403.
Bevir, M. and Rhodes, R. A. W. (2006b) 'Defending Interpretation', *European Political Science*, 5(1): 69–83.
Bevir, M. and Rhodes, R. A. W. (2006) *Governance Stories*, London: Routledge.
Bevir, M. and Rhodes, R. A. W. (2010) *The State as Cultural Practice*, Oxford: Oxford University Press.
Department of Education and Science (1965) *Report of the Committee on Social Studies*, Cmnd 2660, London: HMSO.
Douglas, M. (1986) *How Institutions Think*, London: Routledge and Kegan Paul.
Dovey, H. O. (1986) 'Why National Registration Had to Go', *Public Administration*, 64(4): 459–62.
Eliot, R. (2006) 'An Early Experiment in National Identity Cards: The battle over registration in the first world war', *Twentieth Century British History*, (17)2: 145–76.
Higgs, E. (2004) *The Information State in England*, Basingstoke: Palgrave Macmillan.
House of Commons (1966) *4th Report of the Estimates Committee on Government Statistical Services*, HC 426. London: HMSO.
Mallet, B. (1917) 'The Organisation of Registration in its Bearing on Vital Statistics,' *Journal of the Royal Statistical Society*, 80(1): 1–30.
Mallet, B. (1929) 'Reform of Vital Statistics: Outline of a system of national registration', *Eugenics Review*, 21: 87–94.

Redfern, P. (1987) *A Study of the Future of the Census of Population: Alternative approaches*, Luxembourg: Office for Official Publications of the European Commission.

Redfern, P. (1989) 'Population Registers: Some administrative pros and cons', *Journal of the Royal Statistical Society, Series A*, 152(1): 1–41.

Redfern P. (1990) 'A Population Register or Identity Cards for 1992', *Public Administration*, 68(4): 505–15.

Redfern P. (2004) 'An Alternative View of the 2001 Census and Future Census Taking', *Journal of the Royal Statistical Society, Series A*, 167(2): 209–48.

Smith, M. J. (2008) 'Re-centring British Government: Beliefs, traditions and dilemmas in political science', *Political Studies Review* 6(2): 143–54.

Westin, A. (1967) *Privacy and Freedom*, New York: Atheneum.

9   Interpretivism and Public Policy Research

Helen Sullivan

Introduction

This chapter is about the value of interpretivism to public policy research and by extension to public policymakers. This is a challenging chapter to write in the prevailing context of policy research, which is dominated by positivism and experimental approaches. However, interpretivism offers an important alternative perspective that can help us understand why actors might not always act in the way that positively derived evidence might suggest.

Bevir's and Rhodes's work, beginning with *Interpreting British Governance* (2003), provides a helpful account of the value of interpretivism in practice as well as theory and it also offers pointers to the application of interpretivism. However, while Bevir and Rhodes are prolific authors who have separately and together reminded political science students of governance of interpretivism's potential, it is important to acknowledge the ongoing contribution of the broader interpretivist academic community to public policy research. This community brings together scholars from a wide variety of disciplines including political science and includes many who see interpretivism as making a vital contribution to public policy understanding. The community is supported by the annual international conference – 'Interpretive Policy Analysis' – while the journal *Critical Policy Studies* offers an important home for the development of interpretivist ideas, alongside and in conversation with other approaches. This chapter draws on ideas from that broader community in its discussion of interpretivism and public policy.

The chapter begins with a discussion of the place of interpretivism in public policy research, focusing specifically on the limits of positivism in a political context where argument is key to decision making. The chapter then offers some examples of the way in which interpretivism can be operationalised in public policy research and its value to policymakers. Drawing on the work of the author, the chapter explores three aspects of interpretivism: traditions (following the work of Bevir and Rhodes), situated agency, and practices. The chapter concludes with a discussion of the potential and dilemmas of interpretive approaches and outlines some lines of enquiry for the future that could benefit public policy research.

Interpretivism and Public Policy Research

Public policy and administration is, like other sub-fields of political science, subject to the competing claims of different research paradigms. Interpretivism, with its constructivist–subjectivist epistemology, its association with qualitative methods and its presence across various humanities as well as social science disciplines, is experiencing mixed fortunes. Barely acknowledged in the US, dominated as policy research is there by behaviouralism, interpretivism has a stronger presence in the UK, where there is a tradition of interpretive research in political studies as well as in history. However, here too it has struggled to compete with the positivist wave that aligns well with British empiricism and which has been augmented in recent years by a renewed enthusiasm for experimental research designs in public policy. In continental Europe more variegated research traditions offer fertile ground for interpretivism, though here the influence of positivism is growing, to the extent that interpretivists have formed themselves into a 'counter identity' that stands clearly in opposition to positivism but, some argue, risks marginalisation as a result. By contrast, in Australia interpretivism is now part of the mainstream, largely as a result of the presence of a cluster of influential academics researching and teaching in Australian universities (Boswell and Corbett, 2014). So, while certainly not a dominant force in public policy research, interpretivism has a robust academic base in a number of parts of the world.

The extent to which this academic base and its research influences public policy is a more vexed question, though the longstanding debate about the academic/practitioner divide is much broader than simply interpretivism. The remainder of this chapter draws on debates and research and policy examples from the UK as interpretivism arguably has a longer history here, co-existing (more or less well) with an influential positivist paradigm. Between 1997 and 2010, the New Labour Governments also supported significant investment in public policy research and evaluation as part of their commitment to 'evidence-based policymaking'. This investment aimed to involve researchers more directly in public policymaking and to bring a broader range of researchers into programmes of policy analysis (see Sullivan, 2011 for a discussion of the impact of this investment).

Regardless of its current impact on policy there is an argument to be made for the value of interpretivism to public policy research and to policymakers. This argument highlights the political context and quality of public policymaking and identifies interpretivism as a research approach that can accommodate politics appropriately in its application. Hood and Jackson's *Administrative Argument* (1991) summarised this in the context of the UK, suggesting that public administration here privileges 'concrete factual realism' over 'argument and acceptance'. Concrete factual realism reflects the desire amongst some academics to establish public administration as a science following Herbert Simon's (1946) seminal article on the 'proverbs of administration'. Simon critiqued public administration research that used administrative principles as the basis of scientific theory, and proposed instead studies that had controls and objective measurement of results. This privileging of technical specificity and 'hard' data over values and judgement found considerable support amongst British empiricists and it continues to influence UK policymaking and policy research. It is associated with a hierarchy of methods that regard randomised control trials as the 'gold standard' and situates the researcher at a clear distance from the 'subject' in order to protect objectivity and independence.

However, despite the dominance of this technocratic mentality, alternatives continue to exist. These alternatives emphasise the contested nature of the policymaking process, the ways in which ideas gain currency, not simply, nor indeed sometimes at all, because of the weight of evidence, but because of other factors, and the importance of different mechanisms available in democratic societies for communicating and contesting ideas. This 'political' mentality described by Tivey as processes of 'voting, discussing, expressing views, wheeling and dealing' (1988: 138), cannot simply be subsumed into technical measures and subjected to scientific method, but rather demands a mode of researching and examination able to deal with political processes of 'argument and acceptance' on their own terms. Hood and Jackson (1991) elaborate this position, arguing that new ideas about 'what to do' in public policy are the product of context-specific argumentation between different policy 'doctrines'. These doctrines, which answer the 'generic question of administration' – how to get organised (1991: 3) – recur with striking regularity in public policy debates, and the choices made between them at any given moment do not necessarily emerge from a process of reasoned discussion and debate drawing on 'hard' evaluation evidence, but rather are the result of persuasive argument.

Adopting this position draws researchers' attention to the processes that shape how new ideas emerge and how arguments in support of or against these ideas are developed, promoted, contested, and accepted (Fischer and Forester, 1993). This approach rejects a search for concrete factual realism in favour of looking at 'the array of administrative doctrines, justifications and philosophies [which] ... deserve systematic study ... without necessarily focusing on the universal validity of their truth claims' and at the process by which some doctrines become received ideas (Hood and Jackson, 1991: 22). This kind of research requires a more interpretivist approach, with its emphasis on identifying and elaborating meaning, focusing on actors and agency, and developing theory through insights from practice. Importantly it does not negate the value of positivism but rather points to the importance of utilising approaches that are appropriate to the questions being asked and the subjects under study.

In the UK, at least, the experience of public policy research is not simply the triumph of one paradigm over another. This is illustrated in the example of New Labour (1997–2010). From the outset the Government expressed formal commitment to evidence-based policymaking – a commitment that generated considerable debate but also a great deal of research for policy researchers. However, as I have argued elsewhere (Sullivan, 2011), New Labour's approach was more patterned than the label 'evidence-based policymaking' might suggest. In practice the government drew on old and new mentalities to generate two distinct and potential competing ideas of policy research that served different purposes.

In the first version of policy research, the 'old' mentality of methods-led, British empiricism connected with the 'new' mentality of New Labour's enthusiastic embrace of the 'new public management' (and its focus on performance management tools and techniques, on target setting and measurement, etc.). This privileged policy research as technical expertise through the deployment of ever more sophisticated methods and models and drawing on particular kinds of data (e.g. performance statistics).

In the second version, the 'old' mentality of political argumentation connected with the 'new' mentality of 'stakeholder engagement' in New Labour's policy-making to promote 'policy entrepreneurship'. Here policy research was one of a number of ways in which evidence could be generated and marshalled in support of a particular perspective or policy option. Researchers' agency was expressed through their ability to bend policy towards a particular position or cause.

These manifestations of policy research identify particular roles and therefore responsibilities for researchers. A further potential role is that of researcher as 'the interpreter of interpretations'. In circumstances where multiple interpretations abound but with little formal acknowledgement, part of the researcher's role may be to work with actors to elucidate and elaborate the interpretations in operation. This role could be performed in ways that embrace the identification of the 'technical specialist' or the 'policy entrepreneur' but in each case there is a requirement for the researcher to acknowledge and to declare their involvement in the process of constructing different worldviews.

One of the important implications of Hood and Jackson's focus on the interplay of pre-existing doctrines and actors' argumentation is that interpretations have material consequences, i.e. that (in Hood and Jackson's terms) the doctrinal 'settlement' that ensues from a process of argumentation actively shapes policy choices and local actions. How this happens and the consequences for the design and implementation of public policy are the subject of the remainder of this chapter. Three particular aspects of interpretivism will be examined because they illustrate particular opportunities and challenges for interpretivist research and because they reveal something about the potential and limits of the contribution of Bevir and Rhodes's work. These are traditions, situated agency, and practices.

To illustrate each aspect of interpretivism the chapter will draw on three different research projects, all undertaken during the period of New Labour's programme of reform, 1997–2010. Two of the research projects were commissioned as part of the 'local government modernisation agenda', a policy programme that sought to change the way in which local government was governed, was organised, made decisions, and designed and delivered services. The remaining project was undertaken independently but linked closely to policy research on collaboration undertaken by the author (Williams and Sullivan, 2009).

Policy Ideas and Traditions

Much policy research is concerned with establishing whether or not a policy, or more precisely a policy programme, 'works'. In this case a programme is usually defined by a set of activities linked to priority outcomes, supported by a defined resource. However, on occasion policy research can also be focused on the operationalisation of an idea, again linked to preferred outcomes but without specific activities or resources associated with it. This kind of policy research is difficult to undertake using positivist methods as so much of what is to be examined or evaluated is not clearly defined. However, policymakers retain an appetite for trying to understand what happens to policy ideas, whether or not they 'work' and, less often, why. In such cases interpretivism offers a route to this kind of understanding, as it enables researchers to explore the ways in which ideas are shaped and reshaped by different actors in the policy process and the influences that inform these (re)formulations.

Bevir and Rhodes (2003) identify 'traditions' as a key component in the ways in which individuals make sense of the world and construct meanings to guide their action. They describe traditions (and ideologies) as 'aggregate concepts' that evoke particular kinds of social contexts (2003: 131). Actors compile specific stories or narratives to support their actions. These constructions are never complete and are always subject to challenge by other actors' narratives. Bevir and Rhodes's work has been extensively discussed and critiqued (for example, Finlayson, 2004; Wagenaar, 2012), and, while it is arguable that they offer sufficient specificity for researchers to 'know a tradition if they saw one', and to differentiate between traditions and ideologies, there is something helpful about identifying an assemblage of factors that interact with actors to shape what it is possible to do. In the context of public policy these insights can help us to understand why policy ideas develop in different ways in different times and spaces, and why actors may have such difficulty in reconciling themselves to others' interpretations. They are also useful in enabling different interpretations to be formally delineated and acknowledged, thereby further facilitating discussion about what the different constructions are as well as why they might exist.

My first encounter with Bevir and Rhodes's work was during a period in which I was one of a large number of researchers working to explore the implementation and impact of the 'local government modernisation agenda', an ambitious programme of local government reform in the UK under the New Labour Governments (1997–2010). The Government commissioned evaluations of individual policy programmes but also attempted a meta-evaluation of the whole agenda focusing on a number of broader themes including service improvement, public confidence, accountability, stakeholder engagement, and community leadership.

The meta-evaluation adopted a 'theory of change' approach (Connell and Kubisch, 1998). This approach allows evaluators to examine how and why a programme 'works', drawing from the theory/theories of action that are in operation. A theory of change framework does not specify methods. This means that a range of quantitative and qualitative methods can be used, depending on the programme. The meta-evaluation made use of longitudinal surveys and case studies common across all of the themes, supported by data from the programme-specific evaluations led by other researchers (Bovaird and Martin, 2003).

While this common methods framework was more efficient for the evaluation, it was more or less effective depending on the theme. For example, some of the broader themes such as service improvement were amenable to clear specification of what to measure and how, while others such as community leadership were much less so (Sullivan, 2008). The evaluation dealt with this by focusing on the Government's own definition and elaboration of community leadership. This is contained in the 1998 Local Government White Paper 'Modern Local Government: In touch with the people' (DETR, 1998). The core purpose of local government is defined as being to 'promote the well-being of communities' with local government having a specific role to perform as community leader:

> Community leadership is at the heart of the role of modern local government. Councils are the organisations best placed to take a comprehensive overview of the needs and priorities of their local areas and communities, and lead the work to meet those needs and priorities in the round.
>
> (DETR, 1998: 62)

From this and related material in the White Paper we developed a description for local government's community leadership role:

• Focusing attention on key community priorities. Local authorities need to demonstrate the capacity to set a strategic direction that is shared with other key stakeholders and to represent community priorities beyond the locality.
• Galvanising a range of stakeholders to contribute to delivering these priorities. Local authorities need to generate and/or harness sufficient collaborative capacity amongst local stakeholders to enable 'joined-up' action and the development of new approaches.
• Involving citizens in the process of priority identification and delivery. Local authorities must seek out the diversity of citizen 'voices' and include these in decision making as well as stimulating citizen action to help themselves (Sullivan, 2008: 5).

Early findings from the evaluation revealed two distinct interpretations of the term 'community leadership'. These were the role of the local authority 1) as a strategic leader, acting in an authority-wide capacity, and 2) as democratic champion, acting in support of ward- or neighbourhood-level initiatives. This distinction was clarified in the 2006 Local Government White Paper 'Strong and Prosperous Communities', which referred to local government's 'strategic leadership' and 'community advocacy' roles (DCLG, 2006). The evaluation adopted that distinction and terminology for the remainder of the evaluation period and the findings and conclusions from the evaluation were published in *The State of Governance of Places* report (Sullivan, 2008).

A key conclusion from the report was that

> Community leadership (as strategic leadership) prospered in localities when it became attached to a powerful idea ('place-shaping') which also offered local authorities and local stakeholders the opportunity to develop their own interpretation of community leadership that made sense in their locality.
>
> (2008: 81; see also Lyons, 2007)

This prompted further interrogation of the data to explore the different ideas that were in operation locally regardless of the formal policy position, to examine whether and how these ideas became concrete as operating interpretations, and to explain what facilitated the persistence of these interpretations.

Drawing on relevant academic literature, policy documentation, and the experiences and views of national and local actors, I identified a range of ideas associated with community leadership and detailed four related dominant interpretations of community leadership: as a symbol of change, as a formalisation of local government's enabling role, as an expression of citizen 'voice', and as an expedient device (see Table 9.1).

Bevir and Rhodes's (2003) identification of traditions was particularly helpful to my analysis as it provided a way of situating emergent interpretations in their historical and political contexts. This enabled me to distinguish between emergent interpretations that were transient and developed in response to contemporary concerns, and those interpretations that were connected to a broader understanding and valuing of the role of local government. It also helped to understand more clearly why actors might be attached to a specific interpretation.

Interpretation 1

Community leadership is identified as a symbol of the transformation of local government, representing its radical shift from an old-fashioned institution to a 'modern' one (Lowndes, 2004). Symbols are powerful because their application can shape organisational structures and cultures through the application of new institutional templates (Scott, 1991). The tradition of UK local government as an adaptive institution that has 'has evolved gradually and piecemeal over the centuries', adapting its rules and practices 'in response to changing circumstances' (Wilson and Game, 2002) suggests that symbols are likely to generate change. This tradition also connects a past 'golden age' of local government with the proposed 'modern' future. It references legacies of innovation and enterprise, while at the same time refashioning twenty-first-century community leadership by emphasising the importance of inclusive governance.

Interpretation 2

Here, community leadership is associated with the manifestation of local government as an enabling institution, 'fit for purpose' in the twenty-first century. This institutional position derives both from the scope and scale of local government and the resulting potential to promote 'community well-being' in various sites and at various levels, and the responsibilities contingent on the 'democratic' nature of local government, specifically the responsibility to be both inclusive and representative of local views and to be both transparent and accountable in relation to decision making (Sullivan, 2003). The interpretation is directly linked to a tradition of local self-government in the UK, which considers the protection and promotion of democracy and the delivery of locally appropriate services as equally important (Hill, 1974).

Table 9.1 Interpretations of Community Leadership

Interpretations

	1 Symbol of change	2 Formalisation of local government as 'enabler'	3 Expression of citizen 'voice'	4 Expedient device
Tradition of local government	Adaptive institution	Local self-government	Community empowerment	'Agent' of centralised control
Narrative of community leadership	Modernisation	Community governance	Devolution	New central–local settlement
Storyline	Benchmark for a new era in local governance	Fitness for purpose in complex world	Better decision making and responsive services	Achievement of key outcomes
Impact on local government (1)	Local determination within national framework	Strategic enabler and steward of local values and aspirations	Stronger interactions with communities through multiples sites	Reduced role, increase in alternative governing bodies
Impact on local government (2)	Empty symbol generating cynicism	Managerial coordination and facilitation	Challenge to elected members' legitimacy, conflict within communities	Local resistance and generation of alternative proposals

Source: Sullivan (2008: 145).

Interpretation 3

In this interpretation community leadership is understood as the authentic expression of citizens' aspirations and choices, facilitated by regularised interactions between officials and citizens in their communities, and channelled through local elected members. It accords with a tradition of community empowerment in local government that is fed by concern about the operation of representative bureaucracy and belief in the value of citizen participation beyond the ballot box (Gyford, 1991). Leadership is about creating the conditions for the exercise of community influence, supporting its translation into decisions, coupled with a need to safeguard broader community values. The accompanying narrative is one of devolution – locating influence over decisions at the closest point to citizens on the basis that citizens' community knowledge and experience will secure outcomes that are more appropriate to their needs (Dahl and Tufte, 1973; Lowndes and Sullivan, 2008).

Interpretation 4

Here, community leadership is merely a device, a sleight of hand employed by government to divert local authorities' attention from the fact that their influence is waning as central government exercises greater control and service delivery is undertaken by a proliferation of other agencies. It is situated in a tradition of central government dominance over local government, where the latter is the 'creature' of central government, required to act as an 'agent' in the achievement of policy goals, usually at the expense of its autonomy (Carter and John, 1992). In this context 'community leadership' is offered to local authorities as an 'alternative' to the service delivery function, but in reality it has limited substance. The narrative is one of tension in central–local relations, fuelled by central government's determination to achieve key outcomes in what it considers the most effective manner.

Elaborating these different interpretations helps us understand why policy ideas so often evolve in the process of engagement with different actors. Central actors who hold different interpretations from local actors frequently express this as 'policy failure' and there is no doubt a tension between central and local government in the UK that manifests itself in divergent interpretations linked to different traditions. However, it can also be experienced between different groups of actors in the same locality, where each has an attachment to a different tradition. This matters because the interpretations are not necessarily complementary but can suggest very different organisational arrangements, modes of decision making, and resourcing. Interpretations then have material impacts that inform policy choices and local actions. This can generate conflict between actors, conflict that can be better explained if there is an awareness of the competing interpretations actors hold to and the traditions they draw on in support of them.

The ways in which actors make sense of and meaning from policy ideas is considered in the next section.

Actors and Situated Agency

Interpretive approaches focus on actors and the ways in which they make meaning from their subjective experience. Interpretivism presupposes that actors have agency – the ability to set and pursue their own goals and interests. This suggests that in any given context actors will act differently depending on their motivations. What that looks like and how it happens is an important part of interpretivist inquiry. Bevir and Rhodes's *Interpreting British Governance* (2003) provides an important opening for researchers to develop actor-centred approaches to political science and policy analysis.

'Leadership' and 'collaboration' are integral to twenty-first-century governance and management but, despite a growing literature, understanding about leadership for collaboration is hampered by a lack of specificity and nuance in theory and empirical research. In a review of relevant literature we found that leadership analyses are still concerned with traits (personal characteristics), styles (behaviours), and contingencies (factors that influence effectiveness) though understandings of each have continued to develop. We concluded that coverage of the traits, styles, and situations associated with leadership for collaboration suggests a wide range of possibilities, raising questions about how public leadership for collaboration is shaped in practice (Sullivan *et al.*, 2012).

In response to this, my colleagues and I devised a research project to examine what 'leadership for collaboration' meant and how it was practised (Sullivan *et al.* 2012). The research was conducted in Wales, a small country with a population of less than three million, and a common strategic policy framework for public services based on 'citizen-centred' and 'customer-focused' services delivered in partnership across all sectors (Welsh Assembly Government, 2007; see also 2006). Institutional design, financial incentives, and policy goals were all aligned in support of collaboration as a policy instrument for achieving key outcomes. Together these powerful structural factors combined to offer a framework for public governance and leadership in Wales.

The research aimed to uncover how actors responded to these common policy frameworks and incentives. We used Q methodology for the study as it enables the identification and elaboration of the shared subjectivities of actors in relation to a particular issue, in this case leadership for collaboration. Q method involves presenting respondents with a set of stimuli (statements) and asking them to sort them into preferences using a form of grid. The sorts are correlated then analysed using a by-persons factor analysis that reveals underlying factor groupings within the data. The method is particularly well suited to topics where subjective positions are tacit rather than explicit (Brown, 1980).

The outcomes of the Q-sort revealed that, despite the clear and coherent governance and policy framework for collaboration in Wales, there was significant scope for interpretation by individual leaders. The identification of five distinct configurations of leadership for collaboration suggested that individuals did not perceive themselves to be passive recipients of new ways of organising but rather considered themselves as active participants in the process of design and action – as agents in that process (see Table 9.2).

Table 9.2 Leadership for Collaboration

Leadership for collaboration as:

---

1 Co-governing through inclusive relationships
   Providers and users share in the design and delivery of services; the processes of
   co-governance are as important as the outcomes. Leaders work in the background to
   facilitate others and the processes.
2 Negotiating dynamic complexity
   Collaboration necessary to meet challenge of contemporary context but any response
   is temporary and subject to renegotiation. Leaders need to be active in building and
   managing relationships, but also able to stand back.
3 Judicious influence by elites
   Focus is on maintaining or enhancing organisational resources through actions of
   elite group engaged in shaping action and outcomes.
4 The achievement of key outcomes
   Collaboration required to achieve synergy – outcomes that could not otherwise be
   achieved. Leaders need strategic nous to drive collaboration.
5 Co-governing through expert facilitation
   Processes of co-governance as important as outcomes but emphasis on leaders as
   expert shapers of stakeholders, resources and opportunities to achieve process and
   outcome goals.

Source: Sullivan *et al.*, 2012; adapted from pp. 52–55.

The concept of situated agency is useful as a way of understanding why different interpretations of leadership for collaboration emerge and how that process happens. Situated agency suggests that agency is influenced but not determined by structures, 'emphasizing internalized understandings and frameworks as well as external actions' (Evans, 2002: 248). These influencing factors take many forms. They may be relational, as actions are, at least in part, a product of individual agents' interactions with others. They may be structural, as actors have 'subjective perceptions of the structures they have to negotiate, which affect how they act' (Evans, 2002: 252) These influencing factors may also be temporal – processes of social engagement in which past habits and routines are contextualised and future possibilities envisaged within the contingencies of the present moment (Emirbayer and Mische, 1998).

The concept of situated agency confirms the importance of both macro- and micro-understandings of collaboration as factors that frame actors' expectations of the demands and conditions of leadership (Weick, 1995). The way in which the respondents in the research accepted the Q-sort statements as a representation of the collaborative context in Wales without contesting them is one indication of this.

Importantly, a focus on situated agency allows a range of actor-centred factors to be considered in relation to leadership possibilities. These include reflecting on one's past experiences, assessing the likely balance of power between actors and judging the costs and benefits of a collaborative approach to oneself and one's organisation. Vickers's (1965) concept of 'appreciative systems' offers a helpful way of thinking about how our respondents reacted to the statements in the Q-sort and the influences that shaped them.

What actors do in the context of the meaning they make from any situation and the practices that describe or are associated with expressions of agency is the focus of the next section. However, it is worth reflecting here on the practice of 'local reasoning', the action that Bevir (2010) suggests actors engage in when they need to reflect on or alter their beliefs following contact with a new idea. Local reasoning 'operates through a capacity for creative if situated agency' (2010: 392). If we understand leadership for collaboration as a new idea, then local reasoning alerts us to attend to the ways in which actors appraise possible options in the context of inherited values and commitments. In the Wales study this was illustrated in the differential way in which actors responded to a Q statement that leadership for collaboration 'prioritizes the needs of service users and citizens over the interests of organizations' (Sullivan *et al.*, 2012: 53). While some clearly supported this perspective, others were much more sceptical, suggesting attachment to other values and ideas about the appropriate role of citizens in governance and public services.

The material consequences of interpretations are evident through the exercise of situated agency and its influence on practice. In the Wales study this is illustrated in the way in which respondents' agreement over particular statements generated rather different interpretations of leadership for collaboration. For example, both configurations 1 and 5 in Table 9.2 interpret collaboration as an expression of 'co-governance' between providers and users, leaders and citizens, and value a number of statements the same. However, a key difference between them is that in configuration 5 leaders have much more agency, a clearer role, and the ability to fulfil it. Configuration 1 is much less clear on how leaders build inclusive relationships and also contains uncertainty about how co-governance can operate.

A focus on leadership traits and styles also highlights the variation in roles assigned to leaders in the five configurations. The emphasis is on facilitation but the features are markedly different. Configuration 1 has them as background figures, gently supporting others, while in configuration 5 their facilitative role is more about active shaping. Configuration 2 contains a mix of both, with leaders key to building and managing relationships but not directing. In configurations 3 and 4 leaders are active shapers of the collaboration process but for different ends. One immediate issue arising from these different configurations is the range and diversity of skill sets associated with the exercise of leadership. An obvious question is whether all of these skills can be associated with single leaders or whether they can be present among a number of actors building leadership for collaboration.

While situated agency focuses on what drives and limits action, the acts themselves also warrant investigation in interpretive accounts. The next section explores how interpretivism enables the study of practices.

Actors and Practices

According to Griggs *et al.*,

> People do not only make sense of situations which confront them by reflecting upon them within the context of traditions, belief systems, or ideologies,

they also move about in the world in a more or less effective way by acting upon the situation at hand.

(2014: 15)

These actions or practices may be routine or spontaneous, intimate or public, but in all cases they are:

a move or thrust into an only partly known and knowable world. By acting, by intervening, we extend our intentions and understandings into this indeterminate world without being able to predict how its agency will effectuate itself and impact us.

(Wagenaar, 2012: 92)

Griggs *et al.* outline three premises of a performative account:

*   interventionism – reality is not 'out there' but is 'a product of our ongoing practical engagement with the world';
*   temporal emergence – time and experience bring each other into being, 'the constraints and affordances of the outer world come to us only through our experience of them in emergent time';
*   'interpenetration of the human and the material in the way we act on and understand the world' (2014: 16).

Practice then is a way of making manifest policy realities through the dynamic interaction of human and non-human actors.

This section explores how practices are elucidated in interpretive accounts and the implications for public policy. It focuses on what it is that actors do in the process of designing and enacting policy and the interaction between action and 'situation' in generating practices. In this way it builds on and possibly departs from the contents of *Interpreting British Governance* (Bevir and Rhodes, 2003). The section draws on research into central–local relations undertaken by Steven Griggs and myself (Griggs and Sullivan, 2014) to illustrate how interpretivism can support the examination of practice.

UK central–local relations are of interest because, while there is little doubt that since the mid-1980s local government has become more closely prescribed by central government – dependent on it for much of its finance, and regularly reshaped in terms of its responsibilities, powers, and functions – the extent to which these reforms transformed the relationship between the centre and localities remains contested (Leach and Lowndes, 2007; Sullivan 2010). New Labour's local government modernisation agenda included a commitment to refashion central–local relations, but as with previous reform programmes, the outcomes are the subject of much debate.

Our research identified two dominant interpretations of central–local relations under New Labour. 'State-centric dirigiste' (Fuller and Geddes, 2008) accounts depicted a powerful central state deploying both 'hard' and 'soft' regulatory strategies. By contrast, accounts of 'disciplined pluralism' (Painter, 2005) argued instead in favour of local diversity and the need to manage ambiguity and competing priorities through local political settlements. Neither of these dominant interpretations, though helpful, seemed sufficient to us. So we began to explore an alternative actor-centred approach drawing on King's conception of regulatory intermediaries. This appealed to us because of regulation's increasing prominence as a governmental strategy and its application in central–local relations.

King (2006: 11) identifies 'regulatory intermediaries' as actors who 'occupy the space between the regulator and the regulated' and whose agency permits the distribution and modification of regulation. The political character of central–local relations also suggested that we should not focus on the regulatory intermediation of local auditors or quality assessors, those who may be described as 'technical' actors. Rather, we should examine the regulatory intermediation of senior managers and institutional leaders within local government whose roles include divining and communicating meaning to government and regulators' policy, advice, and guidance and performance regimes, and whose activities may be described as 'political'.

We explored this empirically, drawing on our research into the take-up and use of the local government well-being power introduced in 2000 (Kitchin *et al.*, 2007). This power was particularly relevant as it represented New Labour's attempt to afford local government greater freedom and flexibility to act. The well-being power also provided an interesting paradox as local authorities lobbied for it but then rarely appeared to use it. While lack of use of the power can be explained via both 'state-centric dirigiste' (the power as a form of soft regulation) and 'disciplined pluralist' (the power as one of many instruments available) approaches, neither, we suggest, offers an adequate account of local responses to the power. This is explored further below with specific reference to situated agency and practices.

Our research identified six interpretations of the well-being power. These interpretations were diverse both in terms of judgements about the merits of the power and its utility, and about the value of local government (see Table 9.3).

Taking an actor-centred approach it is possible to associate different interpretations with different groups of actors. These actors may be multiple and diverse, e.g. a broad coalition of actors across the public, private, and voluntary and community sectors – from leaders/mayors through to business managers and voluntary organisation managers – who supported the interpretation of the power as 'a renewal of local government' and encouraged its use. They may be an elite group, e.g. the interpretations of the power as 'a symbol of trust in local government' and as 'an expression of community leadership' attracted local authority executive leaders (political and officer) and strategic officers, with support from peers in other sectors interested in doing things in a different way. In two interpretations – the power as a 'safety net' and as 'not on the agenda' – lawyers played a key role, framing how the power could be used and often limiting understanding about the potential of the power to few others. This reduced the likelihood of the power being identified as a potential resource and serves to illustrate how interpretations can draw boundaries between actors. Finally, in the interpretation of the power as 'not fit for purpose', an elite group of local

Table 9.3 Interpretations of the Well-Being Power

Interpretations / Elements	A Symbol of Trust in Local Government	A Renewal of Local Government	An Expression of Community Leadership	A 'Safety Net'	Not on the Agenda of Local Authorities	Not Fit-for-Purpose
Local authority context	Service focused	Change focused	Partnership focused	Risk focused	Rule focused	Resource focused
Levels of understanding	High among chief executives and leaders	High and distributed throughout authority and partners	High and distributed throughout authority and partners	Limited to chief officers and lawyers	Limited to lawyers	Spread among chief officers, senior lawyers and members of the executive
Take-up and use of the Power	Limited	Power of First Resort	Power of First Resort	Reassurance or 'belt and braces'	Limited – unrecorded	No-use
Main rationales for use or non-use	Instrumental; symbolic (badging)	Symbolic (community leadership; coalition-building)	Instrumental; symbolic (coalition-building)	Instrumental	Instrumental (reassurance); symbolic (badging)	Strategic advantage of existing powers already enable the authority to act
Key players	Executive leadership	From executive leadership through to business managers and partners	Executive leadership and strategy officers	Lawyers	Chief executive and lawyers	Executive leadership

Source: Griggs and Sullivan (2014: 505).

government officers and elected members discouraged its use. We considered these different actors to be 'regulatory intermediaries', because of their ability to shape the distribution of information about the power, and their capacity to modify its meaning.

However, the variation in interpretations and the different groups of actors with agency in each suggests that the positional and professional authority of such actors is insufficient to explain what is happening. We also need to take account of the situation, in this case the particular local contexts or regimes into which the power was introduced. This helps to constitute the spaces and capacity for agency in concert with different actors' ability to develop narratives about the potential of the power that infused it with particular meaning(s). These acts of meaning making are political as they shape the potential and limits to local action and also constitute boundaries such as those between 'central' and 'local', between 'experts' and 'others', and between 'leaders' and 'followers'.

The impact of boundaries was evident from the way in which these 'local' interpretations were constituted through actors' beliefs and experiences about 'the centre'. While actors used the language of 'the centre', their narratives emphasised the multiplicity and incoherence of 'central' perspectives. Departmental actors were identified as ignorant of the power entirely, as not serious about its transformative potential for local government, as unable to coordinate their own activities to help support use of the power, or even in the case of the 'host' department, the Department for Communities and Local Government, to be unable to influence other central departments over the utility of the power (Kitchin *et al.*, 2007: 83). Such claims brought to the surface the differentiated relations central actors (individuals, departments, or programmes) have with localities in ways that are rarely elaborated clearly in reviews of central–local relations (Sullivan, 2005).

The interpretations also constitute, and are constituted by, actors' positioning in relation to central government. The research identified a range of positions: from enthusiastic support (interpretations 2 and 3), and sage acknowledgement (1 and 4) to disappointment (5), and betrayal (6) (Griggs and Sullivan, 2014: 508). Affect imbued the meaning and the positioning of actors. For example, interpreting the well-being power as 'a symbol of trust' illustrated positive affect while negative affect was registered through references to the lack of support (political, technical, resources) for the introduction of the power.

These affective responses emphasise the significance of the power as a political instrument and reveal the power relationships being negotiated and renegotiated through its introduction. Politics and power relations were present in the practices associated with regulatory intermediaries' work. Here our research explored decision making in different localities, specifically the style of senior local government actors. Community leadership practices, e.g. coalition building, collaborative planning, and citizen engagement, offered important insights as they illustrated how local actors could interact and engage with one another. Lawyers' practices were also significant as they could play a key role in shaping how the power was understood in a locality and whether or not it was used:

> Practices here included the prominence of lawyers in key decision making settings, their preparedness to communicate about the power, what they chose to communicate, and the tone they chose to use to communicate in, and even the particular format of their briefings.
>
> (Griggs and Sullivan, 2014: 509)

Evidence from the well-being power research suggests that practices are indivisible from particular interpretations. For example, the interpretation of the power as the renewal of local government envisaged the power as a power of first resort, an instrument to facilitate ambition, associated with practices of coalition building and community leadership. The interpretation of the power as a symbol of trust was reflected in the use of the power as a 'symbolic badge' in which existing initiatives were reframed in the context of the power. These practices are both instrumental and performative, highlighting the use of the power to 'do the right thing.' By contrast, the interpretation of the power as a 'safety net' or legal 'belt and braces' constructed it as an additional tool that local government could use to put beyond doubt their capacity to act on an issue. Practices here were about providing reassurance.

Conclusion

This chapter has examined the contribution of interpretivism to public policy research. Drawing on research undertaken in the UK as part of New Labour's public service 'modernisation' programme, the chapter highlights the ways in which interpretivism can enhance policy research and offer additional insights to policymakers. Focusing on the work of Bevir and Rhodes but also taking account of contributions from the broader community of interpretivist scholars, the chapter explored the analytical potential of 'traditions', 'situated agency', and 'practice' through their application to particular policy ideas and reforms.

For researchers, Bevir and Rhodes's concept of 'traditions' offers a way of situating emergent interpretations in their historical and policy contexts, enabling a clearer identification of those interpretations that have real purchase on actors' motivations and actions. The concept of 'situated agency' coupled with 'local reasoning' provides researchers with analytical tools to identify and delineate the range of influences interacting with actors and to identify why actors in apparently similar contexts may develop different interpretations and responses to policy ideas. Finally the chapter also highlights the potential significance of focusing on 'practices' as conduits for researching 'situated agency'. This demands fine-grained analysis of what it is that evaluators, policymakers, etc. do in the process of making and judging policy and how this is influenced by 'situational' factors. It also allows for the exploration of the same or similar practices across a range of actors, to examine whether and how the operating rationalities of different actors accord with those traditionally assigned to them.

Interpretivism and the empirical examples offered in this chapter demonstrate that 'meaning making' can be as important a part of the policy process as policy design, and can also benefit from interaction with a wide range of stakeholders (including the public). What remains unclear and would benefit from further empirical examination is how a focus on interpretation and the use of interpretive approaches can improve our understanding of how and why individuals and institutions alter their attachment to particular interpretations over time.

Interpretivism challenges policymakers as it doesn't offer them definite and complete responses to questions such as 'what works?' but rather proposes responses that are of necessity incomplete and frequently multiple and contesting. Interpretivism's utility to policymakers is, like all analytical approaches, contingent on the questions being asked and the subjects being researched. Policymakers and researchers have a role in figuring out which questions and which circumstances are appropriate for which approach. Interpretivism's acknowledgement of and engagement with the political is of particular value in public policy where very often 'the right thing to do' is neither evident nor singular but instead a matter of weighing up competing claims and trade-offs.

Arguably the current political climate is hostile to interpretivism. Contemporary governance and policymaking occurs within a context of emergent doubt amongst citizens and other actors at government's capacity to meet the challenges it faces (Sullivan, 2011). Consequently, policy research approaches that appear to offer certainty and clarity and apparently operate beyond politics have regained their appeal. However, interpretivism, through its commitment to better reflecting the messy realities of public policymaking and implementation, offers the prospect of enabling improved understanding of that messiness and providing context-relevant yet analytically generalisable explanations.

References

Bevir, M. (2010) *Democratic Governance*, Princeton, NJ: Princeton University Press.

Bevir, M. and Rhodes, R. A. W. (2003) *Interpreting British Governance*, London: Routledge.

Boswell, J. and Corbett, J. (2014) 'An Antipodean History of Interpretation', *Australian Journal of Public Administration*, 73(3): 296–306.

Bovaird, T. and Martin, S. (2003) 'Evaluating Public Management Reform: Designing a 'joined up' approach to researching the local government modernisation agenda', *Local Government Studies*, 29(4): 17–30.

Brown, S. (1980) *Political Subjectivity: Applications of Q methodology in political science*, New Haven, CT: Yale University Press.

Carter, C. with John, P. (1992) *A New Accord: Promoting constructive relations between central and local government*, York: Joseph Rowntree Foundation.

Connell, J. P. and Kubisch, A. C. (1998) 'Applying a Theory of Change Approach to the Evaluation of Comprehensive Community Initiatives: Progress, prospects and problems', in K. Fulbright-Anderson *et al.* (eds), *New Approaches to Evaluating Community Initiatives: Volume 2 theory, measurement and analysis*, Washington, DC: The Aspen Institute, pp. 15–44.

Dahl, R. and Tufte, E. (1973) *Size and Democracy*, Stanford, CA: Stanford University Press.

DCLG (2006) *Strong and Prosperous Communities*, London: Department for Communities and Local Government.

DETR (1998) *Modern Local Government: In touch with the people*, London: Department of the Environment, Transport and the Regions.

Emirbayer, M. and Mische, A. (1998) 'What is Agency?' *American Journal of Sociology*, 103: 962–1023.

Evans, K. (2002) 'Taking Control of their Lives? Agency in young adult transitions in England and the new Germany', *Journal of Youth Studies*, 5(3): 245–69.

Finlayson, A. (2004) 'The Interpretive Approach in Political Science: A symposium', *British Journal of Politics and International Relations*, 6(2): 129–64.

Fischer, F. and Forester, J. (eds) (1993) *The Argumentative Turn in Policy Analysis and Planning*, Durham, NC: Duke University Press.

Fuller, C. and Geddes, M. (2008) 'Urban Governance Under Neoliberalism: New Labour and the restructuring of state-space', *Antipode*, 40(2): 252–82.

Griggs, S., Norval, A. J., and Wagenaar, H. (2014) 'Introduction: Democracy, conflict and participation in decentred governance', in S. Griggs, A. J. Norval, and H. Wagenaar (eds), *Practices of Freedom: Decentred governance, conflict and democratic participation*, Cambridge: Cambridge University Press, pp. 1–37.

Griggs, S. and Sullivan, H. (2014) 'Puzzling Agency in Centre–Local Relations: Regulatory governance and accounts of change under New Labour', *British Journal of Politics and International Relations*, 16(3): 495–514.

Gyford, J. (1991) *Citizens, Consumers and Councils: Local government and the public*, London: Macmillan.

Hill, D. M. (1974) *Democratic Theory and Local Government*, London: George Allen and Unwin.

Hood, C. and Jackson, M. (1991) *Administrative Argument*, Aldershot: Dartmouth Publishing Company.

Kitchin, H., Griggs, S., Rogers, S., Crawford, C., Mathur, N., Wilson, L., Sullivan, H., and Braybrook, L. (2007) *Formative Evaluation of the Take-up and Implementation of the Well Being Power*, Final Report, 2003–2007, INLOGOV, University of Birmingham and Cities Research Centre, University of the West of England.

King, R. (2006) *The Regulatory State in an Age of Governance: Soft words and big sticks*, Basingstoke: Palgrave Macmillan.

Leach, S. and Lowndes, V. (2007) 'Of Roles and Rules: Analysing the changing relationship between political leaders and chief executives in local government', *Public Policy and Administration*, 22(4): 183–200.

Lowndes, V. (2004) 'Reformers or Recidivists? Has local government really changed?' in G. Stoker and D. Wilson (eds), *British Local Government into the 21st Century*, Basingstoke: Palgrave, pp. 230–46.

Lowndes, V. and Sullivan, H. (2008) 'How Low Can you Go? Rationales and challenges for neighbourhood governance', *Public Administration*, 86(1): 53–74.

Lyons, M. (2007) *Lyons Inquiry into Local Government – Place-Shaping: A shared ambition for the future of local government*, Norwich: The Stationery Office.

Painter, C. (2005) 'Operating Codes in the Emerging System of Local Governance: From 'top-down state' to 'disciplined pluralism'?', *Public Money and Management*, 25(2): 89–98.

Scott, W. R. (1991) 'Unpacking Institutional Arguments', in W. W. Powell and P. J. DiMaggio (eds), *The New Institutionalism in Organizational Analysis*, Chicago, IL: University of Chicago Press, pp. 164–82.

Simon, H. (1946) 'The Proverbs of Administration', *Public Administration Review*, 6(1): 53–67.

Sullivan, H. (2003) 'New Forms of Local Accountability: Coming to terms with many hands?' *Policy and Politics*, 31(3): 353–69.

Sullivan, H. (2005) 'Is Enabling Enough? Tensions and dilemmas in New Labour's strategies for 'joining-up' local governance', *Public Policy and Administration*, 20(4): 10–24.

Sullivan, H. (2008) *The State of Governance of Places: Community leadership and stakeholder engagement*, Final Report of the meta-evaluation of the local government modernisation agenda, Bristol: University of the West of England.

Sullivan, H. (2010) 'Central–Local Relations in the UK', in M. Goldsmith and E. Page (eds), *From Localism to Intergovernmentalism: Changing patterns of central–local relations in Europe*, London: Routledge.

Sullivan, H. (2011) '"Truth" Junkies: Using evaluation in UK public policy', *Policy and Politics*, 39(4): 499–512.

Sullivan, H., Williams, P., and Jeffares, S. (2012) 'Leadership for Collaboration: Situated agency in practice', *Public Management Review*, 14(1): 41–66.

Tivey, L. (1988) *Interpretations of British Politics: The image and the system*, Hemel Hempstead: Harvester Wheatsheaf.

Vickers, G. (1965) *The Art of Judgement: A study of policy making*, London: Chapman and Hall.

Wagenaar, H. (2012) 'Dwellers on the Threshold of Practice: The interpretivism of Bevir and Rhodes', *Critical Policy Studies*, 6(1): 85–99.

Weick, K. A. (1995) *Sensemaking in Organizations*, London: Sage.

Welsh Assembly Government (2006) *Making the Connections: Delivering beyond boundaries*, Cardiff: WAG.

Welsh Assembly Government (2007) *One Wales: A progressive agenda for the government of Wales*, Cardiff: WAG.

Williams, P. and Sullivan, H. (2009) *Getting Collaboration to Work in Wales: Lessons from the NHS and partners*, Wales: National Leadership and Innovation Agency for Healthcare.

Wilson, D. and Game, C. (2002) *Local Government in the United Kingdom*, (3rd edition), Basingstoke: Palgrave.

Conclusion

10 Interpreting British Governance

Ten Years On

Mark Bevir and R. A. W. Rhodes

Introduction

We are grateful to everyone for engaging with our work and, in their different ways, taking the interpretive agenda forward. Obviously there are many points of disagreement, as well as different emphases. There is a temptation to reply to everyone. We resist. The reality is that such exercises exude a defensive air and interest only the protagonist. Indeed, various contributors to this volume mount a defence on our behalf. Thus, Wagenaar (Chapter 7) caustically comments:

> Marsh for example, claims that the notion of 'truth' does not apply to interpretations and chides Bevir and Rhodes for suggesting so (2011: 36). But this shows only that Marsh implicitly adheres to a naïve realist correspondence theory of truth, in which each representation has an exact correspondence somewhere out there in the world (Allen, 1993: 9–10; Wagenaar, 2011: 59). (This is yet another example of the sway that empiricism holds over social scientists of all stripes.) … [A]fter Nietzsche 'Truth' has become 'truth': multifaceted, theoretically loaded, and embedded in historically situated language games and ordinary practice.

Our defence is in safe if overly vigorous hands. So, we do not comment on every chapter or repeat previous replies.[1] The editor enjoined all contributors seriously to seek 'critical engagement with [our] work … with a determined eye towards the future contribution of interpretivism to governance research'. So, we seek to be positive, by identifying common ground and new lines of inquiry. We share the aim of growing the interpretive canon. We take our agenda forward by showing how it opens new empirical topics.

An interpretive approach rejects both comprehensive theory and the related idea that such notions as the state, class, or gender are material objects or emergent structures or social forms (Bevir and Rhodes, 2015). We consider such claims equivalent to Bertrand Russell's China teapot in space.[2] We reject the claim that the '*pre-existence* [of social forms] implies their *autonomy* as possible objects of scientific investigation; and their *causal efficacy* confirms their *reality*' (Jessop, 2005: 42). We reject the idea that the state, for example, is a pre-existing causal structure that can be understood independently of people's beliefs and practices. As MacIntyre (1971: 263) argued:

> It is an obvious truism that no institution or practice is what it is, or does what it does, independent of what anyone whatsoever thinks or feels about it. For institutions are always partially, even if to differing degrees, constituted by what certain people think or feel about them.

Studying the state or other structures is not about building formal theories; it is about telling stories about other people's meanings; it is about narratives of their narratives. As Finlayson and Martin (2006: 167) stress, the object of analysis is not the state but 'a diverse range of agencies, apparatuses and practices producing varied mechanisms of control and varied forms of knowledge that make areas or aspects of social life available for governmental action'. An interpretive political science highlights contests among diverse and contingent meanings. As a result, it privileges distinctive empirical topics, including rule and elite narratives, rationalities and technologies of governance, and resistance and local knowledge. It espouses unearthing whatever the existing literature does not cover. It seeks out whoever is left out of existing accounts. It strives for 'edification' – a way of finding 'new, better, more interesting, more fruitful ways of speaking about' political science (Rorty, 1980: 360). Or to use common parlance, debunking is top of its agenda. We first proposed the '3Rs' of rule, rationalities, and resistance in 2010 (Bevir and Rhodes, 2010: 95–8), and it continues to inform our research agenda.

Rule, Rationalities, and Resistance

Rule

Interpretive theory suggests that political scientists should pay more attention to the high politics of the court; to the traditions against which elites construct their worldviews including their views of their own interests. Court politics (Chapter 4) is the site for ruling elites and their rationalities of governance. We are not subscribing to any notion of a ruling elite or a ruling class. The central elite need not be a uniform group, all the members of which see their interests in the same way, share a common culture, or speak a shared discourse. Our interpretive, decentred approach suggests that political scientists should ask whether different sections of the elite draw on different traditions to construct different narratives about the world, their place within it, and their interests and values. In Britain, for example, the different members of the central elite are inspired by Tory, Whig, Liberal, and Socialist narratives. The dominant narrative in the central civil service used to be the Whig story of the generalist civil servant, spotting snags and muddling through. It has been challenged by a neoliberal managerial narrative that sees civil servants as hands-on, can-do managers trained at business schools, not on the job. But the traditions coexist, sometimes separately but sometimes bumping into one another to create dilemmas. Thus, civil servants continue to believe in the Westminster notions of ministerial accountability to parliament, a centralising idea, even as they decentralise decision making to conform to managerial notions (see also Chapter 4 above; and Bevir and Rhodes, 2016: Part I).

Here, of course, we differ from Diamond *et al.* (Chapter 1) who treat tradition as an essentialist concept. In their view, there is a dominant British political tradition: it is a fixed, even monolithic, entity. Our analysis does not preclude a dominant tradition but it also, and crucially, directs attention to contending elite narratives and to changes in any dominant tradition. We define traditions

> pragmatically depending on the events and actions we want to explain. Political scientists construct traditions in ways appropriate to explaining the particular sets of beliefs and actions in which they are interested. They move back from particular beliefs and actions to traditions made up of linked beliefs and actions handed down from generation to generation.
>
> (Bevir and Rhodes, 2003: 33)

So, when looking at the beliefs and practices of governing elites, we focus on 'situated agents' and contending elite narratives because it is often the dilemmas posed by the contending narratives that underpin change, and it is the change we want to explain. We move back and forth between aggregate concepts such as tradition and the beliefs and practices at play in specific contexts.

Diamond *et al.* (Chapter 1) know there are forces for change:

> the September 2014 Scottish referendum may retrospectively come to be seen as an exogenous shock to this aggregate tradition of a central, power-hoarding approach. The response of both the main parties in the aftermath of the referendum reveals a series of contingencies potentially challenging the key tenets of the British political tradition.

But the debate over Scotland is not a one-off event, an aberration, 'an exogenous shock'. It is the most recent of many manifestations of a contending narrative about British government that is often labelled 'Home Rule'. This long-standing tradition has its roots in Irish independence and the dilemmas it poses are now being played out again in Scotland. Scotland has already gained many powers and more devolution is unavoidable. Nor is 'Home Rule' the only such challenge. British membership of the European Union is a constraint on elite actions – Clifton (2014) talks of the EU 'straightjacketing the state' in the so-called age of austerity. Also, EU membership divides the British elites, and that divide is now long-lived and pervasive in its effects. It is hard to see how a power-hoarding model copes with such major, persistent, and increasingly successful challenges to its authority. So, we insist that even when there is a dominant tradition, other traditions persist and are a wellspring of dilemmas, and therefore of change, for that tradition. To focus on the dominant tradition is to look at British government through the wrong end of a telescope; it excludes too much. Exploring contending elite narratives does not preclude a dominant tradition yet directs attention to the rival traditions.

Andrew Taylor (Chapter 3) offers a variant on well-worn criticisms of our concept of tradition. He alleges 'interpretivism tends to focus on "surface politics" ... to the exclusion of "deep politics" that deals with meanings, beliefs and preferences that influence visible behaviour'. He alleges that 'interpretivists tend to collapse deep politics into a broad concept of tradition'. Deep politics is 'extremely resistant to change' and 'coexists with an open "surface polity" that projects a different configuration of meaning'.

'Deep politics' appears to have two meanings. First, it refers to institutions, 'represented here by organisational cultures and traditions'. As we see organisations as constituted by contending traditions where traditions are embedded beliefs and practices, then all that is at stake here is the label 'deep politics'. However, a critical realist claim could be lurking behind the argument that structures such as institutions are emergent mechanisms that determine people's actions. In other words, institutions have 'causal powers which structure can express in relation to agency' (McAnulla, 2006: 121). But we do not know how structure determines individual actions without passing through intentional consciousness. Why cannot agents change emergent structures? The structure emerges from actions, so, presumably, if all the relevant people change their actions, they will stop producing that structure, so changing it. So, emergent structures are better understood as practices that are embedded, durable but not immovable (see, also, the exchange between Hay (2005) and McAnulla (2005)).

Initially, we had a sense of déjà vu when we revisited these arguments about tradition. However, we realised as we read the several chapters that, although contested, the concept informs much of the analysis (Chapters 2, 3, 4, and 9). So, our lasting impression is, 'look how far we have travelled'. As Fawcett (Chapter 2) points out, even those colleagues 'who remain sceptical about [interpretivism's] core claims ... can no longer ignore its growing influence on the profession, particularly among younger scholars'. Whatever the defects in our analysis of tradition, it is clear the notion has much traction in the analysis of British governance (see, for example: Sullivan, Chapter 9; and Gardner and Lowndes, 2015).

Rationalities: Technologies of Governance

Central elites may construct their world using diverse narratives but they also turn to forms of expertise for specific discourses. Nowadays different traditions of social science influence public policy. Our interpretive approach draws attention to the varied rationalities that inform policies across different sectors and different geographical spaces. Rationalities refer here to the scientific beliefs and associated technologies that govern conduct. The term captures the ways in which governments and other social actors draw on knowledge to construct policies and practices, especially those that regulate and create subjectivities. Britain, like much of the developed world, has witnessed the rise of neoliberal managerial rationalities, commonly referred to as the new public management. It uses a technology of performance measurement and targets that spreads far beyond the central civil service to encompass the control of localities (and for a comprehensive survey see Ferlie *et al.*, 2005).

A good example of rationalities or technologies of governance is provided by Paul Fawcett's (Chapter 2) analysis of metagovernance. He identifies three different approaches to metagovernance including a pluralist approach that emphasises the role of the state as a network manager. His favoured example is Torfing *et al.* (2012: 156–59 and chapter 7) who suggest the state's role is that of 'meta-governor managing and facilitating interactive governance'. Their task is to 'balance autonomy of networks with hands-on intervention'. They have various specific ways of carrying out this balancing act. They can 'campaign for a policy, deploy policy narratives, act as boundary spanners, and form alliance with politicians'. They become 'metagovernors', managing the mix of bureaucracy, markets and networks. The metagoverning public servant has to master some specific skills for managing networks. They include: integrating agendas, representing both your agency and the network, setting broad rules of the game that leave local action to network members, developing clear roles, expectations and responsibilities for all players, agreeing the criteria of success, and sharing the administrative burden. The neo-Weberian approach would accept this tool view of metagoverning but insist that it increases the capacity of the state to act (Bell and Hindmoor, 2009) whereas Torfing *et al.* (2012: 132) would argue that such arrangements constrained that capacity. If they disagree on the continuing importance of hierarchy in state action, they agree there is a new rationality underpinning state action. If its influence is not as pervasive as that of new public management (NPM), nonetheless it now has its own acronym of new public governance (NPG) and there is an extensive literature on 'how to manage your network' (Goldsmith and Eggers, 2004; Agranoff, 2007; Osborne, 2010; Klijn and Koppenjan, 2015).

Resistance and Local Knowledge

Resistance means a refusal to comply with someone: an attempt to prevent something when that someone has the power to enforce compliance. Here, power refers to the constitutive role of tradition in giving us our beliefs and actions, and in making our world. It also refers to the restrictive consequences of the actions of others in defining what we can and cannot do. In these terms, an interpretive approach shows how various actors restrict what others can do in ways that thwart the intentions of policy actors. Interpretive studies can show how local actors are able to draw on their own traditions to resist policies inspired by the narratives of others in the policy cascade. An interpretive approach moves away from the strategies and interactions of central and local elites when it turns its attention to resistance; to the other actors who resist, transform, and thwart the agendas of elites. Interpretive theory draws attention to the diverse traditions and narratives that inspire street-level bureaucrats and citizens. Policies are sites of struggles not just between strategic elites, but between all kinds of actors with different views and ideals, reached against the background of different traditions. Subaltern actors can resist the intentions and policies of elites by consuming them in ways that draw on local traditions and their local reasoning.

So, we need:

- accounts of the local traditions and forms of knowledge with which civil servants, mid-level public managers, and street-level bureaucrats have interpreted and responded to elite policy narratives;
- explorations of the myriad ways in which local actors have interpreted and thus forged practices of governance on the ground.

The notions of local knowledge, storytelling, and performative action are central to the analysis of resistance (see Bevir and Rhodes, 2016: Part II.)

For Geertz (1993c: 75–6):

> If we are to take local knowledge seriously, we need to pay attention to everyday notions such as 'common sense'. Common sense is an integral part of local knowledge and its inherited tacit theories – folk theory – pervade everyday life. It should be viewed as 'a relatively organized body of considered thought'.

In interpretive policy analysis, local knowledge has been defined by Yanow (2004: 12) as 'the very mundane, yet expert understanding of and practical reasoning about local conditions derived from lived experience'. It is 'contextual knowledge', which is 'specific to a local context'. It is tacit knowledge that 'develops out of experience with the situation in question'. As a result, 'local workers ... are far more knowledgeable about the situation at hand than those without such experience or point of view'. Durose (2009: 36) expands on Yanow, suggesting that local knowledge develops 'from their own subjective interpretations or "readings" of a situation', which is passed on in the stories people tell.

In public administration and public policy, the most common example of local knowledge is provided by the work of street-level bureaucrats (see, for example, Maynard-Moody and Musheno, 2003; Vinzant and Crothers, 1998). Thus, street-level police officers are often influenced by organisational traditions that encourage them to set priorities different from those of both their superior officers and elite policymakers. Combating crime is seen as the core of police work, not the 'touchy-feely' areas of community policing. The new police commissioner may want to set an example, cause a stir, and ginger up the troops. But the troops know he or she will be gone in a few years. There will be a new commissioner with new interests and priorities. Similarly, citizens may continue to act on territorial loyalties and identities that bear little resemblance to the administrative units crafted by policymakers (see Sullivan, Chapter 9). However, as Vohnsen (2015) suggests, local knowledge is 'shifty'. It is 'dispersed' and 'not possessed equally by all'. Vohnsen also usefully highlights the complex specificity and contingency of local knowledge: 'what people *know* to be of local relevance in one situation might be different from what they know to be of local relevance in the next situation'. As we know from our personal experiences, some people have little common sense.

Hendrik Wagenaar (Chapter 7) has criticised our use of practice elsewhere (Wagenaar, 2012; Bevir and Rhodes, 2012).[3] We accept that 'the concept of practice has considerable more inner complexity to it' than we have allowed. We find his emphasis on the performative analysis of the concept helpful. Similarly, Helen Sullivan (Chapter 9) observes (citing Griggs, 2014: 15) that people make sense of situations not only by thinking about them in the context of their traditions but also by acting on the situations. We agree with her that 'the concept of "situated agency" coupled with "local reasoning"' provide the analytical tools 'to identify why actors in apparently similar contexts may develop different interpretations and responses to policy ideas'. Also, focusing on practices will provide a fine-grained analysis of 'situated agency'; of 'what it is that evaluators, policymakers, etc. do in the process of making and judging policy (see also Craig, Chapter 5).

Just as Wagenaar and Sullivan extend the notion of practice, so Fawcett (Chapter 2) extends our analysis of storytelling (Bevir, 2011b), stressing the need to understand 'their differential transmission and uptake'. Two features of his research agenda are promising. First, storytelling is not the only metagoverning tool, and exploring alternative ways of steering the state will extend our understanding of the available technologies of governance. Second, examining how speaking truth to power is performed invites us to consider different forms of storytelling, the transmission of stories, and the reasons for their success or failure.

In our view, however the great strength of a focus on stories is that it integrates the analysis of local knowledge and performative action. Storytelling is performative. Rhodes (2011: 273–4 and 276) describes how public servants construct their stories, distinguishing between the language game of constructing the storyline, the performing game of telling the story internally and externally, and the managing game of getting on with everyday business. He also explores 'the appearance of rule' or the ways in which ministers not only make decisions and manage the department but also enact, in public, constitutive and representational rituals that legitimate governmental authority (Rhodes 2011: 105–7 and 287–8). Here performative practices are at the heart of storytelling.

'Blurring Genres': A New Toolkit

In addition, we need to move beyond modernist empiricism as the way of studying rule, rationalities, and resistance. Modernist empiricism treats institutions such as legislatures, constitutions, and executives as discrete, atomised objects to be compared, measured, and classified. It adopts comparisons across time and space as a means of uncovering regularities and probabilistic explanations to be tested against neutral evidence (see Bevir, 2006). In contrast, we argue for the recovery of meaning (Taylor, 1971) and for 'blurring genres' by drawing on the humanities (Geertz, 1993b).

As Geertz (1993b: 21) points out 'there has been an enormous amount of genre mixing in intellectual life.... Social scientists have turned away from a laws and instances ideal of explanation towards a cases and interpretations one'.

They draw on 'analogies drawn from the humanities'. So, 'society is less and less represented as an elaborate machine or quasi-organism and more as a serious game, a sidewalk drama, or a behavioural text'. The task is to recover the meaning of games, dramas, and texts and to tease out their consequences. So, what can we learn from the humanities? The task of blurring genres is an exciting challenge for political scientists. It takes us out of our comfort zone by asking us what we want to know and providing new ways of finding out. It is not about replacing but adding to the political scientists' toolkit. It is about opening a conversation with the humanities that enlarges our organising perspective and broadens our toolkit.

An interpretive approach does not necessarily favour particular methods. It does not prescribe a particular toolkit for producing data but prescribes a particular way of treating data of any type. It should be treated as evidence of the meanings or beliefs embedded in actions. This view of how we should treat data does, of course, have some implications for methods of data collection. It leads, in particular, to greater emphasis on qualitative methods than is usual among political scientists; to historicism and ethnography.

Historicism – Get into the Archives

Human action is historically contingent. It is characterised by change and specificity. We cannot explain social phenomena if we ignore their inherent flux and their concrete links to specific contexts. Such historicist explanations work not by referring to reified correlations, mechanisms, or models, but by describing contingent patterns of meaningful actions in their specific contexts.

Historicists argue that beliefs, actions, and events are profoundly contingent because choice is open and indeterminate. They question the possibility of either a universal theory or ahistorical correlations and typologies. In addition, they argue that, if we are to understand and explain actions and beliefs, we have to grasp how they fit within wider practices and webs of meaning. They emphasise contextualisation in contrast to both deduction and atomisation and analysis. Historicism thus promotes forms of understanding and explanation that are inductive studies of human life in its historical contexts. Historicists do not appeal to fixed principles or to reason and progress to define the relevant contexts and link them to the present. So, historicist explanations are not only temporal in that they move through time; they are also historical in that they locate the phenomena at a specific time.

David Craig (Chapter 5) explores the 'potential synergies' between our approach to historicism and the history of political thought and the hermeneutics of John Dunn. He finds much common ground:

> We all hold more or less well-justified beliefs about the beliefs and sentiments and practical situations of others. We all can and indeed *must* attempt to judge methodologically how it is sound to attribute beliefs or feelings to others. Within a common physical world we are all radical interpreters of one another, assigning beliefs, desires, intentions and meanings simultaneously to

one another and trying to make sense of conduct by solving the resulting simultaneous equations.

(Dunn 1980: 107)

The common ground is not limited to Dunn but extends to others who have been influenced by the 'Cambridge School'. We can only agree, for example, with Geoffrey Hawthorn's (1991: 79) comment that analysis begins with 'particular agents in particular sets of circumstances' (1991: 168); and that:

> Doubts can be thrown on the distinction between structure and agency such that structure is not so much an unchangeable set of affairs, but simply a set of affairs that happened not to have changed much, but which could have been changed.

In Chapter 6, Emily Robinson provides a historicist account of progressive politics in Britain, providing a decentred analysis of this tradition. We welcome her argument that we extend the idea of tradition to include emotions. We need more such historicist studies.[4] For example, Bevir (2011a) unpacks the various strands that fed into the British socialist movement. He shows how Marxism, Fabianism, and ethical socialism developed and competed. Although he allows for the contingency of their fate, he suggests that the dominant ideas in the Labour Party have consistently merged Fabianism with ethical socialism to the exclusion of more pluralist and non-governmental strands of socialist thought. Crucially, he also ends with the claim that these early socialist traditions were transformed by the rise of modernist rationalities that came to dictate so much of Labour Party policy.

Ethnography – Get into the Field

Anthropologists practice ethnography to discover the relevant webs of meaning. Ethnography involves selecting informants, transcribing texts, and keeping field notes. It aims at 'thick descriptions' or 'our own constructions of other people's construction of what they and their compatriots are up to' (Geertz, 1993a: 9). The everyday phrase is 'seeing things from the others' point of view'. The ethnographer provides an interpretation of what others are up to and so of these others' interpretations of the world. Ethnographic studies are often microscopic interpretations of the flow of social discourse. The task is to set down the meanings that particular actions have for social actors and then say what these thick descriptions tells us about the society in which they are found. There is a world of difference between modernist empiricist and interpretive ethnography. The former uses ethnography as a method for collecting data to test political science theories. The latter uses ethnography as a way of recovering beliefs and practices to write narratives of how things work around here.

Such fieldwork is not represented in this book but it has become a prominent part of our research agenda (see, for example, Rhodes *et al.*, 2007; Rhodes, 2011, 2015; Rhodes and Tiernan, 2014; Bevir and Rhodes, 2016: Part II). The work has explored the everyday life of ministers and permanent secretaries in British government departments; the role of the Chief of Staff to the Australian Prime Minister; and advice to ministers in Australia, Britain, Canada, and New Zealand. One general lesson we have drawn from these studies is that there are many ways of 'being there'. There is a clash between 'deep hanging out', or intensive fieldwork, and 'hit-and-run' ethnography (Geertz, 2001: 110). Ethnographic practice has become more varied, even baroque. So, ethnographers 'study-up', and 'follow through' by conducting 'yo-yo-research' in 'multi-local' sites. Practice is no longer limited to participant observation. Fieldwork is done by teams, often in collaboration with a client and involves taking 'ethnographic snapshots' at a particular time in several locations. In a phrase, we have 'hit-and-run' ethnography. But it is not an either/or choice. The relevant skills include both deep hanging out *and* hit-and-run ethnography. As well as parti-cipant observation, we can use focus groups, para-ethnography, and visual eth-nography (see Rhodes, 2014). Truly, ethnographers are *bricoleurs* employing a ragbag of tools; what works is best.

Conclusions

Interpretivism is a broad church but its members have shared concerns with the philosophical underpinnings of the human sciences and the recovery of meaning. It deconstructs the mainstream, and suggests new topics of research: the study of elite narratives, technologies of governance, and resistance rooted in local know-ledge. In the earlier chapters, the contributors have identified a detailed research agenda for interpretivism. It encompasses:

- court politics, elite narratives, and their associated traditions;
- metagovernance as an emerging technology of governance, to which we would add the mass-privatisation of public services in the so-called 'franchise state';
- the exploration of local knowledge and traditions through stories of resist-ance that recover the beliefs and practices of local actors.

Interpretivism is no mere fashion, but a burgeoning, blooming profusion of ideas and research.

Interpretivism also encourages genre blurring and drawing on the humanities for such methods of analysis as historicism and ethnography. It looks for gaps in the existing literature. It seeks to give voice to those left out of existing accounts. It is a distinct, distinctive and varied research agenda and, as our colleagues in this volume clearly demonstrate, the interpretive adventure takes many forms, although storytelling and the analysis of performative action are areas of shared interest. However, we do not look for agreement. We look for engagement, and that is here aplenty.

It is commonplace for our critics to reject the claim that political science is modernist empiricist. Rather, they claim, it is eclectic. We would love to be wrong but see little evidence to support their view. For example, looking at the subfield of public administration and its leading journals, such as *Journal of Public Administration Research and Theory* and *Governance*, there are few interpretive articles. Rather, there is a turn to rational choice theory and quantitative studies, not interpretivism. Or, more broadly, Auyero and Joseph (2007) examined 1,000 articles published in the *American Journal of Political Science* and the *American Political Science Review* between 1996 and 2005. They found that 'only one article relies on ethnography as a data-production technique' (2007: 2). Exceptions there may be, but the dominant idiom of present-day political science in Britain and America is modernist empiricism or, if you prefer, naturalism. So, the future is not necessarily sunny for interpretivism in political science. Nor is it all doom and gloom. The Political Studies Association of the UK has a thriving Interpretive Political Science specialist group. There is the Critical Policy Analysis group with its annual conference on 'Interpretive Policy Analysis' and its journal *Critical Policy Studies*. The question of whether there will be an interpretive turn in political science in the coming years remains unresolved. We have no crystal ball. We can only state and defend our position, and wait. We look forward to assessing where we are in another ten years.

In his introduction Nick Turnbull distinguishes between our work 'as an endeavour to do something interesting and innovative in British political science, particularly in the often dry field of governance, public policy, and public administration' and 'as an altogether more challenging and confrontational effort to establish interpretivism as an analytical framework, one which rejects some of the established and valued aspects of British political science'. Of course, we do both. But the point bears restatement. Emily Robinson (Chapter 6) enters a caution to our ambition. She fears we seek to create 'interpretive political science as a discipline'. Heaven forfend. Perhaps she teases us (at least we hope so). We challenge the empiricist tradition in British political science. We take the discipline back to its roots in history and philosophy. We are advocates of a historicist philosophy, not a discipline, and we favour blurring genres. Willingly, we concede that much of what we say is commonplace in other disciplines. We do insist that it is not the everyday language of political scientists and that we can and should learn from the historians, ethnographers, and philosophers working in the interpretive idiom. If we sought to create a discipline, it would not be in the mould of the modernist empiricism of present-day American political science but 'a glorious interdisciplinary set of practices'.

Notes

1 See, for example, Bevir and Rhodes (2004, 2006, 2008a, 2008b, and 2012) and the overview by Turnbull (Introduction, this volume).
2 Given the tendency to reify (perhaps deify) structure in much political science, Russell's repudiation of Christian dogma has resonance:

> Many orthodox people speak as though it were the business of sceptics to disprove received dogmas rather than of dogmatists to prove them. This is, of course, a mistake. If I were to suggest that between the Earth and Mars there is a China teapot revolving about the sun in an elliptical orbit, nobody would be able to disprove my assertion provided I were careful to add that the teapot is too small to be

revealed even by our most powerful telescopes. But if I were to go on to say that, since my assertion cannot be disproved, it is intolerable presumption on the part of human reason to doubt it, I should rightly be thought to be talking nonsense.

(Russell 1997: 547–8)

3　However, we note, with a tinge of disappointment, that he continues to ignore our more recent work on traditions (Bevir, 2011a) and everyday practices (Rhodes, 2011).
4　In passing, we welcome the demonstration in Taylor (Chapter 3) and Bellamy and 6 (Chapter 8) that the analysis of archival documents is an important tool in identifying and describing beliefs and practices.

References

Agranoff, R. (2007) *Managing within Networks: Adding value to public organizations*, Washington, DC: Georgetown University Press.

Auyero, J. and Joseph, L. (2007) 'Introduction: Politics under the ethnographic Microscope', in L. Joseph, M. Mahler, and J. Auyero (eds), *New Perspectives on Political Ethnography*, New York: Springer: 1–13.

Bell, S. and Hindmoor, A. (2009) *Rethinking Governance: The centrality of the state in modern society*, Cambridge: Cambridge University Press.

Bevir, M. (2006) 'Political Studies as Narrative and Science, 1880–2000', *Political Studies*, 54(3): 583–606.

Bevir, M. (2011a) *The Making of British Socialism*, Princeton, NJ: Princeton University Press.

Bevir, M. (2011b) 'Public Administration as Storytelling', *Public Administration*, 89(1): 183–95.

Bevir, M. and Rhodes, R. A. W. (2003) *Interpreting British Governance*, London: Routledge.

Bevir, M. and Rhodes, R. A. W. (2004) 'Interpretation as Method, Explanation and Critique', *British Journal of Politics and International Relations*, 6(2): 156–64.

Bevir, M. and Rhodes, R. A. W. (2006) *Governance Stories*, Abingdon: Routledge.

Bevir, M. and Rhodes, R. A. W. (2008a) 'Politics as Cultural Practice' *Political Studies Review*, 6(2): 170–77.

Bevir, M. and Rhodes, R. A. W. (2008b) 'The Differentiated Polity as Narrative', *British Journal of Politics and International Relations*, 10(4): 729–34.

Bevir, M. and Rhodes, R. A. W. (2010) *The State as Cultural Practice*, Oxford: Oxford University Press.

Bevir, M. and Rhodes, R. A. W. (2012) 'Interpretivism and the Analysis of Traditions and Practices', *Critical Policy Studies*, 6(2): 201–08.

Bevir, M. and Rhodes, R. A. W. (2015) 'Interpretive Political Science: Mapping the field', in M. Bevir and R. A. W. Rhodes (eds), *The Routledge Handbook of Interpretive Political Science*, Abingdon: Routledge: 3–27.

Bevir, M. and Rhodes, R. A. W. (2016) *Rethinking Governance: Ruling, rationalities and resistance*, Abingdon: Routledge.

Clifton, J. (2014) 'Beyond Hollowing Out: Straitjacketing the state', *the Political Quarterly*, 85(4): 437–44.

Dunn, J. (1980) *Political Obligation in its Historical Context*, Cambridge: Cambridge University Press.

Durose, C. (2009) 'Front line Workers and "Local Knowledge": Neighbourhood stories in contemporary UK local governance', *Public Administration*, 87(1): 35–49.

Ferlie, E., Lynn, L. E., and Pollitt, C. (eds) (2005) *The Oxford Handbook of Public Management*, Oxford: Oxford University Press.

Finlayson, A. and Martin, J. (2006) 'Post-structuralism', in C. Hay, M. Lister, and D. Marsh (eds), *The State: Theory and issues*, Houndmills, Basingstoke: Palgrave Macmillan: 155–71.

Gardner, A. and Lowndes, V. (2016, forthcoming) 'Negotiating Austerity and Local Traditions', in M. Bevir and M. Rhodes (eds), *Rethinking Governance*, Abingdon: Routledge.

Geertz, C. (1993a) [1973] 'Thick Descriptions: Towards an interpretive theory of culture', in his *The Interpretation of Cultures*, London: Fontana: 3–30.

Geertz, C. (1993b) [1983] 'Blurred Genres: The refiguration of social thought', in his *Local Knowledge: Further essays in interpretive anthropology*, New York: Basic Books: 19–35.

Geertz, C. (1993c) [1983] 'Common Sense as a Cultural System', in his *Local Knowledge: Further essays in interpretive anthropology*, London: Fontana: 73–93.

Geertz, C. (2001) 'The State of the Art', in his *Available Light: Anthropological reflections on philosophical topics*, 3rd edition, Princeton, NJ: Princeton University Press, pp. 89–142.

Goldsmith, S. and Eggers, W. D. (2004) *Governing by Networks*, Washington, DC: Brookings Institution Press.

Griggs, S., Norval, A. J., and Wagenaar, H. (2014) 'Introduction: Democracy, conflict and participation in decentred governance', in S. Griggs, A. J. Norval, and H. Wagenaar (eds), *Practices of Freedom: Decentred governance, conflict and democratic participation*, Cambridge: Cambridge University Press, pp. 1–37.

Hawthorn, G. (1991) *Plausible Worlds: Possibility and understanding in history and the social sciences*, Cambridge: Cambridge University Press.

Hay, C. (2005) 'Making Hay ... or Clutching at Ontological Straws? Notes on realism, as-if-realism and actualism', *Politics*: 25(1): 39–45.

Jessop, B. (2005) 'Critical Realism and the Strategic-Relational Approach', *New Formations*, 56(1): 40–53.

Klijn, E.-H. and Koppenjan, J. (2015) *Governance Networks in the Public Sector: A network approach to public problem solving, policy making and service delivery*, Abingdon: Routledge.

Marsh, D. (2011) 'The New Orthodoxy: The differentiated polity model', *Public Administration*, 89(1): 32–48.

Maynard-Moody, S. and Musheno, M. (2003) *Cops, Teachers, Counsellors: Stories from the front lines of public service*, Ann Arbor, MI: the University of Michigan Press.

McAnulla, S. (2005) 'Making Hay with Actualism? The need for a realist concept of structure', *Politics*, 25(1): 31–8.

McAnulla, S. (2006) 'Challenging the New Interpretivist Approach: Towards a critical realist alternative', *British Politics*, 1(1): 113–38.

MacIntyre, A. (1971) *Against the Self-Images of the Age: Essays on ideology and philosophy*, London: Duckworth.

Osborne, S. P. (2010) 'Introduction, The (New) Public Governance: A suitable case for treatment', in S. Osborne (ed.), *The New Public Governance: Emerging perspectives on the theory and practice of public governance*, London: Routledge and Taylor and Francis, pp. 1–16.

Rhodes, R. A. W. (2011) *Everyday Life in British Government*, Oxford: Oxford University Press.

Rhodes, R. A. W. (2014) 'Genre Blurring in Public Administration: What can we learn from the humanities?' *Australian Journal of Public Administration*, 73(4): 317–30.

Rhodes, R. A. W. (2015) 'Ethnography', in M. Bevir and R. A. W. Rhodes (eds), *The Routledge Handbook of Interpretive Political Science*, Abingdon: Routledge: 171–85.

Rhodes, R. A. W., 't Hart, P., and Noordegraaf, M. (eds) (2007) *Observing Government Elites: Up close and personal*, Basingstoke: Palgrave-Macmillan.

Rhodes, R. A. W. and Tiernan, A. (2014) *Lessons of Governing: A profile of prime ministers' chiefs of staff*, Melbourne: Melbourne University Press.

Rorty, R. (1980) *Philosophy and the Mirror of Nature*, Oxford: Blackwell.

Russell, B. (1997) *The Collected Papers of Bertrand Russell, Vol. 11: Last philosophical testament, 1943–68*, edited by John Slater and Peter Köllner, London: Routledge.

Taylor, C. (1971) 'Interpretation and the Sciences of Man', *Review of Metaphysics*, 25(1): 3–51.

Torfing, J., Peters, B. G., Pierre, J., and Sørensen, E. (2012) *Interactive Governance: Advancing the paradigm*, Oxford: Oxford University Press.

Vinzant, J. C. and Crothers, L. (1998) *Street Level Leadership: Discretion and legitimacy in front line public services*, Washington, DC: Georgetown University Press.

Vohnsen, N. H. (2015) 'Street-level Planning: The shifty nature of "local knowledge and practice"', *Journal of Organizational Ethnography*, 3(3): 147–61.

Wagenaar, H. (2011) *Meaning in Action: Interpretation and dialogue in policy analysis*, Armonk, NY: M. E. Sharpe.

Wagenaar, H. (2012) 'Dwellers on the Threshold of Practice: The interpretivism of Bevir and Rhodes', *Critical Policy Studies*, 6(1): 85–99.

Yanow, D. (2004) 'Translating Local Knowledge at Organisational Peripheries', *British Journal of Management*, 15(1): 9–25.

Index

Page numbers in *italics* denote tables, those in **bold** denote figures.